UNDER ASSAULT

UNDER ASSAULT

INTERFERENCE AND ESPIONAGE
IN CHINA'S SECRET WAR
AGAINST CANADA

DENNIS MOLINARO

RANDOM HOUSE CANADA

PUBLISHED BY RANDOM HOUSE CANADA

Random House Canada, an imprint of Penguin Random House Canada Limited
320 Front Street West, Suite 1400
Toronto, Ontario, M5V 3B6, Canada
penguinrandomhouse.ca

Random House Canada and colophon are registered trademarks of Penguin Random House LLC.

The authorized representative in the EU for product safety and compliance is Penguin Random House Ireland, Morrison Chambers, 32 Nassau Street, Dublin D02 YH68, Ireland. https://eu-contact.penguin.ie

Library and Archives Canada Cataloguing in Publication

Title: Under assault: interference and espionage in China's secret war against Canada / Dennis Molinaro.
Names: Molinaro, Dennis G., author
Description: Includes bibliographical references and index.
Identifiers: Canadiana (print) 20250115654 | Canadiana (ebook) 20250115689 | ISBN 9781039011700 (hardcover) | ISBN 9781039011717 (EPUB)
Subjects: LCSH: Espionage, Chinese—Canada. | LCSH: Canada—Foreign relations—China. | LCSH: China—Foreign relations—Canada.
Classification: LCC FC251.C5 M65 2025 | DDC 327.71051—dc23

Photo in chapter six, page 186, supplied courtesy of the author.

Text design: Dylan Browne
Cover design: Dylan Browne
Image credits: (figures) pressmaster, (dust texture) Ivan, (abstract texture) BNMK0819 / all Adobe Stock
Typeset in Garamond Premier by Sean Tai

Printed in Canada

2 4 6 8 9 7 5 3 1

Penguin
Random House
RANDOM HOUSE CANADA

CONTENTS

FOREWORD

WHEN I FIRST started advocating for Canada to recognize its problem with foreign interference, in 2020, journalists and policy-makers were quick to dismiss the diaspora's concerns with surveillance and safety. They stopped short of calling us paranoid conspiracy theorists to our faces. At the time, few in Ottawa understood that the Chinese authorities were targeting community members in Canada, or that foreign interference represented an existential threat to Canadian liberal democratic society. Whether the collective dismissal came from ignorance or wilful neglect, the reality is that foreign state actors and their influence are evident across Canadian institutions. Those speaking up against Beijing become top targets of the Chinese party-state, which fears that diaspora communities have the potential to threaten its one-party regime.

Since at least the 1990s, the Chinese Communist Party (CCP) has turned its totalitarian governance outwards. Long before I entered advocacy, diaspora community members were sounding the alarm over their experiences with transnational repression and Beijing's attempts to assert influence and control overseas communities. We know that agents mobilize pro-Beijing supporters on the WeChat social networking app, encourage the use of physical and online violence against publicly outspoken dissidents and organize counter-demonstrations to disrupt dissident communities hosting solidarity protests in Canada. This is all part of the united front strategy developed by the CCP in the early twentieth century to combat warlords and the Nationalists during the formation of the People's Republic of China (PRC), and also to use against regions that contested CCP rule after China's civil war. It has long since become institutionalized, and dissident communities are very familiar with the united front playbook. In response, we diligently collect chat records, photographs, videos and other evidence and submit it to the police in hopes that perpetrators will be held accountable. Even when criminal activities such as harassment, intimidation and assaults are recorded, with perpetrators identifiable on video, Canadian police agencies do not press charges. Community members rarely, if ever, receive briefings from Canadian policing and intelligence institutions.

My first report on foreign interference was published in 2020, a case study based on a weekend of events across the globe to show solidarity with Hong Kong, hosted by Hong Kongers. My colleagues and I recorded the tactics, slogans and timelines used by the Chinese party-state in its coordination of intimidation and harassment campaigns in eight Canadian cities and nine other countries. Over the weekend, we observed standardized practices across all these locations. Organizers of counter-demonstrations issued the same flags, signs and equipment to attendees. After my group, Alliance Canada Hong Kong, published this report and provided briefings to Canadian policy-makers and politicians, many were shaken by the report's findings. Few questioned the integrity of the report or whether its authors were experiencing confirmation bias. It was clear from the response that foreign interference and transnational repression were not well understood outside the community. However, at the time, politicians and officials were reluctant to spend their political capital on the issue.

By 2023, that was changing. The topic of foreign interference began to dominate media headlines, with allegations that the People's Republic of China, among other nations, was interfering in Canadian democratic institutions and electoral processes. Since then, foreign interference has continued to be a high-profile topic in Parliament, media and public discourse. Canadians are justifiably concerned about the integrity of Canada's democratic institutions and electoral processes.

Foreign interference has broad implications for Canadian society and neoliberal democratic norms. While transnational repression disproportionately impacts diaspora communities and our families back home, foreign interference pervades all sectors of Canadian society. Diaspora communities have long observed united front actors building relationships with academics, business leaders, policy-makers and politicians. Through building personal relationships and lucrative agreements, and encouraging grassroots pro-Beijing sentiments, a network of united front actors and proxies has sustained an environment of influence that enables Chinese state actors to blur the line between traditional forms of diplomatic influence and outright foreign interference.

The interference revelations of 2023 and '24 did not come as a shock to the diaspora communities. As a dissident, I felt my years of advocacy were validated by the reports published by the Canadian NSICOP and NSIRA government-initiated investigations into interference, as well as the public inquiry of 2024. I hoped to find a sense of closure from these reports, and yet I can't help but question: Is it a fair exchange that our pain and trauma sparked change in the Canadian national security apparatus?

Across the country, international students from the PRC were concerned that the education office of the PRC embassy would cancel their travel documents, study permits and scholarships for participating in a pro-democracy protest. These students wrapped themselves in layers of jackets, masks and scarves while protesting, holding up signs to hide their identities and avoid being photographed. A small business had to allocate additional staff and funding to install surveillance cameras after pro-Beijing individuals vandalized the store's Lennon Wall and pro-democracy display, intimidating workers and customers. In the days leading up to solidarity protests across Canada during 2019 and 2020, activists cleaned up dead rats and vandalism around their properties. Dissidents have sacrificed contact with their family members in the PRC, hoping their loved ones are safer this way.

Over the last few years, I have shared my traumatic experiences of transnational repression to raise attention about what is happening in Canada. You will read about some of these experiences in the pages that follow. Each time I speak out about them, I am met with attacks by critics and receive even more harassment. From an eager and passionate community advocate, I became a cold, cynical researcher. I am not alone. Many in the diaspora community have lost trust in Canadian institutions after experiencing years of neglect and gaslighting. Once the community has lost its trust, it will take substantive work to rebuild and regain their confidence.

Reflecting on the political discourse, I find it difficult not to be angry when watching officials and politicians make a sharp about-face in their attitude towards interference, when I still remember their cold, uninterested response as I pled for their attention and support only a short time ago. Their recent and suddenly strong stance against foreign interference is too obviously meant to capitalize on political support from Canadians. I hear the RCMP and national security institutions discuss the "safety of diaspora" while my peers and I continue to survive transnational suppression without formalized support or resources.

Foreign interference acts like a double-edged sword. At one extreme, it leaves diaspora communities marginalized by both the Chinese authorities and Canadian institutions. In the absence of a strategic and coordinated approach to counter foreign interference, diaspora communities will remain vulnerable to influence and intimidation from foreign state actors and their proxies while Canadian institutions fail to provide safeguards.

At the other extreme, foreign interference can be used as a racist and Sinophobic weapon against Chinese and East Asian communities. The national security apparatus may exacerbate this dynamic if it approaches diaspora communities without a clear understanding of the reality they face, caught between malign foreign interference and domestic suspicion. Rather than providing a sense of safety, a reckless turn towards a policing- and enforcement-centric approach will further alienate diaspora communities.

In an increasingly globalized and technological world, repressive regimes are motivated to improve and expand their transnational repression. As Canada moves to confront the threat of foreign interference, we must also look back and understand how we arrived at today's precarious situation.

Cherie Wong
Founder of Alliance Canada Hong Kong

INTRODUCTION

I KNEW RUSSIA. I knew the Cold War like I knew the back of my hand. I was a historian of intelligence and a university professor, and when I joined the intelligence world in 2018 as an intelligence analyst, I took it as a given that I would be working on the Russia file. Instead, my focus quickly became centred on the PRC. Now inside Canada's security and intelligence establishment, I was shocked at the threat posed by one of Canada's largest trading partners. I quickly came to believe that confronting the PRC was vastly more urgent than any threat presented by our former Cold War antagonist.

Canadians have become alarmed about the foreign interference threat posed by the PRC, but they don't yet understand it. This needs to change. Counterterrorism has been the primary security focus of the Western world for the past twenty-odd years, and the counter-intelligence effort traditionally aimed at countering Cold War–style state spying differs from foreign interference. However, the PRC remains the most persistent and largest foreign power covertly interfering in the political operations and civic life of Western nations. Canadians have many unanswered questions. This isn't to say Canadians have met only silence on the subject, but much of the analysis to date has been written by journalists and rooted in their particular angles on the issue. There have been academic books on the Canada–China relationship, but the broader picture of the PRC's targeting of Canada, from its beginnings to the present, remains untold. With the perspective I developed in my time in intelligence work, combined with my training as a professional historian and academic, I hope to fill that need.

This book is not a recollection of my time in Canadian intelligence or a revelation of specific intelligence files. I do not divulge classified material or "name names." The entire book was researched and created using publicly verifiable sources. All my comments, conclusions and analysis are derived from those sources. Instead, this book identifies and illustrates a long-standing pattern of failure in Canadian political circles to understand what our own intelligence service has been trying for decades to tell us. The result is, I hope, a realistic appraisal of Canada's relationship with China, by way of China's secret operations against Canada over the last fifty years. I hope readers will come away from this book knowing far more about China's secret operations, how and why they have been so successful, and what Canada's failure to stand up to this threat says about the country.

———

The book will reveal how for decades, Canadian leaders have engaged with a China they convinced themselves they knew and understood. They saw China's potential as a profitable trading partner and counterweight to Canada's often lopsided relationship with the United States. They saw a country they thought would one day adopt democracy and the rule of law and become a trusted partner in Asia. Under the rule of the CCP, the PRC would become none of these things. It would instead use Canada to help develop its economy, build its military—especially in equipping the People's Liberation Army (PLA) with modern technology—and accelerate its quest to supplant the United States as the world's dominant power.

A number of China commentators claim the country changed once President Xi Jinping, a fervent nationalist, took power in 2012, which could suggest that up until then Canada's hopes for a prosperous partnership with China were no illusion. Certainly, Xi ramped up the PRC's espionage and foreign interference, and the militancy of Chinese diplomacy; but, as this book will show, he was more accelerant than catalyst. Xi didn't mastermind the horrors of the Cultural Revolution or order 1989's Tiananmen Square massacre. Even if commentators thought these horrors did not reflect China's forward-looking attitude in the decades between Tiananmen Square and Xi's ascent to power, during this time the PRC was consistently engaging in secret operations to steal technology and influence Western politicians. But blinded by optimism and perhaps even greed, Canada's political leaders saw only the China they wanted to believe in.

Americans had adopted a far more realistic view of the PRC. The US still had an obligation to Taiwan and sought to prosecute those stealing its technology. It came around quickly to the threats China posed to its sovereignty and interests. But the US did not share Canada's cultural needs. It wasn't concerned with being recognized by other powers or with convincing the world of its independence (needs Canada often exhibits). China correctly understood these flaws in the Canadian character and played to them.

Canada's political class was desperate to build trade relations, so desperate that they often attributed early PRC interference to immigrant-community infighting. Long before Xi Jinping escalated interference, Canada had created a permissive environment for espionage and covert influence by failing to impose any cost on their perpetrators. That environment had grown out of government's immature understanding of the role and function of intelligence, and its refusal to accept a view of China that clashed with government's multilateral aspirations. Policy-makers didn't so much ignore intelligence on China as refuse to accept any intelligence that was at odds with their views. For decades, this hurt no one in Canada more than Chinese Canadians themselves.

The book relies on a mixture of archival sources, media reports and dozens of interviews with people from within the communities targeted by China, the civil service, political parties and Parliament (MPs). Security was a real concern while I was writing this book. Sometimes I had to meet community members in secret and rely on underground networks to put me in touch with people who wanted to tell their stories. I had confrontations with people in the community who, I think, wanted me not to talk to groups the PRC opposed. I even had a cellphone spontaneously reformat itself just hours after I talked to one of the PRC's most hated pro-democracy activists. Sometimes I met my interview subjects in remote locations, and some didn't want me using their names because they feared for their careers, their reputations and, for some, their safety.

———

What is foreign interference? I sometimes want to answer, You'll know it when you see it. Hopefully, new laws passed during the writing of this book will help untangle the different definitions used by Canada's security institutions. The Royal Canadian Mounted Police (RCMP) use a definition from Canada's Criminal

Code that is better suited to describing Cold War–era espionage, while the Canadian Security Intelligence Service (CSIS) uses a broader definition. My interpretation stems from CSIS's 2024 Public Report. I define it as covert actions through which one state is trying to advance its interests in another state. I am often asked, How is influence different from lobbying? What makes it interference? It's the *covert* part that's different, and the fact that it's a foreign state doing the influencing and its target is not a diplomatic representative of our government. A corporation in Canada might secretly lobby government for its interests, and in doing so it may even run afoul of lobbying laws. But when a state is secretly trying to influence members of a foreign public or government—and to do so outside established diplomatic channels—that's interference. The fact that a foreign state is orchestrating this influence in secret often means its interests are to the detriment of Canada's. For instance, a corporation might break lobbying laws when trying to get a development deal done, which is clearly a crime. But a foreign country trying secretly to build relationships with academics to acquire technology that could help that country corner the market in that tech and use it to build weapons that the country might then use against you or your allies constitutes interference. These are the types of things the PRC has been accused of doing in Western countries.

Influencing can also occur in the open without its benefit to the PRC being fully apparent. China has openly courted academics, for instance, with the stated aim of building academic partnerships. Yet Western intelligence services have warned that the real aim of some of these partnerships has been to acquire intellectual property intended for military use. The manipulation, deception and covert elements implicit in this kind of foreign interference might seem indistinguishable from traditional espionage. But it operates in more of a grey zone; the theft is not exactly secret, nor is it transparent. Historically, it hasn't even been illegal. If someone gives you what you're after, that's not stealing. But if someone is hiding their intentions about why they want something, it's deceptive.

The same applies to interference in areas other than technology. PRC interference may seek to influence a politician to pass policy that benefits the PRC, and individuals who are hiding their connections to the PRC state can be employed to silence critics of the CCP in the diaspora community. But sometimes people engaged in foreign interference in the community don't hide their state connections, affording them added clout with which to threaten and intimidate people into submission. Remarkably, even these foreign interference activities historically have not been illegal in Canada, and they are a key element of how the PRC has been able to continue to extend its influence for over half a century.[1]

As the book will show, from the days of Canada's recognition of the PRC in 1970, the government in Beijing has been using Canada. When the former Republic of China government assumed control of Taiwan following its civil war with Mao's Communist forces, the new Communist government of mainland China—the PRC—wanted the world to see it as the only true China, and for Taiwan to be isolated diplomatically. Even before he became prime minister, Pierre Trudeau was a willing ally in this effort, and he helped set the stage for successive Canadian governments to see only the China they wanted to see rather than the one that was using Canada to further its interests. Recently declassified documents I will discuss in this book suggest he may have been the first Canadian PM targeted by PRC foreign interference. Not only that, but the undertaking and successful execution of Canada's recognition of China also appears to have been a major foreign interference operation by China.

As I've suggested, the PRC's interference in Canada hasn't been a secret to all Canadians. Canada's recognition of the PRC left Chinese Canadians fearing that their own government had opened the country's doors to the CCP, whose terrors these Canadians had fled. Through the 1980s and '90s, the CCP targeted Chinese-Canadian communities directly through harassment and intimidation. Politicians paid little attention to a conflict few of them understood, seeing only some indecipherable internal dispute within the community. Profitable business opportunities in China were of much greater and more comprehensible interest, despite what Tiananmen Square suggested was the CCP's true attitude towards becoming a free and open society. A Canadian culture of policy-makers receiving intelligence but not acting on it, or even choosing to believe they never saw it, appeared to take root. Interviews I conducted with people connected to the top levels of government in the 1990s paint a shocking picture of how politicians of that time viewed foreign interference. Recently declassified archival documents also reveal the degree to which PRC state officials even worked with organized crime to interfere with Canadian citizens of Chinese origin and descent.

Little changed in the 2000s with the transition to the Stephen Harper–led Conservative government. While it initially sought to take a tougher line with the PRC and its human rights record, this determination ultimately gave way to the tantalizing prospect of more business and tourism dollars. At the same time, China began to wage its cyber warfare, dismantling a Canadian tech giant, as we shall see, as well as using Canada to steal some of the Western world's most important military secrets.

As Canada entered the 2010s, the tactics began to shift, and while traditional espionage and cyberattacks still occurred, China had begun to ramp up its targeting of academic institutions. China exploited the academic principles of intellectual freedom and international partnerships to strengthen the capabilities of its military and biomedical industries. I have spoken with academics who were approached to assist PRC companies, and I will explain how the PRC tried to recruit scientists to assist the Chinese military in its research on pandemic viruses.

Justin Trudeau's time in the Prime Minister's Office has proven to be the most confrontational yet, but hardly by design. His government's initial goal was to strengthen relations with China with a free trade deal and even an extradition treaty much desired by Beijing. Those dreams were dashed by hostage diplomacy upon the kidnapping of two Canadians, Michael Spavor and Michael Kovrig. The PM himself appears to have been a target of interference, as a private fundraiser after his election in 2015 was attended in significant numbers by individuals who appear to be connected to the PRC state. Soon, intelligence leaks to the media spurred the creation of reviews to formally investigate PRC interference and its role in two federal elections. One review revealed that some MPs had "wittingly" betrayed Canada.

While I'm confident the journey ahead will be eye-opening, it might frustrate you. Time and again, different decisions should and could have been made and interference taken more seriously. It is a necessary journey, though, and one that I hope will convince readers of the need to prevent their politicians from thinking Canada can ever go back to business as usual when it comes to the PRC, if truly there ever was such a thing.

ONE

OTTAWA GUARANTEES

Canada's Early History with China

THE CHINA OF the 1960s and '70s was very different from the world-beating economy we know in the twenty-first century. Poverty, famine and ideological battles afflicted the country and its people. Modern-day China emerged from the Communist Revolution led by Mao Zedong in 1949. Mao's victory resulted in the exile of the government, led by Chiang Kai-shek, to the island of Taiwan. In the years that followed—the Cold War years—China occupied a grey zone with the West. It engaged in border clashes with the Soviets while exporting Mao's brand of Communism through proxy wars in Korea and Vietnam and by supporting Communist allies throughout Southeast Asia. China was both an enemy of the West and a possible ally and bulwark against Russia. After the United States and Russia came close to nuclear midnight in 1962 with the Cuban Missile Crisis, the Cold War entered a period of détente. By the 1970s, the US and Canada were looking to ease global tensions. They both had plans to finally recognize that the Republic of China (ROC), then confined to Taiwan, was no longer the governing power of the mainland, thus making diplomatic relations with a CCP-controlled China inevitable. Canada, and specifically Prime Minister Pierre Trudeau, was influential in leading efforts to recognize the new China. Canadians have long accepted that their country's recognition further promoted peace in the Cold War. This may be the story that has often been told, but it's not the whole story. This version of history downplays the CCP's less peaceful goals and its use of Canada in achieving them. I want to present a reality that I believe is closer to the whole story. I say "closer" because much of what we know about those years is still locked up in Canada's government archives. But thanks to a recent declassification of documents, the real story of the recognition of China is closer to being fully understood.

Canada's recognition of post-revolutionary China had a lot to do with Canada's relationship with the United States. It also stemmed from a blind romanticism; Canada was unable or unwilling to see the PRC's real purpose in encouraging Canada to recognize the legitimacy of its government. China wanted to establish relations and further trade with the United States, but the Americans opposed the Communists' usurpation of the former government. Recognition from Canada was a convenient and expedient way to normalize Communist China's role in the global order and encourage the United States to finally accept the transfer of power.

But how and why did Canada accept this role? The answer lies with Pierre Trudeau. Recently declassified Foreign Affairs documents about Canada's role in the recognition of China reveal that China may have targeted Trudeau with foreign interference and influence operations. From day one of Canada's relationship with the PRC, Canada, its people and its leaders have been interference targets of the CCP.

———

Canadian relations with China date back to the 1880s, when Chinese immigrants arrived on Canada's west coast as sojourners looking for work. Some were in search of gold and participated in the gold rushes of the nineteenth century. Others helped build the BC section of the Canadian Pacific Railway. It was perilous work that had many Chinese people living in degrading conditions. By 1885, with the railway nearly done, Canada imposed a head tax on Chinese immigrants. Restrictions on immigration increased over time, until Canada imposed the Chinese Exclusion Act of 1923, which prevented further Chinese from immigrating and denied citizenship to others who were already here.

Canadians were also going to China, though most of them were Christian missionaries bound for the Chinese countryside. Generations of missionaries remained in the country throughout the world wars and China's civil war. Their children, raised in China and fluent in Mandarin and Chinese culture, were commonly known as Mish kids. The Methodist influences contributed to the Mish kids mixing religion with quasi-socialist leanings. Several grew up to occupy roles in the Canadian government, like long-time diplomat Arthur Menzies, who shared the same United Church background as men like Lester Pearson, O.D. Skelton, Vincent Massey and Hume Wong. When Mao and his CCP engaged in civil war against Chiang and the Nationalist Party, or Kuomintang, which had ruled China with a dictatorial hand, the Mish kids sympathized with the revolutionary leader's Communist ideology.[1]

The Communists had come together in 1921, originally as an entity within the Nationalist Party. These political opponents entered into a united front to combat local warlords who were preventing the formation of a central government, but co-operation

ceased in 1927 when the Nationalists betrayed the Communists
and expelled them from the party. By 1931, Chiang found himself
dealing with multiple enemies. Japan had invaded Manchuria, in
northeast China. He was now fighting both the Japanese and the
Communists. During these battles, one Canadian had a lasting
impact on the CCP. Dr. Norman Bethune was a member of the
Communist Party of Canada. Bethune travelled to Spain to offer
medical aid to Republican fighters in the Spanish Civil War and
to China to do the same for the Communists. When not tending
to injured Communist fighters, he treated people in rural communities. He died in 1939 after slicing his finger during surgery and
contracting an infection. Praised by Mao for his efforts, Bethune
has been memorialized in China ever since.

A second united front formed to combat Japan but did not last
long, as the Communists gained support in the countryside and
corruption within the Nationalist Party kept eroding its support
amongst the people. US forces continued to back Chiang's party
as a means of curtailing Communism, but the end of the Second
World War sparked civil war again, and the Communists were now
winning. The US and other powers had supported China during
the Second World War to counter Japan, but by the end of the war,
the US initially tried to mediate a cease fire between the warring
Nationalists and the Communists. General George C. Marshall
was sent by President Truman to China in 1945 to act as a special
emissary. At the same time, the US still supported the Nationalists.
These interventions by foreign powers, as China expert Maochun
Yu reveals, did not stop the civil war. Instead they indirectly contributed to a Communist victory by reducing Chiang's legitimacy
and his ability to control rival factions. By 1947, Chiang and his
ROC government had retreated to Taiwan. On October 1, 1949,

Mao proclaimed victory on the mainland and established the People's Republic of China.[2]

Western policy towards the nascent PRC was driven by the United States. The US and Canada found themselves in combat against Chinese forces after hostilities broke out in Korea between the Communist North Korean forces and the UN-backed South. The Korean War cemented American support of Taiwan as a bulwark against the spread of Communism. The US would view the ROC as China's legitimate government-in-exile for decades to come. Canada would be persuaded to change its view much sooner.

The postwar decades saw a rising sense of nationalism in Canada, and its relationship with the new China resembled other Canadian attempts to diversify its foreign policy, independent of the country's place in the Americans' orbit. For instance, after the US placed an embargo on trade with Communist Cuba, Canada maintained a trading relationship with the island nation, mainly out of fear that Canada would be viewed internationally as a vassal of the US if it followed suit. Similarly, in 1958, Prime Minister John Diefenbaker began trading wheat to China, which the PRC needed desperately because of failed Communist policies like Mao's Great Leap Forward, which had led to mass starvation. By 1961, these wheat sales would balloon to $422 million, despite the Americans maintaining a strict trade embargo on China.

Canada's early attempts to normalize relations with China were not well received by the Americans. During Louis St. Laurent's Liberal government, then–foreign minister Lester Pearson floated the idea of recognizing the PRC and the CCP as its legitimate government past US president Dwight Eisenhower. Canadian diplomat Chester Ronning recounted Eisenhower's reaction: "The

President blew up and asked how Canada could think of recognizing 'Communist China, whose hands were dripping with the blood of Americans killed in Korea.'"

Diefenbaker's wheat trade with China continued. The deals were mainly the result of the work of Alvin Hamilton from the Department of Trade and Commerce. But Hamilton ran into a snag. US sanctions on the PRC left the country with little currency to buy Canadian wheat. Canada solved that problem by lending China money. Hamilton was subsequently praised by the PRC's first and long-time premier, Zhou Enlai. Trade expanded in the years following, as would Hamilton's China brief. After he left government, Hamilton turned to advertising trade with China within Canada, and travelled abroad to convince other countries to do the same, before eventually taking up a role in Beijing as a trade "adviser." Zhou shared with Hamilton that, before his time as premier was over, he wanted to "bring the United States and China back into some form of harmony."[3]

Imagine how this looked to the US, during the height of the Cold War, as the Americans were facing down the existential threat of Soviet expansion. Chinese forces had killed Canadians and Americans a decade earlier in the Korean War, and now China was selling weapons to Communist forces in Vietnam so they could kill more Americans—and the Canadian who had arranged the wheat deals to feed the Chinese public got a plum job in Beijing as an adviser.

———

While using Canada to pressure the United States into recognizing its legitimacy, China was waging a war internally against ideological opponents.

During the 1960s, Mao was focused on his Cultural Revolution, which rooted out what he viewed to be "counter-revolutionaries" along with the old customs and ways he thought threatened the Communist revolution. In reality, he was killing his opponents, and his purge led to the deaths of millions of people, with reports of mass killings and even cannibalism. Mao believed his revolution would be successful only if it achieved world revolution and confronted the West. This was the main task of China's foreign relations, and China found itself in conflict with a Soviet neighbour no longer toeing its own Stalinist party line.

The PRC believed that the end of US imperialism and Soviet Communism was approaching, and that China's export of revolution across the globe could hasten that change. Enemies were everywhere. Mao proclaimed that "power emerges from the barrel of a gun," and China supported armed struggles in Asia (such as in Vietnam, Laos and later Cambodia), Africa and Latin America. Even into 1972 it supported anti-government guerrillas operating in Mexico. Military support aside, China organized with rural farmers against their governments and engaged students in subversive activity. A new international "united front" was taking shape in the PRC's foreign interference playbook. In 1967, China's backing of several provincial rebellions led the Cambodian government to request that China cease distributing propaganda through CCP-supported schools. China replied by claiming that overseas Chinese should be permitted "freedom of speech" and to "love" the PRC. In Mongolia and Burma (Myanmar), the CCP continued to rely on Chinese students to distribute CCP propaganda through its network of schools.[4]

The CCP's global revolution was not producing timely results. Its steadfast commitment to Communist governance and ideological export was isolating the newly minted nation and leaving it vulnerable to the expansionist aims of the much more developed Soviet Union. A closer relationship to the US could help discourage Soviet designs on the PRC while giving the Americans a regional check on the Soviets. Russian defectors were informing US intelligence that a Sino-Soviet split had occurred, and the prospects of exploiting this rift were too tempting to ignore. While the US collected intelligence on border skirmishes between the two sides, they also heard from senior Russian officials that the PRC had used the Soviet Union to help build the PRC state with military aid and advisers placed throughout the CCP government. The Soviets had come to believe that the PRC sought to supplant their hegemony in the region and would use a US partnership to overtake the Americans as the world's dominant superpower. Meanwhile, Soviet defectors and officials warned that the biggest mistake the US could make would be to aid the PRC with military equipment and technology, because the PRC aspired to restore the country to the top of the international hierarchy. The PRC was employing a Chinese stratagem of "kill with a borrowed sword"—that is, using the power of another to attack. To the Americans' detriment, the strategy left the US thinking and behaving much like its northern neighbour. The Americans found these warnings far-fetched and, even if serious, far less pressing than the need to counter Soviet aggression. The Americans chose to see the threat as they believed it to be, not as it actually was. The Russians had tried to warn them what was coming, but the US had too many reasons not to listen to its then primary rival.[5]

The military was spearheading the PRC's approach to the United States. Author Michael Pillsbury details how in 1969 Mao summoned four generals who believed China needed to assert itself against the Soviets. The generals believed that the US strategy reflected a Chinese proverb of "sitting on top of the mountain to watch a fight between two tigers," meaning that the US was waiting for the Soviets and PRC to wear each other down. Their view reflected their own "borrowed sword" stratagem. To counter the US and Soviets, the generals mused that the PRC should study the non-aggression pact Stalin negotiated with Hitler, as well as stories from the Warring States period of Chinese history, in all of which a lesser power cunningly overtakes a hegemon through duplicity.

Ultimately, more significant border clashes with the Soviets in 1969 led Mao to initiate contact with Nixon. The US did not understand that China still viewed it as an enemy and a tool to help counter the Soviets. The PRC view was reflected in Secretary of State Henry Kissinger's meeting with Premier Zhou Enlai in 1971. Zhou told Kissinger's interpreter that "America is the *ba*." The term was repeated by Mao and later his successor, Deng Xiaoping. Many Mandarin words don't have a direct equivalent in English. Kissinger's translator told him Enlai had said, "America is the leader." But *ba* has a specific Chinese historical meaning: *tyrant*.

Years later, acclaimed China expert Michael Pillsbury asked the translator if he ever told Kissinger what *ba* meant in this context.

"No," he replied.

"Why?"

"It would have upset him."[6]

————

In Canada, the PRC saw a small country desperate to carve out its own space in the world while resenting the American dominance that encroached on it culturally, politically and economically. The CCP would take full advantage.

In 1964, France recognized the CCP-led China, and the Liberal Party of Canada wanted to follow suit. The PRC's goal of international recognition received a tremendous boost from a newly elected member of Parliament from Outremont, Quebec, named Pierre Trudeau. He believed recognition was in line with the Liberal party platform and that if Canada worked directly with China, "it would be harder for the Americans to stop us." Trudeau would pick up on previous government efforts to recognize the PRC, as well as his personal streak of anti-Americanism, which was enabled by his government and typified much of his career in government. In 1973, for instance, during Trudeau's first tenure as PM, his Liberal government passed a motion condemning the "prolonging" of hostilities in Vietnam. He continually sought a "third" option to diversify Canadian trade away from the US, referencing the ever-present threat of US economic "imperialism." Trudeau had visited China twice, once in 1945 and again in 1960. His public views in the wake of his CCP-directed introductions to China served the Beijing government's interests well. In one instance, he declared he "did not dislike the people of Taiwan, only its government," with which he claimed he'd had personal experience while visiting China in the 1940s.[7] Ambitious, intelligent and influential, Trudeau was a perfect mark for a foreign interference operation that may have begun years before he was elected.

In 1960, Trudeau documented his second trip to China in a book co-authored with Jacques Hébert titled *Two Innocents in Red China*. Trudeau wasn't in government yet, but the PRC likely saw him as a rising star in law and politics with Communist sympathies, which made him an ideal cultivation target. Despite the authors' view of themselves and their journey of discovery, the title conjures an image of two people who are oblivious to the realities of the great Asian civilization. The book glorifies the PRC as the pair enjoy guided tours in the care of their Chinese hosts. They visit a prison where they are "welcomed" by a garden "planted with greenery and fine fragrant trees" and see only one guard. "This is a prison?" they ask. They are told prisoners here contemplate their wrongs, which enables the prison to focus on reintegrating them into society. They find "no bolts, no locks on the cell doors." Next they visit a commune that contains workers in various forms of industry and agriculture, but also restaurants, clinics and shops. They are told by their hosts that the state plans the commune, and the people elect representatives who discuss any changes that are needed before the state decides what those changes will be.

Marvelling at everything they witness, Trudeau and Hébert request to see how China treats its minorities. They are taken to the Institute of the Minorities of China. In this charming building bustling with professors and students, they open one door and find:

> a Tibetan girl of seventeen, with a very pretty face framed in two braids of black hair; she is playing the cello. In the next room we find an adorable Korean girl with enormous eyes who sings a folksong of her country at our request. . . . We speak to a Tibetan girl of less than twenty. "What will you do after you graduate?"
>
> "What will be best for the country—what the party decides."[8]

After being dazzled by the library, which contains Marxist texts but also the works of other authors, including a book Trudeau himself had authored about a fractious asbestos strike in 1949 in Quebec's Eastern Townships, the pair concludes:

in comparison with China, all the peoples of the earth are minorities, and . . . there would be some profit in pondering on the underlying attitudes of the Chinese Communists when they confront the minority problem . . . [W]e had been tempted to dismiss as mere cold-war tactics the solicitude professed by the Chinese government towards colonial or exploited peoples throughout the world. But today's tour obliges us to reconsider the question: for we have witnessed the respectful caution with which the Chinese tackle the problem of their ethnic groups . . . [T]he present facts lead us to the conclusion that in the eyes of the Communist government the best way of integrating the minorities into the New China is not to try and assimilate them but—on the contrary, while respecting them—to seek to make them understand the blessings of Marxism.[9]

The book fawns over multiple facets of life and politics in the PRC. Perhaps not surprisingly, the pair were not shown the results of China's occupation of Tibet and the bodies of the thousands killed by the PRC when the PLA entered Lhasa in 1959, only a year earlier, and dissolved the government of the Dalai Lama. That demonstrated another way the PRC had been dealing with the "minority problem." It's a wonder how millions were imprisoned and killed during the Cultural Revolution of the 1960s, given there were only garden prisons with no locks or doors. Or how the Great Leap Forward, which was underway while Trudeau was in China (with those communes designed by Mao to advance the country from an agrarian society into an industrial one), could have led to the mass famine that killed tens of millions of people, given how successful the communes appeared to be during Trudeau's tour. Somehow, he'd missed all the millions who were dying. But perhaps the most shocking element of this book was that it was co-authored by a man who would become the prime minister of Canada and take the lead in officially recognizing the PRC.[10]

How and why did Trudeau receive this guided tour? Clearly, his government hosts wanted to convince Trudeau that China was becoming a Communist utopia. And Trudeau, left-leaning and concerned about US "imperialism," fit the mould of a person of influence China could use to achieve its aims of achieving US recognition and support. Are readers of Trudeau and Hébert's book really meant to believe that Trudeau's previous book just happened to end up on the shelves of a PRC library he was visiting?

By the time Trudeau became PM in 1968, he believed that recognizing China was essential to ending its isolation and thus promoting a more peaceful global order. It also represented an enormous trade opportunity. The US had become more open to the idea of recognizing China, likely due to the intelligence they had gathered on the Sino-Soviet split, but Assistant Secretary of State William Bundy summoned Canada's ambassador to emphasize that Taiwan had to be supported nonetheless. "We have to prevent Taiwan from falling into the hands of the communists," he insisted. Diplomatic recognition of China could disturb the power balance in the region, and threaten not only the ROC but Japan as well. In the eyes of the US, dealing with China was a "necessary evil," but not one that could come at the expense of sacrificing Taiwan.

France had recognized the PRC in 1964 for economic reasons, but also because France wanted to prove that it could still play a role in shaping international affairs. The French government made no statement about Taiwan, only that it recognized the PRC as the government of China. The ROC subsequently broke off relations with France. In 1968, the Canadian plan was to recognize China without giving up official relations with Taiwan, and yet Canada would shift on this. By the time recognition happened in 1970, Canada would move from a "One China, one Taiwan" policy to a "One China" policy.[11]

———

In May 1968, Trudeau publicly stated that he intended to recognize the PRC. The first negotiation sessions at which the terms of that recognition would be decided began in February 1969 in Stockholm, Sweden. From the beginning, the PRC negotiators were clear on Taiwan: The island had to be recognized as an "inalienable" part of China, and all relations with the "Chiang Kai-shek gang," as PRC officials often called the ROC, had to be severed. Canada's desire to discuss the practicalities of recognition—trade, citizenship, the rights of diplomats—was met with talk of political principles. Canada had arrived with no real understanding of the PRC's intentions.

Initially, China's Ministry of Foreign Affairs (MFA) was unsure whether Canada was acting "as a surrogate for the Americans." But it concluded that Canada's foreign policy was "somewhat independent," and so its representatives could negotiate on Taiwan's status, regardless of Washington's hard line on the island's independence. Belgium and Italy had also expressed interest in recognizing China, but China had chosen to deal with Canada first. The MFA explained this decision years later, stating that "since Canada was linked to the Americans, and because the United States was our main target, we preferred Canada."[12] The CCP government wasn't interested in recognition to end isolation (as Trudeau and the Canadians kept telling themselves). It faced the threat of the Soviet military and could use the US to support its defence, even though the US was an enemy. It would be China's turn to sit on a mountain and watch two tigers fight. Mao also needed to establish that only the PRC was China; there was no other China that could be supported. Closer to home, Mao needed to cement his power over the still-fledgling PRC. Insofar as he could advance all these goals in the recognition talks, Canada was proving to be the useful idiot.

During negotiations, the PRC team quoted Foreign Affairs Minister Mitchell Sharp's statements in the House of Commons in order to demonstrate that Canada in fact had a pro-Taiwan or Two China policy. Clearly determined to assure them of Canada's stance, in July 1969 Sharp responded in Parliament to a planted question. His response was, in essence, meant for the ears of the PRC. Sharp clearly stated that Canada's goal was to "recognize one government of China" and not wade into issues of territorial claims. The PRC reacted positively to Sharp's answer.[13]

If the Canadians were naive about their negotiating partners, they were less so about their geographic neighbour. Early in the talks, Sharp authored a report that explained how the push to recognize the PRC might do serious damage to the ROC, which could infuriate the Americans. He mused about whether a "chain reaction" might occur in which other states "followed our example," thereby expanding the anger towards Canada, but he also thought other countries could follow Canada's road map to PRC recognition. For instance, the Japanese might also take issue with Canada's position, because China remained a major security issue for them; they did not need Mao feeling emboldened as he surveyed the region from the rising vantage point of his country's rapidly globalizing economy. Further, Sharp warned that in the future the

PRC could link trade to political relations and could scale back trade should they not approve of a Canadian policy. He thought the presence of an embassy in China could help direct China to Canadian business, and vice versa. It appears that Sharp, even as he was taking measures in Parliament to assuage the concerns of his PRC negotiating partners, had a knack for predicting the Canada–China relationship to come.[14]

The PRC paused negotiation meetings in the fall of 1969 because Canada did not vote in favour of China's admission to the UN. After the pause, in the ninth meeting, Canada attempted to walk a fine line between the rival positions of its most powerful ally and its new partner in Asia. Canada stated it would take "note" of the PRC's position that Taiwan is part of the PRC's territory. In the eyes of the PRC, this statement constituted agreement with their principle that there is only one China and Taiwan is a part of it. They dismissed Canada's apparent hedging on the position by claiming, "Canada did not want to make [its new position] public." The PRC believed it now had an agreement other countries could follow.

The English version of the eventual joint communiqué makes Canada's attempt to skate down the middle of this point of global disagreement very public: "The Chinese Government reaffirms that Taiwan is an inalienable part of the territory of the People's Republic of China. The Canadian Government takes note of this position of the Chinese government. The Canadian Government recognizes the Government of the People's Republic of China as the sole legal Government of China." However, in Mandarin the phrase for "recognize" can also mean "admits." None of this mattered, ultimately. So long as Canada's taking "note" didn't challenge the PRC's position on Taiwan, the PRC could do as it wished.

In November 2010, at a conference in Shanghai on the fortieth anniversary of Canada's recognition of China, two PRC diplomats reviewed the record surrounding the negotiations. They claimed the PRC leadership had in fact known a great deal about the Canadian prime minister's views. But how? In 1960, the PRC government had presented a younger Trudeau with a highly curated view of China that appeared to influence his view of the nation for many years to come. And of course, once he was in office, they did their research on his attitudes and statements, as PRC ministry officials admitted decades later, and so would have been familiar with his disinclination to make decisions based on the probable American response. But negotiations ended so favourably for the PRC, we have to ask how its negotiators had been so effective in bending the Canadian prime minister to their desires. The answer might be found with an individual named Paul Lin.

———

In mid-century British Columbia, student politics were frequently occupied with the issue of Japanese imperialism, particularly as China came under attack by Japan. Among the most vocal of students was Paul Lin, a child of Chinese immigrants who came to Canada in the late 1880s. He grew up in BC and travelled to the US to study engineering, but switched to law as his pro-China advocacy evolved during the 1940s. He changed his name to Paul Ta-Kuang Lin, a more "proper" Chinese name, as Lin himself put it. By 1948, he was opposed to the Nationalist Party and an avid supporter of the CCP. He eventually moved to the newly formed PRC with his family.

In China, Lin took advantage of extended family ties to enter the good graces of the CCP. His oldest brother married a woman named Pearl Sun. She was the granddaughter of the revolutionary Sun Yat-sen, who overthrew the Qing dynasty in 1911 and so paved the way for the CCP's eventual rise to power. Lin now had a family connection to an early founder of modern-day China. Sun's widow, Soong Ching Ling, would go on to serve as Lin's conduit to the party, because Lin's wife, Eileen, was related to a long-time adviser of Soong's brother. Lin thus had two major connections to a couple that was influential in the rise of the modern-day CCP, one through his brother and one through his wife. Connections and introductions were made, and Soong became a guiding influence on Lin and introduced him to senior government officials. Lin left the country before the Cultural Revolution took hold, but not before taking a post at the new Huaqiao University, founded in 1960 by PRC premier Zhou Enlai. This university was designed to promote and encourage overseas Chinese to come to China to teach and bring their knowledge to assist the country.

When Lin returned to Canada in 1964, he drew the attention of domestic intelligence, then handled by the RCMP Security Service, as well as interest from the US Central Intelligence Agency (CIA). Presumably, both services were concerned about Lin's connections to the CCP government. Lin took up a post at a new Centre for East Asian Studies at Montreal's McGill University in 1965 as an assistant professor. In 1968, he was contacted by newly elected PM Trudeau's foreign policy adviser, Ivan Head, and was asked to submit policy papers on China for the government, which he did. Lin began publicly commenting on the need to recognize the PRC as China. The outspoken professor's knowledge of China eventually caught the attention of American scholars who were seeking a way to thaw relations between Washington and Beijing.

In 2010, the CIA declassified a 1973 memo about Lin written by Richard Soloman of the National Security Council (NSC). The memo contained a report written by a man named Harned Pettus Hoose. Hoose had been a consultant to the NSC and a promoter of doing business with China. He also fancied himself a freelance agent. In his report, Hoose described Lin's house and study, indicating he'd visited them. He claimed Lin told him he was a "close friend" of Zhou Enlai and "very close" to the governing circles in the PRC, and that he had large sums of money in his possession. He also appeared to broker business dealings between Canadian firms and China. Hoose stated that Lin "should be regarded as a total PRC supporter . . . [H]e can be useful to some U.S. companies in establishing contact with PRC trading officials . . . but should be regarded by the U.S. as potentially very dangerous." Soloman was annoyed by Hoose, who had clearly been sending these types of reports before, and did not appreciate Hoose's volunteer work. Soloman mockingly referred to the information as Hoose's "intelligence report." More surprising than the findings of the report was that Soloman mentioned he had brought it to the attention of the CIA, "and there [was] nothing in it not already known to the Agency." This admission, from CIA files, is startling because it means the CIA had a larger file on Lin already, and it knew about his ties to the PRC government and his ability to arrange deals in the PRC. The CIA was already closely watching this Canadian.[15]

While the attention paid by intelligence agencies to Lin has been known publicly since 2010, what I discovered more recently through freedom of information requests and recently declassified documents is that Lin may have been directly influencing Pierre Trudeau and working directly with PRC officials during the recognition talks, something Canadian government officials didn't know until the talks were well underway. What's more, I found out even more on Lin and his connection to the CCP—much more.

During the negotiations, the Canadian embassy in Stockholm began regularly producing what they called "China Logs," an attempt to keep track of the events surrounding the recognition talks hosted in that city. They logged any known contact made by anyone with representatives of the two sides. These logs were sent to the Undersecretary of State for External Affairs. The twentieth iteration of these logs, which covered the period from July 2 to August 7, 1970, documented an encounter between a Swedish reporter from Sveriges Radio known only as Pier and Robert Edmonds, a Canadian diplomat working on the talks. Edmonds wanted the meeting with the reporter to be kept on background and not recorded.

On two previous occasions the embassy had been approached by media (such as Al Simon of Voice of America) and asked about the presence of a "special envoy" that was sent from Canada to Peking. On both occasions, the Canadians claimed to have no knowledge of such an envoy. The subject of this "special envoy" was about to be broached a third time. But as it turns out, it wasn't Edmonds who ended up leaking confidential information to the reporter, it was the other way around.

Pier asked Edmonds about the nature of the talks and if they were proceeding well, but then switched gears. He said that in May he'd attended a seminar in Austria, focused on China. Among the diplomats, academics and journalists in attendance was Paul Lin. Lin approached Pier at the seminar and asked if he could arrange an invitation to Stockholm, which Pier claimed he could easily do. Lin was asking Pier to help him get into Stockholm without anyone knowing. Afterwards, the conversation didn't sit well with Pier, and he clearly had to say something about it. Pier "confided" to Edmonds that he had information for Government of Canada officials only, meaning he did not want to publish it. He wanted to warn the Canadian government about what he knew. He stated that "Lin had obtained a visa to visit China and had been seen at the Hsing Chao Hotel in Peking at the same time as Ambassador Wang Tung"—one of China's negotiators in Stockholm—"was in Peking." Pier believed "that Lin had a close personal connection with Prime Minister Trudeau" and, in his talk with Edmonds, wondered if they had met when Trudeau was in China in 1960.

Edmonds denied any knowledge of Lin's relationship to Trudeau. But Pier wasn't asking—he was telling. He continued, saying Lin might be working as an "intermediary between the Canadian and Chinese Governments, with close access to both." Clearly at a loss as to how to react to what Pier was telling him, Edmonds denied knowing anything about it.[16]

When did Lin meet Trudeau? The government had approached him for policy papers on China in 1968, shortly after Trudeau was elected. Why? What did they need Lin for? Was it just an attempt to get Lin some credibility as an adviser to government? Could Lin have met Trudeau while Trudeau was in China in 1960? By that time, Lin had already courted friendships and relations with senior government officials as well as people with links to the founders of the CCP and PRC. It is certainly a strong possibility. Trudeau and Hébert documented in their book that they attended a banquet celebrating the PRC's founding on October 1, which Premier Zhou Enlai attended and spoke at, and Lin was close to Zhou by then and still in the country. That banquet hosted five thousand people, of whom half were foreigners. If Lin did, in fact, meet Trudeau in China, this banquet would have been the ideal occasion for it to happen. Given that Trudeau and Hébert were the PRC's guests and had met CCP leaders, a fellow academic with Lin's pedigree, and who was close to CCP leadership, would have been a logical introduction to make to the two visiting Canadians.[17]

Pier's questions were dismissed by Edmonds, but officials must have been worried when Edmonds shared what the Swedish journalist had told him. The embassy dispatched a secret memo back home to External Affairs, detailing the Pier conversation. It read, "Pier also mentioned that he had met Paul Lin of McGill at a seminar on China in Austria in May. Lin had asked for help in getting invitation to visit STKM [Stockholm], which Pier provided. Subsequently, Pier said (For CDN Govt Info Only) Lin obtained Visa for PRC and had been seen at Hsing Chao Hotel Peking during period of Wang Tungs [sic] return." The next sentence was underlined in the original archived copy: "Pier believed Lin had close personal connection with PM Trudeau."

Why was Lin trying to arrange a way of getting himself quietly into Stockholm while the talks were underway? Why was Lin travelling to the PRC and seen at a hotel at the same time as the Chinese ambassador involved in the talks? Pier was not publishing this information; he wanted only for the Canadian government to be aware of it. I interpret Pier's tone to be one of concern, and I can detect no reason for him to lie. But nowhere in the official histories of the recognition talks is there mention of Lin being involved. In Lin's memoir he recounts how he was accused by the opposition Progressive Conservatives of being friends with Trudeau and involved in the talks. He continually denied ever knowing Trudeau before 1970, and Trudeau did the same, even though the PM had invited Lin for dinner in 1968 (Lin said he did not attend).

The media had caught on to Lin's presence as well. According to Lin, the Montreal *Gazette* reported on February 28, 1969, that Ottawa sources alleged Lin had flown "undercover" to China earlier in the year to act as Trudeau's secret emissary to Beijing. The *Gazette* claimed it was Lin who brought back word that China would not go forward with talks if Canada retained relations with "the Nationalists."[18] If that's the case, it is clear why Lin was secretly trying to get a visa: He didn't want his role in the talks publicly known. Pier's secret message to the Canadian government then raises the strong possibility that Lin may not only have been a secret emissary for Canada but may also have been secretly working for the PRC to influence the Canadian government and Pierre Trudeau, in the talks or likely even earlier. Pier's tip, Lin's surveillance by the CIA, the surveillance by the RCMP dating back to 1964 and the *Gazette*'s story all point in that direction.[19]

If it's true that Lin was contacting the PM with direction from Beijing, it means that from day one of Canada's official relationship with the PRC, it had been a target of foreign interference. Trudeau could have been a target because of his promising career trajectory and rising status. And given that he attended a banquet in China with thousands of other foreigners, he most certainly was not the only Westerner that China had set its sights on.

Back to what I discovered in declassified files, specifically on Lin. I obtained nine hundred newly declassified pages of Lin's RCMP Security Service file from CSIS. Was he a spy and secretly working for China? According to the RCMP Security Service, yes, he was.

Lin's file is heavily redacted, but what is clear is that Lin was a surveillance target of the Security Service. He was under what appears to be constant surveillance. His appearances in media were logged, and surveillance reports tracking his movements are found throughout his file. In August of 1970, the director general of the RCMP Security Service, John Starnes, wrote to Don F. Wall, secretary of the Security Panel within the Privy Council Office. He stated that Lin "is known to us [RCMP]" and that he is "[redacted] known to have a direct link to the Central Committee of the Communist Party of China." Starnes noted that Lin returned to Canada in 1964, but it's the reason for Lin's return, as Starnes reported it, that is truly shocking. "It is established," Starnes wrote, "that he [Lin] returned to Canada on an assignment for the Chinese Communist authorities. We believe Lin's principal role here to be that of an 'agent of influence,' an advocate on behalf of Communist China." In essence, the RCMP had established that Paul Lin was tasked with conducting foreign interference in Canada. Other details are redacted, but Lin was publicly speaking about recognizing China during this period. It appears likely, then, that Lin was indeed secretly working to influence Canada to recognize the PRC. But why? The RCMP file indicates that the Security Service viewed Lin as supportive of the Communist Party, but also that he was involved in an extramarital affair. It isn't clear if he fell for a honeypot trap (in which a person is baited into a sexual relationship and forced into the service of a state under the threat of blackmail), or if he was the one using the woman to engage in intelligence operations on his behalf. The RCMP seemed to think it was the latter.

The RCMP documented in a report that Lin was meeting a "female" and that they had "prearranged meetings either in Ottawa or Montreal, and they had devised a system of establishing contact with each other secretly," which contributed to the Security Service's inability to identify the woman until November of 1969. They witnessed the pair dining at the Bonaventure Hotel, and embracing and kissing. The Security Service noted that "the investigation might have been terminated at that point with the conclusion that it was nothing more than an extramarital 'affair' except for one other factor." A passage is then redacted in the report, and it then continues on about how the woman was "doing an errand for Lin." They continued watching the pair, noticed more "clandestine meetings" and kept watching, "especially when Lin's intelligence background" was taken into consideration. The file doesn't explain the comment about Lin's "intelligence background." They next saw the pair meet in Toronto in December 1969 at the Four Seasons Hotel and noted that "they are known to have had sexual intercourse on that occasion." Starnes's concerns about this relationship are redacted in his letter to the Privy Council Office (PCO), but he also told the PCO that sources in the case were very "delicate" and knowledge of it should be restricted to "need-to-know." The Security Service viewed the relationship as one where Lin was tasking this woman to carry out activities on his behalf.

In another letter to the PCO, the RCMP assistant commissioner of the Directorate of Security and Intelligence, L.R. Parent, detailed that the secret sexual relationship Lin was involved in was still continuing in 1971. He stated that he was writing to the PCO after they requested an update on Lin, "a known agent of the Chinese Communist Intelligence Service." Lin was in China in the summer of 1970, and the Security Service noted he was "permitted to travel widely throughout the country" and had lengthy meetings with Premier Zhou Enlai and even met with Mao in September 1970, one month before Canada recognized China.

In February of 1971, the RCMP also learned that Lin was seeking to draw "influential Canadian Government Officials" closer to the PRC, but that "he failed" because the Department of External Affairs and PCO were briefed about his plans. Their surveillance also helped to block him and others over whom he "had a potential intelligence hold" from getting access to sensitive government information. But the RCMP did note that Lin's role as "an agent of influence" had "increased" since the creation of the PRC embassy. He often acted as a "gatekeeper" to the embassy for Americans and academics, journalists and professionals.

Lin would continue in this role under the watch of the Security Service. In May 1973, the Security Service prepared a summary on Lin for the Privy Council and deputy ministers of External Affairs, Immigration and Industry. It details that the Security Service believed Lin was "tasked for his agent of influence role to cultivate influential leaders of Canadian society and to create a climate of public opinion favourable to eventual diplomatic recognition of the PRC. In this respect his activities were not solely confined to Canada but were also directed at the USA." In other words, PRC foreign interference against Canada began with Lin and Canada's recognition of China, which then assisted the PRC with getting recognition from the US. The summary continues detailing how Lin spent more and more time in the US on a "lecture circuit" that cultivated academics and politicians to persuade US public opinion in favour of China. The Security Service assessed that the US was Lin's next target. He took two trips to China that he claimed were for book research, but the Security Service believed they were to receive more tasking on his influence mission. They noted how his "counsel and advice has been sought by an increasing number of US and Canadian notable persons wishing to obtain PRC visas and business recommendations and contacts." They remarked that he sought to use art and cultural and friendship groups to expose

Canadians to China so that they could be brought to, quoting Lin, "our way of thinking about China." The summary states that he received "preferential" treatment in China, the kind reserved for high-ranking officials. Notwithstanding his Canadian birth and citizenship, the Security Service cautioned that they believed Lin was the PRC's "loyal and dedicated servant."

The RCMP went on to warn the officials that they:

> should be under no illusion when dealing with Lin that his foremost interests and activities are primarily those that will promote the welfare and interests of the PRC, and they should be alert to the fact that he uses his academic position and expertise on China to cultivate high level contacts as a "talent spotter" of individuals who are, or who may in future be, of special use to the PRC.

The RCMP even noted that he attempted to arrange a meeting with Trudeau in 1968 about recognition for China, but was unsuccessful in that attempt. This, despite Lin claiming he did not know Trudeau and that the government contacted him first.

My examination of Lin's file covered the years 1970 to 1977, but it was clear based on not only what I saw, but what files remain redacted, that Lin was a high-profile and sensitive target of investigation for decades, presumably because of his ability to influence leading Canadian and Americans. So much of his file is redacted, and so many questions remain: What did government officials know of Lin? Clearly some were briefed, as was the PCO. What did the PM know of Lin's activities? Did they all choose to ignore these briefings the RCMP gave? If so, why? Lin went on to help create the Canada China Business Council. Did later prime ministers and government officials know of Lin's past activities? The historical record clearly reveals that Canadian, and likely American, intelligence believed quite certainly that Lin was working for the PRC and engaging in foreign interference in North America. (The details are still redacted.) But if so, Lin's greatest achievement may have been the recognition of the PRC, likely China's first big interference operation against the West. Given the number of individuals he could have steered towards the PRC since, it is little wonder he was treated with such esteem in China.[20]

On October 13, 1970, Foreign Affairs Minister Mitchell Sharp read out the communiqué detailing the terms Canada and the PRC had agreed to, and the negotiations officially concluded. Canada had recognized the PRC and moved from the "One China, one Taiwan" principle to the PRC's One China principle. Japanese papers, citing a Japanese government source one month prior to recognition, reported exactly the direction Canada would end up taking in acquiescing to the PRC's position and consequently dismissing Taiwan's claim to independence. Japan also claimed Canada would now support a United Nations resolution that would see the PRC take the place of the Nationalist Chinese government in the UN. What did the Japanese believe China was seeking? According to the government source, "China is bent on driving a wedge into the unity of the west and consolidating its position in the world community." The source also claimed that Canada was burdened by a surplus of wheat and that recognizing China gave it a stable export market in which to sell it.[21]

Had Canada been outnegotiated? Yes. It had abandoned Taiwan with little given in return. It seemed to have little idea how strategically China had identified Canada as a means to pressure the United States towards recognition. In his memoir, Sharp gave

Canada a pat on the back, claiming, "It is not often that Canada leads the world. Our recognition led a procession of some 30 other countries who very shortly thereafter followed our example." Further, the Canadians had viewed the talks as a point of pride in that they managed to achieve recognition in spite of US opposition. Trudeau even compared himself to a European leader of the past: "Like Frederick of Prussia, I act first, and then I find learned men who will prove I was acting out of right."[22] But the question wasn't whether Trudeau had acted first. It was whether the PM had led the world—or been led down the path towards recognition by foreign interference. Given the revelations about Lin, it appears the latter is likely.

In 2008, Chen Yonglin, the first secretary of the Chinese embassy in Australia, defected to his host country. He knows very well what the aims of China's embassy and foreign missions are. Chen granted me multiple interviews for this book. During one, we discussed the PRC concept of "old friends." He told me these are people whom "China trusts. They will not speak badly of China" and will defend it and its interests. A "friend" of China is trusted—a business partner, for example—but an "old friend" is even more than that. Old friends have a close and lasting connection to the PRC; not to the people of China, but to the CCP. Chen told me he recalled reading a file on North American and Oceanic Affairs while he was still working with the foreign ministry. Within that file he noted that among the many "old friends" of China—such as a former US secretary of state—were two prominent Canadians. One was Pierre Trudeau.

According to Chen Wenzhao, the former PRC ambassador to New Zealand, when Premier Zhou Enlai told Mao that Canada had agreed to recognize the PRC, Mao laughed and stated, "Now we have a friend in America's backyard!" Chen also explained the significance of the recognition and what Mao meant, in case it was unclear. "Canada was America's ally. The establishment of diplomatic relations with Canada broke a hole in the backyard of America. And that was piece of slap [*sic*] on America's anti-China policy of 'two Chinas' and 'one China and one Taiwan.'" Canada, he added, had created a "Canadian formula" for other countries that could be used to recognize China and "circumvent" the "status of Taiwan." China was pleased.[23]

———

The Chinese diaspora now feared the worst. With the PRC opening an embassy in Ottawa, concerns about spying came to the fore. Accusations were levied of the PRC using community and cultural organizations to engage in influence and espionage.

The Edmund Burke Society was a conservative and virulently anti-Communist organization in this period. Its persistence in monitoring for Communism yielded unexpected finds for historians. The Canadian government zeroed in on a press release from the group printed in Mandarin and aimed at the Chinese community. It claimed that Chinese cultural groups were assisting the PRC in "brainwashing" the overseas Chinese. It named the Sino-Canadian United Association as one such group. The group claimed to promote the culture of the "mother country," with mid-autumn festivals, parades and an "Overseas Chinese Service Center" under the auspices of University Settlement House, a non-profit community social service group. The authors of the Edmund Burke Society press release questioned which "mother country" of the Chinese diaspora in Canada was being promoted, the PRC or the

ROC—the latter being the only "mother country" of the diaspora before 1970. Another such group the Burke Society mentioned was the Mangsheung Child Care Society, which was denouncing other Chinese organizations that opposed the PRC's entrance to the UN.

Concerns about PRC influence and spying were echoed by members of the Chinese-Canadian community themselves. Shanghai-born Louis Tehang was a Catholic priest in Toronto. He told a local Chinese-language paper that the PRC was already attempting to "turn Toronto's Chinatown into a Maoist stronghold." He claimed that organized-crime groups were smuggling "narcotics and jade" into Toronto and Montreal, and the proceeds were being used to fund PRC influence efforts. He claimed to have been personally threatened twice, that the community was already worried about the activities of "Maoist agents" and that recognition would enable the PRC to "openly swoop down on the city's Chinese community." Others told the *China Town News* that recognizing the PRC was a "slap in the face to any of the Chinese here who escaped the Maoists to come to Canada." Others feared being associated with the Communists. One who expressed that concern was Doug Chin, president of the Chinese Canadian Association, who said that "the public image is certain to change. They might think we're all Communists and it could mean a great deal of surveillance by the police."[24]

In the English sections of other Chinese-Canadian community papers, the fears of PRC surveillance of the community continued through late 1970. In the paper *Progress*, people expressed concern the PRC would use "blackmail" against the community and that "the embassy and consulates which will undoubtedly be set up will likely become centres to coordinate the activities of Red spies in this country . . . [E]spionage on a large scale will be sure to result." The paper viewed Trudeau's claim that the world would be unable to ignore the country of 700 million as "unadulterated nonsense. It can only be floated by someone mesmerized by the extra trade dollars that are expected to float Canada's way." And though Canada could receive more trade, the authors also stated that it would have to deal with new "propaganda centres which will spew forth hatred of all things western." Given what we know today about PRC operations (as you will continue to read), it is shocking to see how accurately these people foresaw the degrees of interference yet to come.

A Vietnamese newspaper that served the pro-Communist Vietminh offered its own take on recognition by Canada—and a sample of the attitudes Canadian Chinese were facing from CCP-backed antagonists. *The National Salvation* claimed that "amidst a big crowd in a foreign country, 'Taiwan ambassador' showed his face like a lone dog, with its ears down . . . [H]e wept of his dismissal and his retirement, of accusations coming from all corners of the world, of more kick-out [*sic*] coming from other countries . . . [H]is boss Chiang was overwhelmed with pains and sorrows . . . [G]loomy-faced master Nick [Nixon]sat in the White House with tears rolling down from his swollen eyes."

W.C. Wong, chairman of the Ontario Chinese Benevolent Association, received a letter from the deputy minister of foreign affairs. It was an attempt to placate the fears of the Chinese-Canadian community, and it made an extraordinary promise—one that would prove hollow in the years to come: "Ottawa guarantees that immigrants in Canada would be totally protected and will not be interfered with by any foreign representatives with the recognition of the Peking regime."[25]

Around the world, PRC chargés were calling up Canadian ambassadors in their respective countries in an effort to build positive relations. They asked detailed questions about their embassies and their staff's views on various subjects, including the United States. This sudden desire to cultivate relationships looks, in retrospect, a lot like intelligence collection.

Canada also became aware of activities of the new PRC mission in Ottawa. In November 1970, just one month after official recognition of the PRC, A.J. Andrew of External Affairs noted in a memo to E.R. Rettie in the Security and Intelligence division of External Affairs that he did not want to "lay down the law" too quickly with the PRC and wanted to see their "form" before "blowing the whistle." He was making reference to the fact that the PRC mission was already at work trying to "penetrate and manipulate" the Chinese-Canadian community, exactly as the community said it would. The better strategy, Andrew thought, was to warn the community. That way, word would get back to the PRC mission that the government knew what was going on, and the community would be relieved to know it was being protected. Andrew also claimed the government was expecting the PRC to conduct an anti-Taiwan campaign in Canada (he did not elaborate as to how he knew this), but he did not think Canada should do anything about it, since Canada no longer recognized Taiwan. He was much more worried about the PRC engaging in an anti-American campaign due to the Vietnam War, a campaign he felt Canada should absolutely oppose.[26]

The mission made an unexpected request. The Chinese news service NCNA (New China News Agency, known today as Xinhua News Agency) already had an office in Canada, but the mission asked if they could relocate it to the embassy and extend diplomatic status to its staff. The service reporters would not be considered press until after they arrived in Canada, according to the PRC. External Affairs sarcastically referred to these reporters as "diplomats" in its internal memos and opposed the idea. Andrew went so far as to say it was "likely" that the PRC would "try to conceal the true functions of their 'journalist-diplomats.'" The RCMP Security Service weighed in on the embassy request as well. It argued the reporters shouldn't have diplomatic immunity, nor should their quarters be protected by diplomatic conventions. It sounded as if the PRC wanted the journalists in the embassy so they would have diplomatic immunity if they were accused of spying. In any event, the question of the news service being housed in the embassy was already moot; the RCMP claimed it had reliable intelligence that NCNA would not set up in the embassy but instead would occupy a space in downtown Ottawa.[27]

Chen Yonglin, the PRC defector in Australia, told me Xinhua News Agency was used by the PRC to engage in spying abroad. I heard as much when I interviewed Cheuk Kwan, co-chair of the Toronto Association for Democracy in China, which I did multiple times for this book. In a memorably matter-of-fact way, he talked about the use of PRC missions as interference centres, as if this was something that had been known for years. He spoke as someone who had experienced the pain of being targeted by the PRC for a long time, but also as someone who wouldn't be intimidated into silence. He claimed he knew first-hand that the PRC was using Xinhua as a vehicle for spying because of his time in Hong Kong. He told me that when he was an activist in Hong Kong in the 1990s, when it was still under UK control, Xinhua had set up offices there so reporters could collect information for the PRC. With no official embassy in Hong Kong, Xinhua was fulfilling that role, and it would continue fulfilling that role into the new century.

I spoke to Canadian journalist and author Mark Bourrie, who told me of his experiences after being hired by Xinhua in the winter of 2010. Bourrie's frustration was evident as we talked. It was a common sentiment I picked up during my interviews for this book, as the stories people were desperately trying to tell went ignored despite the gravity of what they revealed.

Bourrie described to me some odd experiences that caused him to think something was not right about his job. Xinhua, Bourrie told me, was operated by "husband-and-wife" teams who would arrive in Canada and then swap out after a time. One such supervisor claimed he had a diplomatic passport and was concerned about attracting any attention to himself; he had absolutely no knowledge of Canada or journalism and could not write stories. However, two subjects obsessed him. One was the religious group Falun Gong (FG), which the PRC had outlawed. Bourrie's supervisor wanted him to write stories about "illegal evil cults" in Canada, such as FG (the group is not illegal in Canada, nor does it appear to be evil). Bourrie refused to do this. His supervisor was dumbfounded as to how FG could exist in Canada and incensed that Bourrie would not write about it. His supervisor also wanted stories reporting that Canada viewed PRC policies positively. And he wanted Bourrie to collect names when FG protesters appeared at press conferences with visiting Chinese leaders. Again and again, Bourrie refused.

The journalist reached his limit in 2012 when the Dalai Lama came to Ottawa. The Tibetan leader in exile had a private meeting with Prime Minister Harper, and Bourrie's supervisor was enraged. He said to Bourrie, "I wanna know what happened in that meeting," and the journalist shot back: "Stephen Harper's not gonna tell me. I don't know, and I'm not gonna find out." Bourrie asked his supervisor, "What are you doing with this stuff?" Bourrie had written some stories on the visit, but they were not appearing on any news wires in China. So where were they going? His supervisor replied, "This is for Beijing." Bourrie quit after the visit and informed the Parliamentary Press Gallery that he had been asked to spy for Xinhua. The gallery told him it was not going to get involved. Stephen Harper made frequent trips to the Arctic, and Bourrie's supervisor went along and was caught taking pictures of the interior of Harper's helicopter. He was banned from the prime minister's future trips.

In 2017, a former high-ranking CSIS officer told the Montreal newspaper *La Presse* that many journalists working for the PRC in outlets like the *People's Daily* and Xinhua are "spies," and that they are a focus of the Five Eyes intelligence network (an intelligence-sharing alliance between Canada, the US, the UK, Australia and New Zealand). Xinhua was founded by the CCP in 1931 and remained under the control of the PRC's State Council. The agency and its staff participated in Mao's Long March in 1934 to avoid capture by the Nationalists. Mao penned over a hundred articles and commentaries for Xinhua, and the service proudly proclaims that it acts as the "ears, eyes, throat and tongue" of all Chinese people. This is not to say that many operating within the service are not legitimate journalists, nor that the service itself is not a news organization and is only a front for spying, but executive control of the organization rests with the CCP, so it can be compelled to do what Beijing wants.

But even if Xinhua reporters were collecting intelligence for the PRC, what would be the harm in one of them working as a reporter in the Parliamentary Press Gallery? Its members are hardly in the habit of keeping government secrets. Bourrie: "There's no security vetting, for anybody" who is admitted to the press gallery. He went on to say:

When you're a member of the gallery . . . what it does give
you is a pass that opens pretty much every door in Ottawa to
a certain level. You can get into most government buildings.
It gives you borrowing privileges at the Library of
Parliament . . . As a member of the press gallery you can
assign parliament researchers, who are usually PhDs, to do all
your research on a certain issue. So if you were interested in
how Canada's electrical system was regulated, you could just
ask the Library of Parliament and they could whip you up a
memo and the whole thing is right there for you if you're
doing open-source intelligence . . . You can get within standing distance, or overhearing distance, of the prime minister of
Canada all the time . . . If you were looking to develop relationships . . . [being a member of the press gallery] gives you
opportunities of access to staffers, ministers, MPs, everybody,
senior public servants . . . military, lots of stuff that's open to
media and not the public . . . budgetary briefings that are off
the record. It's more than the right to cover Parliament; it
gives you almost as much access to move along the Hill as a
ministerial staffer would have.

Xinhua was granted status in the press gallery by Secretary of
State for External Affairs Paul Martin Sr. in 1964, and it appears
to have been under watch since before 1970, given the RCMP's
comments. Ultimately, its press gallery credentials were not
renewed—but that didn't happen until 2021. For fifty-seven years,
despite the suspicions harboured by Canadian authorities, the
outlet had the type of access described by Bourrie. Its access was
finally revoked after the PRC embassy failed to send in a renewal

form. It was a clerical error, not spying, that led to Xinhua's removal from the gallery.[28]

———

From the moment the PRC was granted an official mission in Canada, that embassy began foreign interference activity against the Chinese-Canadian community, exactly as the community had feared. The government had reason to suspect that Xinhua journalists were in on it. The PRC's recognition by Canada set the stage for other countries to adopt the PRC's One China policy, grant it access to the UN and get it closer to the US, as the PRC wanted. Even though he was an "old friend" of the PRC, Pierre Trudeau may actually have been the first Canadian prime minister targeted by China for foreign interference. The PRC's interference efforts to achieve recognition appeared to pay off. All of this is *the start* of Canada's official relationship with the PRC. It wouldn't get better.

Even when Canada recognized that the PRC had begun pressuring the Chinese-Canadian community, rather than confront the mission, the government decided to warn the community. A community that was already warning the government of PRC activities did not need further warning of what it already knew; it needed the harassment and interference to stop. But the PRC would continue its activities against the community unabated as Canadian lawmakers persisted in seeing China in the way they wanted to see it, even when the roar of tanks and the smell of gunfire were about to fill the streets of Beijing on a late spring night.

TWO

A SYMBIOTIC RELATIONSHIP

Foreign Interference and Trade

IN 1979, THE United States finally joined Canada and many other countries in recognizing the PRC, effectively starting a race to capitalize on the enormous economic opportunity of a developing China. That shift led many to turn a blind eye to the PRC's decidedly undemocratic treatment of its own citizens and its interference efforts abroad.

Canada continued its promotion of Beijing's One China policy under Prime Minister Brian Mulroney, who took office in 1984, although his government's fervour for building relations with the PRC was not quite as pronounced as Trudeau's. The PRC tried to preserve its Communist style of government, ironically by allowing more foreign capitalist investment, but this infusion also contributed to youth demanding pro-democratic reforms, which the CCP was unwilling to consider. On June 4, 1989, the world would witness the lengths to which the government was willing to go in order to preserve itself, when tanks and soldiers stormed Tiananmen Square and killed thousands of protesters.

The massacre forced the West to hit pause on building business and political ties with the PRC, and many countries imposed sanctions on trade. But under the government of Jean Chrétien, elected in 1993, Canada eagerly sought an end to these sanctions and would rapidly expand business partnerships with China. The PRC, in turn, would expand its interference operations in Canada. Canadian governments continued to see only what they wanted to see when they looked at the PRC. This continued even when signs emerged of co-operation between PRC officials and organized crime. I conducted interviews with several people connected to the top levels of government throughout the final decades of the twentieth century. The level of complacency they revealed among politicians in this era who were presented with intelligence of foreign interference was shocking, and their failure to respond appears to have set in motion a culture that would persist for decades.

On October 25, 1971, the United Nations General Assembly voted against US efforts to keep the ROC as a member of the UN and in favour of the PRC joining as the only China, with 76 votes in favour of Resolution 2758, 35 against and 17 abstentions The United States voted against the resolution. Canada voted in favour. Taiwan was expelled. The remainder of the 1970s left the Americans seeking ways to continue to support their ally against the PRC.

The PRC next set its sights on the International Olympic Committee (IOC) in an attempt to gain admittance to the 1976 Games in Montreal. While the Olympic Games are often portrayed as a means of bringing countries together, they are frequently used as a vehicle for political messaging and protests. The PRC was aiming to use that international stage to further isolate Taiwan and assert the CCP's status as China's only true government. But for the PRC to succeed, it would need to become part of the IOC, assemble a team able to compete, and pressure the IOC to expel Taiwan. It would end up achieving most of these goals with Canada's help.

———

Taiwan was already facing difficulties competing in the Olympics. In 1960, it was refused participation under the name ROC and so participated as Formosa, a colonial name it had abandoned after the Kuomintang assumed control. But since then, it had resumed calling itself the ROC at the Games and competed under China's pre-war flag and anthem. Since the next Games were to be held in Canada, officials reasoned the PRC's Canadian "friends" should help China gain IOC membership and have Taiwan removed. Beginning in 1974, staff at the Canadian embassy in Beijing were subjected to steady and repeated influence attempts by the PRC. Canadian government officials responded with a non-interference stance and instructed embassy staff to remind PRC officials that states could not lobby an independent sports organization like the IOC. The PRC was undeterred. Its officials even noted that Canada not helping China would be "regrettable" for Sino-Canadian relations.[1]

By 1975, China had secured broad international support to join the IOC, though it still hadn't formally applied. Remarkably, Lord Killanin, head of the IOC, initiated discussions with nations that supported the PRC's admittance, even in the absence of its application. Canada's IOC rep, James Worrall, met with Killanin and Arthur Andrew, the former Canadian ambassador in Stockholm and deputy foreign affairs minister. Andrew reminded the IOC representatives that Canada recognized the Communist government in Beijing as China's only legal government. In essence, he asserted the PRC's One China policy and thus asserted its corollary as well: that Taiwan had no right to call itself the ROC. So much for the Canadian position of non-interference with an international sports organization.

Andrew expressed support for the PRC's IOC admittance, though he did not say that Canada, as host, would forbid Taiwan from participating if it called itself the ROC, allowing only that Canada's response would be a "ministerial decision." Andrew was counting on the IOC to work out an arrangement with China with respect to how Taiwan represented itself at the Games. If he revealed Canada's position on the matter too early, the IOC could respond by moving the Games out of Montreal. As Andrew stated years later in an interview, "We had to defend our position, our One China policy. The Americans had other ideas. They had not established relations with the PRC and did not yet have a One China policy. They wanted the ROC to go as 'China' to Montreal, and they had support in the IOC." Andrew believed the IOC had thought Canada would give in to American pressure, but "Trudeau was adamant." Canada had assisted the PRC in asserting its One China policy through recognition from other countries, and now it would assist it in promoting that policy via the Olympic Games, and it would do so in direct opposition to its closest ally, the United States. And the PM, who may have been a target of PRC interference years earlier, was the one "adamant" that the ROC not be in the Games.

———

While the PRC was pushing Canada towards its Olympic position, Ottawa was well aware the PRC was spying on the United States. Upon Canada's recognition of the PRC, fears had emerged that its embassies and consulates would be used as spy stations. *The Detroit News* had questioned openly whether the PRC had established a base from which to spy more easily on the United States. On May 1, 1975, the CBC reported an incident involving a Chinese diplomat and spying on the United States by China. A Washington-based source told the CBC that a PRC diplomat in Canada had been crossing the border weekly to collect industrial and military intelligence put together by PRC spies in the US. Once the diplomat returned with the intelligence, it was transmitted to Peking though the PRC embassy in Ottawa. The CBC report did not mention how long this had been going on.

The FBI had discovered the operation but did not want to damage PRC relations ahead of an upcoming visit to China by President Gerald Ford, so the matter was left for Canada to deal with. Ottawa had no pressing reason why it could not declare the diplomat *persona non grata* and have him sent back to China. But the Trudeau government did not do that. Instead, it quietly asked if the diplomat could go back home, and China agreed to recall him. The Canadian government would not even publicly say why the diplomat went home.[2] In spite of clear evidence that the PRC's new relationship with Canada had immediately been seized upon as a means to spy on the United States, Canada would go on to support China's Olympic position and oppose the US on Taiwan's participation.

In May 1976, any lingering doubts about Canada's PRC support were about to be removed. Mitchell Sharp, now house leader and head of the Privy Council Office, told the IOC that since it hadn't settled the China/Taiwan issue, the Canadian government would. Canada was going to tell an independent sporting organization what it should do about a member in good standing, out of respect for the policies of a non-member that was, at this point, not even participating in the Games. Sharp declared the government's position to be that Taiwan athletes could not participate if they used the name ROC or China.

Killanin pounced. He reminded Canada that it was the IOC that had authority over "Olympic territory," and Canada's actions were in contravention of Olympic principles of not discriminating against any country or person based on their political affiliation. He also reminded Canada that being on an Olympic committee, as Taiwan was, was not tantamount to political recognition, and added that Taiwan was not claiming to represent athletes on the mainland, nor did it claim sovereignty over any area governed by the PRC. Killanin went so far as to compare Canada's actions to the exclusion of Jewish athletes by Hitler in the 1936 Games, and argued it was Canada that was making the Games political by attempting to influence and set the rules regarding Taiwan.

Canada wasn't going to budge. When it became clear that Canada would not allow the athletes to compete, a compromise was reached: The Taiwanese athletes who were already in Canada under US passports could attend the opening ceremonies, wave the ROC flag and play the national anthem, but then would have to withdraw from the Games. Trudeau disparaged Taiwan and the compromise: "They [ROC athletes] can fly whatever flag they want, and play whatever little tune they want, but let them not call themselves representatives of China."[3]

Taiwan refused the offer and withdrew entirely from the Games. Recognizing that Taiwan was not, however, removed from the IOC, the PRC ambassador called Canada's stance—one taken under influence and in defiance of its original position of non-interference, in opposition to its closest ally and in contradiction of the apolitical spirit of the Olympic Games—merely "somewhat helpful." Because Taiwan was still in the IOC and calling itself China, the ambassador remarked, "Canada had essentially failed."[4]

———

By the 1980s, the Cultural Revolution era in China had passed and Deng Xiaoping was ruling the country after Mao's death. The Cultural Revolution had left China poor, with millions impoverished and millions more dead at the hands of revolutionary zeal. Deng was now experimenting with a new type of Communism, one that would begin welcoming foreign investment and free markets, dabbling with privatization and establishing closer trade relations with the outside world. Other major economies were noticing and investing, including Japan, the United States and countries in Europe. Despite its leading work on recognition, Canada was beginning to worry it was going to miss out on Chinese business opportunities. The deals that other countries were making often had ties to aid. For instance, Japan would lend China billions and get access to development projects; in turn, Japanese products were winning over Chinese customers. Aid for trade was becoming the mantra for anyone doing business with the PRC.

One of the biggest supporters of Canada joining the aid-for-trade train was Paul Desmarais, head of Quebec's Power Corporation. Energy was an area of major need for development in China. In the wake of the Cultural Revolution, Desmarais was hard at work building relations with PRC government officials. It was a familiar strategy for him; Desmarais had courted relations with government officials in many countries as he built his financial and corporate empire. Desmarais and Power Corp. was a favourite subject of Canadian media, often regarding the level of influence he and his company could wield over Canadian politicians. Author Peter C. Newman wrote that plans for Pierre Trudeau's candidacy were launched in 1968 in the offices of Power Corporation, and two months after winning, Trudeau flew out to meet Desmarais at Murray Bay. But he had the ear of more than one Canadian prime minister.

In 1972, Desmarais hired a young Brian Mulroney as a labour lawyer to represent him in a dispute the industrialist was having with the newspaper *La Presse*. According to author and academic Robert Hacket, Desmarais later supported Mulroney in his Progressive Conservative party leadership bid, and Mulroney apparently repaid the support. In 1990, he appointed Desmarais's brother-in-law to the Senate, and in 1993 he appointed his own brother to the Senate, who, upon his exit from politics, returned to Power Corporation's law firm, Ogilvy Renault.

But Desmarais's connections did not stop there. Paul Desmarais's son André married France Chrétien, thereby becoming the son-in-law of Jean Chrétien, who was at the time the minister of justice and attorney general. Desmarais's niece landed a job in the Prime Minister's Office (PMO), and his nephew became an ambassador to Washington. At the age of twenty-eight, a young Paul Martin Jr. joined Power Corporation. The future minister of finance and prime minister was appointed vice-president by Desmarais. Martin became president of Power Corporation's shipping subsiciary, Canada Steamship Lines Inc., in 1974 before Desmarais sold it to him in 1981. Both Mulroney and Trudeau would go on to also serve on Power Corporation's advisory boards after leaving politics. That makes for close personal, and in three cases professional, connections between Demarais and four Canadian prime ministers.[5]

Desmarais wanted the Canadian government to support a trade relationship with China. He argued that foreign competitors were getting into China and securing business deals ahead of Canadian companies. Desmarais served as the president of the newly formed Canada China Business Council, a group that also owed Paul Lin for its creation in 1978. Lin was known for his ability to connect Canadian business officials to Chinese political figures and by the

RCMP as an "agent of influence" and "talent spotter" for the PRC. It was not difficult to foresee the path ahead: Canada was going to provide aid to China in an attempt to sweeten trade prospects.

China had begun accepting aid from Canada in a limited fashion in the 1970s, and it was also now a member of the World Bank and International Monetary Fund. With Deng opening the country for business, accepting aid from capitalist countries was no longer taboo. By the early 1980s, the Canadian International Development Agency (CIDA) was preparing to launch an aid program for China. The initiative was not without controversy. Some CIDA officers did not want CIDA funds to be masked as aid when in fact they would be used as an incentive for trade deals. Regardless, the Canadian government was primed to go ahead. The perception of a China that was moving away from Communism was driving Western willingness to engage through business, so much so that the pursuit of profit seemed to be influencing government policy, instead of government first determining whether China was truly in the process of separating its future from its Communist past.

In 1981, Ottawa cabled plans to the Canadian ambassador in Beijing, Michel Gauvin, that would see Ottawa start a five-year aid-for-trade program with Beijing worth $75 to $100 million in federal funding. Gauvin was Canada's first ambassador without a direct tie to China. His predecessor, Arthur Menzies, was a Mish kid. Gauvin was known for expressing himself directly, and while he had grown fond of the Chinese people, he stated unequivocally, "I opposed the PRC government system." Gauvin was critical of aid to the PRC, but instead of working with him, his subordinates in the embassy told the first secretary of the embassy, Michael Frolic, that "we had to contain him. Aid to China was going to happen." Gauvin thought the PRC did not fit the model of a country in need

of aid; it possessed too many untapped resources of its own and a
population that was too well trained and too literate, with, from
his perspective, too few signs of liberal change from the government. He wanted Canada to wait and see how other countries fared
in business dealings with China. He noted later that there existed
a "mentality in Ottawa that favors China. Before helping the communists, and don't forget they are communists, why not first help
out friends?" Gauvin posed some tough last-minute questions to
his superiors in Ottawa that included whether it was right to
provide aid to a country that "spies" on Canada's diplomats and
"restricts" their movement in the country. He questioned how
Canada was going to deal with the "non-existence" of human rights
in China. He also questioned:

> How do we reconcile giving aid to a country that gives prior-
> ity to the development of nuclear weapons over economic
> development and the raising of the standard of living of its
> citizens? Why should we assume that China will not revert to
> hard Marxism-Leninism and abandon the course of reform?

Gauvin just wanted time and to see more healthy skepticism
from the government, and he wasn't convinced that assuming
China was going to reform and abandon Communism was wise.
Canada's aid package went through anyway. Gauvin was right to
ask these questions; China didn't need the aid. But Canada ignored
his concerns. (Canada still sends aid dollars to China, now the
second-largest economy in the world.)

Listening to Gauvin could have helped Canada avoid the mess
of foreign interference it finds itself in today. But the diplomat

carried no weight with the prime minister. Trudeau said rather dismissively of Gauvin:

> He was some sort of military hero. I can't even remember appointing him. He was a stubborn man. I would have thought our China policy was secure enough to endure him. There may have been some others who thought giving aid to a communist country was a bad idea, but I don't recall their names.[6]

———

Robin Sears has advised multiple political parties and levels of government on China and business. When I interviewed Sears for this book, he suspected that very little intelligence was ever provided to the federal government on Chinese interference activity in Canada. Even as the aid money and trade flowed in ever-increasing volumes, he told me, a "deliberate blindness" was at work in Ottawa—"deliberate" because, if you were in politics during the 1970s and '80s in Vancouver or Toronto, the interference was obvious.

When campaigning, he heard stories of tremendous pressure from the CCP on ROC supporters—which the majority of Chinese refugees were. As Sears put it, people "would tell you about it." Intelligence assessments of the period bear out Sears's claims. One from 1986 states that "the PRC government has continued its efforts to influence the many large Chinese communities abroad and to exploit these communities for its economic and political purposes. In Canada, as in many other western countries, the PRC uses both overt political activities and covert intelligence operations." Another assessment from 1988 made it clear that, of the non–Soviet bloc countries, the PRC "will present the greatest espionage threat to Canada," with its main focus being PRC reunification and "industrial modernization." It predicted that in the following year "competing interests between the Chinese intelligence services and the Taiwanese intelligence services for influence and control over the Chinese-Canadian communities will continue."[7] As foreign agents targeted Canadians, the government continued to devote its attention to doing business and staying aligned with China.

When Brian Mulroney entered office in 1984, he visited China and expanded the CIDA budget and the number of low-cost loans made available to China. The Canadian economy was sagging. In 1987, Mulroney released his government's "China Strategy." It consisted of fourteen recommendations covering multiple aspects of the relationship, from training officials in Mandarin to increasing dialogue on international issues. At the heart of the strategy was trade. To expand trade with China, everyone had to work together, the business community and government, across departments, all aiming to expand the trade of goods beyond staples such as wheat. In the entirety of the China Strategy, human rights occupied only two sentences at the end of the document. Mulroney would recollect in his memoirs that he mentioned human rights during his China visits, but not in a "spirit of hostility." Besides, the strategy's communication plan did not consider human rights in China to be a "major problem." It seemed to let Mulroney's government off the hook of addressing this issue, because "although China's record on human and civil rights is a relatively poor one, Canadians seem prepared to overlook this area of concern."[8]

Much of the China Strategy depended on China continuing to "modernize." But the country was showing signs of instability, with inflation spiking at 20 percent, high unemployment and revelations of corruption within the party. It was also bitterly divided between those who opposed the end of the Marxist state and those who argued socialism had to continue to evolve. Hu Yaobang was a popular reformer in the CCP who was admired by youth and university students, but he lost his position in the party in January 1987. In April 1989, Hu died suddenly, and his death would trigger a domestic crisis of historic proportions.

———

On the night of June 3, 1989, Sheng Xue and her friends were protesting in the streets of Beijing. The death of Hu sparked waves of street protests and sit-ins by university students clamouring for democratic reform. In the growing crowds of Beijing and in the government offices of the watching world, people sensed this could be the moment when democracy finally arrived in China. That sense of hope and optimism would prove sadly misplaced.

Xue agreed to an interview with me. We arranged our meeting through a network of intermediaries. She told me she was one of six individuals greatly despised by the CCP for their activism. And Xue didn't shy away from the party's disdain. As I listened to her tell the tale of June 4, 1989, and even of returning to the PRC to protest during the Beijing Olympics in 2008, I was instantly struck by the determination and courage in her voice. As easygoing as she appeared, she conveyed a sense that "that's just what you do" when fighting for something you believe in.

Xue told me she was drawn to social causes in her youth. She lived within a kilometre of Tiananmen Square, the epicentre of the student protests. She remembered how, as the night of June 3 went on and more soldiers were arriving, the protests became more violent. "We saw students throwing bottles with gasoline at troop transports" en route to the square. Well after midnight, Xue and her friends kept inching forward as fires blazed in the streets and on military vehicles. Amid the swirling smoke and the smell of burning gasoline, Xue remembered, she and her friends thought they were hearing fireworks from Tiananmen Square, now quite close. "We won!" people were shouting in jubilation. Xue then saw bicycles and tricycles heading her way from the square. "They were carrying people," she recalled, people who had been shot, and fellow students were racing to get them to the hospital. Jubilation turned to horror. Realizing what was happening, Xue and her friends fled to her family's apartment. But she just could not sleep, knowing what was going on out there. "We had to get to the square," she told me. And so, despite the military firing on students, Xue and her friends set out again and this time made it there. She recalled the enormous plaza filled with tanks and remembered thinking, "This is war."

She and other students began shouting at nearby military vehicles. A soldier noticed them and opened fire. "There was nowhere to go," she recalled, out in the open square. They dropped to the ground. Xue saw that some of the others around her were bleeding. She looked up at the soldier, and she told me she will never forget the sight. "He was just a boy," she said, young and likely terrified. Xue and her friends managed to get to nearby tricycles and load wounded protesters on them to make their way to the hospital.

One month later, Xue's student visa to Canada arrived and she would leave her homeland for good. "I've been busy ever since," she said, fighting for democratic reform in the PRC. She attempted to go back twice to protest but was turned away, though not before being interrogated. The morning after my interview with Xue, my phone automatically reformatted itself. To date I have no explanation for the malfunction, which had never happened to me before.

The images of People's Liberation Army troops firing at students left the Western world outraged and dismayed. Paul Lin, the academic who appeared to have assisted with PRC recognition and was close to the regime, reacted with anger that night on CBC, saying later: "The Chinese government had committed a crime against the people . . . [I]t was my duty to 'speak truth to power' on behalf of friends and colleagues in China who had been silenced by the government's violence." For a friend of the CCP like Lin to speak out, clearly a line had been crossed. The government called for Canadians to leave China. Canadian journalist John Fraser, who had participated in activism with the Chinese democracy activist Wei Jingsheng in 1978, wrote in *The Globe and Mail* that "for 12 years the world had turned a blind eye to the dark and evil side of the Beijing regime as it embraced the notion that a brutal, totalitarian oligarchy was capable of dwindling into benign quietude. The terror that has descended on China is neither new, nor unpredictable." Despite the international outrage, in the days following the Tiananmen Square massacre, China went on the hunt for student activists and executed others. No longer looking to take the lead on China, Canada awaited the American response.

President George H.W. Bush had maintained cordial relations with Beijing and claimed he wanted to avoid punishing the Chinese people for the crackdown at Tiananmen Square. The Americans implemented economic sanctions and a pause on high-level meetings, although the Bush administration would secretly meet with PRC officials on two occasions to discuss international security. Canada followed with its own sanctions, and Foreign Minister Joe Clark delivered Canada's position on June 30, saying that it could no longer be "business as usual" with Beijing, but neither could the sentiment of Canada's response be "anti-China." The government suspended and cancelled projects with ties to the PLA and government leaders responsible for the murders. No planned visits with Chinese officials would go ahead, and student visas would be extended. PRC premier Li Peng responded to Canada's position by telling Canada's ambassador, "We don't need you."[9]

In the aftermath of the massacre, the PRC moved to silence Chinese students in Canada who expressed support for peers back home. On June 16, Joe Clark announced in the House of Commons that PRC officials posing as diplomats might be spying on students. When Clark brought these points directly to the PRC ambassador, he denied everything. Clark claimed these officials used their positions in the PRC mission to draw up lists of students who supported the democracy movement and had them photographed at demonstrations, and then initiated harassment campaigns against them and others in the Chinese community who supported them. Clark also revealed in Parliament that several Chinese diplomats from the Ottawa embassy and a consulate had asked for political asylum. He offered to make it easier for students to stay in Canada, while the opposition Liberals claimed the government had an obligation to make public any further intelligence it had, given the Ministry of State Security (MSS) was operating in the country. Clark did not offer more.[10]

The Americans buckled. Perhaps sensing that it had no choice but to deal with the PRC in the international arena, or maybe because it could not resist the business opportunities, or both, the US government gradually normalized relations with Beijing. Canada followed its lead. In 1993, Brian Mulroney hosted a private dinner with Vice Premier Zhu Rongji. Mulroney would recall in his memoirs that "Paul Desmarais was one of the leaders of the Canadian business community who saw that China would be the key economic player on the world stage in the coming quarter century. At his suggestion, I hosted a dinner at 24 Sussex for Chinese Vice Premier (and later Premier) Zhu Rongji . . . During a subsequent visit to China, after leaving office, I was told that my family and I would forever be welcome in China, because of the positive signal I had sent with that invitation." This dinner was also attended by Desmarais's son André. The next day, Paul Desmarais would continue to send signals to the PRC and the Canadian government by hosting another private meal with Zhu and a dozen business leaders. Despite the carnage at Tiananmen Square, the Western world and the PRC were soon back to "business as usual."

A Liberal government took power in Canada in the fall of 1993. In March 1994, Foreign Minister André Ouellet made it clear, as he put it, that he was not going to get "bogged down by Tiananmen Square when dealing with China." It was now time to "take advantage of the opportunities there." It had been less than five years since Xue had watched her fellow students be murdered in the streets of Beijing, but maybe Canada's response shouldn't have been a surprise. PRC defector Chen Yonglin had told me that while with the PRC foreign ministry he had once seen the list of "old friends" of the PRC, which included two Canadians. One, as you know, was Pierre Trudeau. The other was Jean Chrétien.[11]

Shortly after being elected prime minister in 1993, Jean Chrétien told Senator Jack Austin, who was then president of the Canada China Business Council (CCBC), "Let's go to China to lead a trade mission." Within eight months, Chrétien would lead his first "Team Canada" trade trip to China. Nine premiers would join him, along with four hundred representatives of the Canadian business community, the latter group organized by the CCBC. Relations with Beijing were restored, and trade with China was now the government's priority. As Chrétien later explained, "We were ready to sell everything from subway cars to CANDU nuclear reactors in Asia's colossal markets." A Canada-wide fear of missing out was driving this fervour. Paul Desmarais had even flown to China right after Tiananmen. Indeed, Pierre Trudeau had visited China with his sons Alexandre and Justin while Mulroney was still prime minister, in 1990. Just one year after the slaughter at Tiananmen, the Trudeaus were taking a guided tour in China with CCP officials and taking photos in the square.

Human rights were not a priority of this mission. Chrétien famously quipped that he could not tell the premier of Saskatchewan what to do, so how could he tell a country of 1.2 billion people what to do? His oft-quoted line was misleading. Of course he could tell the premier of Saskatchewan or the president of China what to do. Neither had to listen to him, but he could have made clear what Canada's stance was on human rights, especially given this was the first large-scale trip to China since Tiananmen. Chrétien chose not to make human rights an issue; he was there to sell. The government's stance did not go unnoticed by the press, with even *The Washington Post* reporting that trade in Asia was being billed as the Canadian government's key foreign policy issue, and "human rights violations, while still officially a Canadian concern, are unofficially bygones."[12]

In April 1994, Vice Premier Zou Jiahua travelled to Canada. His official agenda was small, but the significance of his visit was anything but. Behind the scenes, Zou was in the country to discuss the potential purchase of two CANDU nuclear reactors. Right before Zou's arrival, the PRC made a special request: They wanted him to visit a Canadian nuclear facility so he could see the reactor working. Assistant Deputy Minister of Foreign Affairs and International Trade Howard Balloch received the request and set up the site visit "secretly." As he would recollect, he decided to "not advise Foreign Affairs Minister André Ouellet," and told his deputy minister he was taking Zou to Canada's Darlington nuclear facility "without any press or public knowing about it." If the PRC had made this request officially, it is highly unlikely it would have stayed quiet or even been approved because of national security concerns. After Zou and his team arrived at Darlington, just minutes east of Toronto, he asked a number of "highly technical questions." Canada would later announce, on November 8 in Beijing, that the Team Canada mission had sold China two CANDU reactors.

I interviewed a former senior government official with extensive personal knowledge of the deal, but I agreed to keep their identity confidential. I asked if Canada had any red flags about providing China with this nuclear technology. "Of course there were red flags," they said. The individual told me, in their opinion, that they felt there was always an immediate concern that China was going to reverse-engineer the technology. The deal went through anyway because the "prevailing logic" at the time was that Canada was continually advancing and creating improved nuclear technology, and so by committing to this model of CANDU reactor, the PRC would find itself a few steps behind. What this attitude seemed to overlook was that China's capacity for research and development would soon surpass Canada's.[13]

If these red flags didn't stop Canada from selling the PRC nuclear technology, why would the Liberal government think any differently about intelligence-related technology? In July 1994, CTV News was reporting that in January of that year the Canadian company Canadair had been planning on selling "spy planes" to China. Two hundred million dollars' worth of the planes would be sold to China's military. In the documents CTV obtained, the minutes of a meeting written by Ted Lippman, deputy director of foreign affairs East Asia division, state that Foreign Affairs had "approved a loosening of Canada's position on military sales to China, in that all sales are now to be reviewed on a case-by-case basis and approved at the ministerial level." Canadair would install Israeli-produced spy equipment in the planes, but if Canadian export rules posed a problem, diplomats suggested the company send the planes to Israel or elsewhere to have the spy technology installed and then ship the planes to the PRC from there. PRC officials claimed to know nothing of this, and the company denied it was going to sell the planes. Meanwhile, the government confirmed the sale had been discussed and they were just waiting on Canadair to apply for an export permit. It is uncertain whether this deal ever happened, but what amazed me about this story was that Canadian government officials were comfortable discussing how to circumvent their own country's export rules in order to sell Western military surveillance equipment to the PRC—or at least they were until CTV broke the story. By the mid-nineties, nothing seemed to be off limits with China, not even nuclear and surveillance technology.

Five years later, the United States would reveal why selling this tech to China was such a serious problem. Reports appeared on May 15, 1999, indicating that China had been secretly testing stolen

American neutron bomb technology. US intelligence claimed that the technology gains China had made through spying had given Beijing the "ability to develop nuclear weapons similar to the United States, substantially updating an arsenal that just a few years ago trailed America's by decades."[14] Maybe Canada wasn't directly responsible for this, but it didn't help that China had been using its Canadian embassy as a conduit for information gathered by PRC spies in the US. And it didn't help that Canada sold China nuclear technology on the conceit that Canada would always maintain its technological lead.

Putting Team Canada together took most of 1994. The government appointed Raymond Chan, the first Chinese-Canadian government minister, to work with Chinese communities in Canada and assist with advertising trade; he was named Canada's first secretary of state for the Asia-Pacific region. The team landed in Beijing on November 5. Some premiers started handing out their Team Canada shirts, while Chrétien went off for his private and public meetings with Chinese leaders and signed bilateral agreements, such as the deal on Canada–China nuclear co-operation that would allow for the CANDU sale. The trip was spun as a success for inking $8.5 billion worth of deals. The Chrétien government would send three more, smaller, Team Canada trips to China, with the last taking place in 2001.

Were the security risks worth it? Between 1995 and 2003, Canada's exports to China rose 37.4 percent. But in the same period, Canada's imports from China quadrupled. In 1995, Canada's trade deficit with China barely hit $1.2 billion. By 2003, it had blown up to almost $13.8 billion. China's thirst for commodities helped build new factories, office towers and residential buildings, and it boosted Canada's commodities exports. But those shiny new Chinese factories were selling manufactured goods back to Canada, and by 2004 Chinese capital goods imports surpassed commercial goods imports. Just ten years after Team Canada secured the sale of two CANDU reactors, China was selling Canada 44 percent more goods like electronic equipment and mechanical machinery than consumer products. So much for the idea that Canada would remain a step ahead of China in technology. Trade with China in the period represented a win for some individual Canadians and Canadian companies, who got richer, but it was hardly a win for the country as a whole.[15]

People who took part in the 1994 trip told me that while Chrétien may have been the face of Team Canada, the Desmarais family was running the show. As an illustration of the family's level of influence in China, Robin Sears recalled being part of a trip to China led by Paul Desmarais Sr. in the fall of 1993 that included the former PM Brian Mulroney. One of Desmarais's assistants asked Robin Sears if he could pass on the details of the family's private flight to PRC officials. Sears commented that private flights were not permitted to China, to which the assistant replied with a chuckle, "Just make the call." As Sears discovered, Desmarais private flights were permitted, and André Desmarais could meet privately at the time with China's leaders. The CCP had agreed to allow the Desmarais delegation to rent out the Diaoyutai State Guesthouse and surrounding gardens. It had housed Chinese emperors for eight hundred years and was usually reserved for CCP leaders to say goodbye to foreign dignitaries. Sears found it "unimaginable" that such a thing could not only be asked for but permitted.

What business was the family doing in China that allowed for all this? I was told by several people close to government leaders that the Desmarais family was investing in companies in China that would later invest in Canada, and that they had the "best Sherpa in Jean Chrétien," in that his outreach to China provided them with more business opportunities. People were hesitant to discuss what the family owned in China. My research found that the family's business ventures in China are reported to include assets they acquired from the China International Trust Investment Corporation, a "conglomerate" that the Communist Party owned, and that held significant assets outside China. Power Corporation also held over a quarter of one of China's largest asset managers, China Asset Management Corp., which managed $245 billion worth of international Chinese assets.[16]

The family's influence in China was observed by the RCMP as well. At the family's Laurentian retreat, a security detail observed two life-sized terracotta soldiers. They were discovered in China in 1974 near Xi'an and were part of the collection of seven thousand terracotta soldiers that is now a major tourist attraction. Two were sitting in the Desmarais mansion. When PRC leaders visited the family at their retreat, they made no public mention of their stay, only their meetings with political leaders in Canada.[17]

The smiling faces in Team Canada press scrums and Beijing conference rooms during trade announcements led no one to imagine the ever-increasing rate of interference back in Canada, such as the theft of information from the United States. But while Canada's leaders were handing out Team Canada shirts, foreign interference was going far beyond using Canada as a spy outpost on America's doorstep. Declassified documents suggest that the PRC mission in Canada was also assisting an alien smuggling ring.

———

In the early 1990s, the RCMP had become concerned about PRC nationals connected to Chinese organized-crime groups, or Triads, purchasing passports in the Caribbean and South and Central America that allowed them to skirt Canada's visa system. Thousands of PRC nationals were shelling out tens of thousands of dollars to purchase the passports of countries from which Canada did not require a travel visa, which they would subsequently use to enter Canada. The RCMP was monitoring the activities of several people linked to organized-crime groups in Canada, such as the Wa Hop To Triad society, the Tong Yuei, the Big Circle Boys and the 14K. With the help of Hong Kong police, the RCMP had also become aware that in 1990 the consul general in Hong Kong had worked with crime syndicates to smuggle more than twenty thousand PRC nationals into Panama. All that was required to get Panamanian citizenship—and thus a passport—was investment in the country and part-time residency. The scheme didn't appear unique to Panama. People seeking to enter Canada without having to apply for a visa could acquire a passport via Panama, Venezuela or several other countries in the region.

These schemes were so large the RCMP had no way of knowing how many organized-crime members had entered Canada. As one of their reports put it, "The fact remains that someone in Hong Kong, Taiwan, or PRC who is unable to obtain a visa because of their criminal background could, for example, purchase one of the 3,000 St. Kitts and Navis [sic] passports for U.S. $25000, which would give them visa exempt status to enter Canada or any other commonwealth country, without fear that the visa procedures may uncover their criminal activity." This could apply not only to organized-crime members but to anyone seeking to hide their background.

According to the RCMP, the looming 1997 handover of Hong Kong from the British to the Chinese had created a market for these investment-for-passport schemes. As a result, a relationship was emerging between the PRC state and organized crime, with Hong Kong stability being a major motivator. According to Michel Juneau-Katsuya, a former member of Canadian intelligence, a defector from the MSS had told Australian intelligence services that since the 1980s the MSS was being tasked with establishing partnerships with Hong Kong Triads in order to assist the PRC with maintaining an orderly handover of Hong Kong once the British were out.[18] It is not difficult to imagine the benefits such an arrangement could have for both parties. Presumably, the Triad gangs would be permitted to continue their illegal operations, and the PRC state could gain the benefits of their underground networks and street-level muscle.

The melding of organized criminal activity with PRC state officials also appeared in Canada. In a March 24, 1992, intelligence report, Toronto police documented that a number of PRC nationals who had claimed refugee status in Canada wanted to return to the PRC before their immigration hearings. Given the RCMP's concerns about organized-crime members wanting to get in and out of Canada, there is a strong possibility that some of these individuals fell into that category. Toronto police explained that a person would buy a passport from an alien smuggling syndicate for $3,000 and stay in China for about three months before coming back, and Immigration Canada would never know they'd left. To pull this off, a member of the PRC consulate in Toronto, identified in the report as Siu Cheung (believed to be a nickname), assisted the crime group. A photo of the prospective traveller and the purchased passport would be given to Cheung, who would then issue a replacement passport with all the same information but with the new traveller's photo inside. Cheung was given $1,500 per document. The syndicate would buy the passports from landed immigrants, who would later report them stolen to police. Alternatively, the group would steal them from driver examination centres, as Chinese immigrants would use passports there for ID. It is hard to imagine that this activity was not known about in the consulate.[19]

But the question remained, how was intelligence like this being received by Ottawa? I asked Sears for his insights, and he didn't think intelligence was playing much of a role in Ottawa's decisions. He speculated that "the degree to which we were knowledgeable, at any official level," on PRC intelligence activities was "pretty thin." Intelligence briefings that may have been given may also have been ignored; but it is equally plausible that politicians were just not told because of information breakdowns.

Many on that first Team Canada trip, for instance, would have believed that China was emerging from its authoritarian past, hoping perhaps that Tiananmen Square represented the last gasp of another, more repressive era. Most were oblivious to the ways in which China was trying to influence foreigners. Sears felt Canada was lacking the sophistication of its Western peers in dealing with China. The Canada–China story, he believed, "is filled with missed cues and things we chose to ignore." Deep suspicions were not present.

———

I wanted to get to the bottom of the Canada–China relationship, so I spoke next with several former senior public officials from the 1990s as well as a Liberal party official who had direct connections to government leaders. Given their high offices, these officials asked me not to disclose their identities, which I have respected. They all conveyed the same sense that Canadian governments were blinkered by a romanticized idea of a modernizing China.

One official recounted an episode they claimed was the "most shameful" they could recall. A Chinese leader had come to Ottawa, and upon arriving for meetings at the Château Laurier, they were met with protesters across the street. Inside the hotel, Canadian officials had blackout blinds pulled down so Chinese dignitaries would not have to see the protesters. The individual who shared this with me was a high-level public servant and felt that Canada was hiding free expression to make members of an authoritarian regime feel more comfortable. This debilitating attitude was endemic to the time. A high-ranking Liberal party official of the era told me that in terms of Canada and the intelligence it received on China, the culture was one in which "we want to know, but we don't want to act on it. We don't want to deal with the nuances of intelligence because it's not 'very Canadian.'"

I was told this culture had pervaded both Liberal and Conservative governments, and that government leaders continually gave the impression to public officials that when it came to receiving intelligence, they wanted "plausible deniability," a sorely abused term that I'll come back to shortly. I asked the senior Liberal party officials I interviewed whether Canada had been naive in its dealings with China, particularly in the 1990s. "Who wasn't [naive]?" came the response. "It was like US manufacturers going to China to make things cheap to send to America and one morning no one coming to work in your factory, and five blocks away a new factory exactly the same goes up and [your employees are] all working for them . . . Well, what did you expect?" Another person replied, quite directly, "Of course, no question."

More surprising was Ottawa's indifference. I was told that the "perennial complaint [among the intelligence community] within Ottawa at the time was that Canada had intelligence, communicated it, and nothing was ever done with it or about it." This complaint came up numerous times in my interviews and conversations. (It is unclear what, if any, intelligence the individuals saw or had access to not being in government. They did not say, and I did not ask so as to avoid any violations of the law.) One of my Liberal party interview subjects made it quite clear what they thought about the government's response to intelligence: "I don't think Canada has been let down by our intelligence forces. Canada has been let down by the politicians receiving their intelligence." Intelligence on China was not taken seriously until later in the 1990s, but even then, "depending on ministers and who is in charge in PCO, leaders like intelligence but are too afraid to do anything about it."

It took Canada many years to realize the PRC always had a hidden agenda of collecting information about people. I interviewed people who went on the Team Canada trade missions, including the largest one, in 1994. I wanted to know what their awareness of China was, and if they had even considered that the PRC might use the trip to entrap people or collect intelligence. When it came to guarding oneself overseas, these same interview subjects told me it was known that some men going over to China "indulged" when it came to sex, and that the odds were high that if you were "going up an elevator in Hong Kong with a hooker, you'd find someone from Toronto going up the same elevator." People worried afterwards that they had been set up and recorded, and I was told there were "officials on these trips who would say, 'You gotta watch yourself,'" but their advice was ignored. Former politicians told me they believed at least one sitting politician at the time was compromised in this way.

I asked these senior Liberal party officials whether people running for office in the 1990s were courted by organizations with close ties to the CCP. One interview subject with whom I spoke for several hours told me, "At the party level there's so much bullshit, it's a fact of life when people want to become important and close to the centre, that's why this stuff [influence] goes on." But my interview subjects claimed they did not think these Chinese organizations sought to influence nominations so much as influence ministers themselves. "Absolutely," this went on, I was told, and the ministers' receptiveness to these attempts was connected to their desire for "status," in that even people who were already high-ranking members of the federal government of a G7 country were often driven by a need to feel important.

I will never forget how all this shady activity of foreign governments influencing the political process was explained to me. The frankness of the conversation still leaves me shaking my head in disbelief about how high-ranking officials at the time appeared to justify it all. I was told, "In the nineties, the Chinese were around, but so were the Indians, the Italians and the Russians . . . They wanted Liberals or Conservatives, whoever was in power, but we wanted their votes, so it was a symbiotic relationship . . . Commercially, it was advantageous." That phrase stuck with me: foreign governments seeking to influence politicians, and the politicians were okay with it because they wanted the votes, all just a "symbiotic relationship." But did people not know they were effectively being bought?

"Undue influence?" one interview subject replied. "People knew, but we're the boy scouts of the world, and Canadians see that now." The insinuation here was that people did know these relationships could be nefarious, but that Canada projected an assumption of innocence on the world and struggled to see the nefarious activity for what it was. But I had to ask specifically about Jean Chrétien's relationship with China. Some media commentators have stated that past Canadian governments and PMs had been compromised. China referred publicly to Chrétien as an "old friend" during a trip he made to the PRC in 2023. Across the board, my interview subjects couldn't explain why Chrétien often spoke highly of the PRC despite its record on human rights and interference. Even some current Liberal MPs at the time of writing could not understand the former PM's praise for the PRC—and they hated it.

I asked a very senior party official of the period who knew Chrétien personally what they thought of the possibility he was compromised in some way by the PRC. After a long pause, they replied, "He wasn't compromised from an intelligence point of view. Was he compromised from a commercial point of view? Absolutely."[20]

My interview subject never elaborated on what they meant by "commercial point of view." They stressed that they didn't think the former PM was one to give up state secrets, and I had encountered no reason to think or suggest otherwise. I did not have more clarity and was never able to secure an interview with the former PM to find out, despite my requests. The disconnect between business opportunities with China and security concerns appears to have pervaded the culture of the Canadian government in the 1980s and '90s. I suspect this is what my subject was referring to in the case of the former PM. People were co-operating, building relationships that were mutually beneficial; how could they jeopardize that headway with talk of security or human rights?

The disconnect shocked me as a former member of the intelligence world. People had largely failed to anticipate how being "compromised" in terms of business could translate into being "compromised" in other areas. From my point of view, being indebted was being indebted, whether you could put a precise dollar figure on it or you had a more general sense of owing someone (or some country) for your financial success. Sooner or later, should that state require a policy decision to go its way, the bill could come due.

———

If there was any truth to what these individuals were saying, it meant that Ottawa had a juvenile approach to intelligence and the intelligence cycle. This is brought into stark relief when contrasted with a strategy US president Dwight Eisenhower had refined in the 1950s. Plausible deniability was a concept that enabled the president to take action on certain issues, but the orders would not be on the record or directly tied to him. US involvement in these events was also expected to be hidden. A covert action like the Guatemalan coup of 1954 is just one example of this. The concept meant the government's actions could not be linked to the president—*but actions were taken*. Plausible deniability was not a concept that revolved around a government receiving intelligence and not acting on it; that's called risk aversion or, worse, negligence.

But neglect of intelligence was the logic of the time is what I was told, and it looked to continue into Canada's dealings with China in the twenty-first century. As we'll see in the next chapter, it was this stubborn belief in a PRC that Canadian governments and business leaders wanted to think they were dealing with that led to the dismantling of a Canadian tech giant by the PRC and paved the way for a Chinese tech giant to take its place atop the world stage.

THREE

"WE WERE OUR
OWN WORST ENEMIES"

The Collapse of a Canadian Tech Giant

ON JANUARY 21, 2000, Nortel Networks became Canada's first company to break $200 billion in market value. One Toronto market analyst boasted in the press that he'd rated Nortel as his top technology stock pick. The tech giant's impressive rise was tied to the rapid growth of the internet and the skyrocketing demand for the network equipment Nortel could provide. The analyst John Wilson claimed that Nortel would continue to be "the dominant player in optical networking, both in terms of technology and market position." The year 2000 was the height of Nortel's dominance. It had a global workforce of ninety thousand people and a market value of C$367 billion, which meant that a single Canadian company was responsible for more than 35 percent of the Toronto Stock Exchange's benchmark stock market index.

The value of the company could be measured in more than dollars. Nortel dominated the corporate sector in Ottawa and had a burgeoning research site with former employees launching start-ups all around it. It was attracting talent from all over the world and creating the framework for the next generations of internet technology, 4G and 5G. It was a leader in fibre-optic transmission, had thousands of fibre-optic and wireless patents and was inventing things like wireless touchscreens a decade before anyone had heard of an iPhone. Ottawa was hosting tech-industry galas with guests who'd flown in on private jets and arrived in lineups of luxury sports cars, while big-tech money was flaunted all over the city. It was a Canadian success story and a Canadian corporate hero.

Yet on January 14, 2009, almost nine years to the day after hitting its record high, Nortel was filing for bankruptcy protection. Its stock price had sunk below a dollar. In the same year, the Chinese telecommunications company Huawei would report a 133 percent rise in profits and become the second-largest supplier of telecom equipment in the world, behind only Ericsson.[1]

How could a corporate star that was rising so quickly collapse so profoundly in such a short period of time? Plenty of ink has been devoted to explaining Nortel's fall. A study conducted in 2007 by professors Timothy Fogerty, Michel Magnan, Garen Markarian and Serge Bohjalian identified some of the "usual suspects" of corporate failures, such as a drastically overpaid CEO, a board of directors that could not function, overvaluation and news that all was not well with Nortel's books. Another study from the University of Ottawa came to similar conclusions. On its face, the causes of the failure seemed pretty straightforward, but some saw much more happening beneath the surface in Nortel's sudden collapse. Systems analyst Brian Shields was with Nortel at the time, and he believes that hacking, and the theft of company trade secrets, was instrumental in Nortel's demise—hacking that was traced back to China.[2]

––––

For three years, Paul Martin's Liberal government kept the China relationship as it was during his predecessor Jean Chrétien's time in office. But when Stephen Harper's Conservatives defeated

Martin in 2006, right in the middle of Nortel's battles with hacking, they immediately sought a complete reset in relations with China. Bilateral engagements were cancelled, and instead of discussing human rights with China behind closed doors, which really only benefited the CCP, the new Harper government publicly called out China for its human rights abuses. In advance of a meeting with Chinese president Hu Jintao, Harper claimed that doing business with China should not come at the expense of human rights. Defending his stance, he told reporters, "I think Canadians want us to promote our trade relations worldwide . . . but I don't think Canadians want us to sell out our values, our beliefs in democracy, freedom and human rights. They don't want us to sell out to the almighty dollar."[3] Anyone who had been involved in the Liberal China policy was no longer consulted, and the Canada China Business Council was to be ignored by the new government. Harper's new adviser on China policy was from Tibet. The new Chinese ambassador was not received by the foreign affairs minister for eight months, which was an exceptionally long time in diplomatic circles. This looked to be an actual reset with China, one in which Canada would be more assertive in defending its interests and values.

The PRC was not pleased with this new version of Canada. A diplomat in the Canadian embassy was quoted as saying, "The Chinese immediately want to know when the next federal election would be held, saying these were not Mulroney Conservatives," while the PRC's foreign ministry was telling Canadian diplomats, "If the Liberals come back, things will be okay, we'll still have difference, but not like this." The PRC had begun to equate friendly relations with Canada with the Liberal Party, no doubt largely due to the Team Canada missions and their attempts to sell China anything, even if the goods or technology were tied to areas of national security.

In 2007, Foreign Affairs Minister Peter MacKay travelled to China. But rather than new trade and businesses deals, MacKay's focus was on human rights, and he highlighted cases of Canadian citizens like Huseyin Celil who were imprisoned in China. The PRC resented what it deemed to be "interference" in its affairs. Further irritating Beijing, Harper met with the Dalai Lama that same year, in his office. A Tibetan flag was on display. But by 2008, the Harper government's stance was faltering. "China specialists" within government were aghast and did not know where the relationship was headed, believing that Canada's foreign policy had lost its new-found ethical bearings. Ministers were calling publicly for a "solid partnership" with China and a boost in trade. The Harper government even halted its prohibition against working with the CCBC. The relationship was beginning to shift back to what many in and around government considered normal.

Beijing tested the resolve of its international peers and partners in March 2008, when riots in Tibet precipitated a violent response by Beijing. In an apparent protest, Harper and other heads of state declined to attend the opening ceremonies of the Olympic Games in Beijing. The crackdown in Tibet was yet another candid illustration of how the CCP regime regarded human rights. But the West's response amounted to more of a blip than a principled stand. Scholars of Canada–China relations noted that the Conservatives had hoped their hard line on China would help them when it came to votes in the fall 2008 election, but it had the opposite effect. As my interview subjects pointed out, pro-CCP groups had sought to court both Liberals and Conservatives, "whoever was in power." It's plausible these groups sought to punish the Conservatives in the fall 2008 election. Harper finally broached the possibility of a trip to China. He had crossed the pro-CCP groups and the business community, whose interests had taken a hit because of the government's stance. Facing re-election, the Harper Conservatives were pushed right back to the long-standing Liberal position: Canada was seeking more trade with China.

The push for trade occurred alongside the financial crisis of 2008. The Harper government feared that an economic slump in the US was going to affect Canada's financial health, and so trade diversification again became a driving consideration. But instead of diversifying trade with like-minded democracies, Canada went begging at the doorstep of the Communist state that had been engaged in foreign interference and espionage against Canada and the US for the past thirty years. International Trade Minister Stockwell Day, Foreign Affairs Minister Lawrence Cannon, Finance Minister Jim Flaherty and Transport Minister John Baird all made trips to China within a few months. Day, who had been a fierce critic of China and a defender of human rights, announced that Canada was going to open trade offices in six Chinese cities. Further, Canada would work with China on several industries, including aerospace, communication technology and pharmaceuticals. The media even called Day the "Canadian Marco Polo" when he returned a changed man and avid supporter of engaging with the PRC.[4]

The die was now cast for Harper to visit the PRC. While hoping to announce and secure "deliverables" for media and public consumption, the government emphasized one item in particular. Canada wanted to get approved destination status (ADS), which would permit travel for Chinese tourist organizations and could be valued at hundreds of millions annually. In 2023, *The Wall Street*

Journal reported that PRC spies posing as tourists had gained access to US military bases over one hundred times. When confronted by officials, the culprits had a rehearsed script of being lost tourists.[5] It is unlikely that this was a new tactic. In any case, security concerns don't seem to have played a role in shaping Canada's ADS agreement. Government officials made that clear by insisting that getting ADS was more or less a condition of Harper visiting the PRC. But the other major takeaway from the visit would be a joint statement from China and Canada that in essence marked the much-desired reset of relations and emphasized co-operation. The draft statement included mention of ADS, and upon reviewing the statement, PRC officials did not omit it, a promising sign for the Harper government.

Where did human rights fit in the draft? It appeared as follows: "Both sides acknowledge that differing histories and national conditions can create some distinct points of view on issues such as human rights," and these can be solved "on the basis of equality and respect." In other words, human rights was back to being a quiet affair discussed by Canadian and PRC leaders behind closed doors.

During his visit, Harper met with Wu Bangguo, chairman of the National People's Congress Standing Committee. Wu reminded everyone that the two states must "respect each other's core interests, each other's sovereignty, territorial integrity, and choice of development." Harper stated that his trip was "fruitful."

Chinese media praised the visit and stated that Harper had even claimed Canada would hand over Lai Changxing. Lai was wanted by the PRC for financial crimes and corruption. He was a well-known smuggler who made tens of millions in China working in the black market. Lai was also believed to have corrupted dozens, involving the highest echelons of the CCP. He had fled to Canada and was living in Vancouver. While the CCP wanted him back to face charges, Canada could not by law deport someone who could face the death penalty, and China had already executed others in Lai's network. Lai had claimed the CCP's interest in him was political. His claim likely has credence, because the extent of Lai's smuggling and bribery was so far-reaching it is highly likely the CCP knew of it and tolerated it for years before turning on him, for whatever reason. While Harper made no mention of Lai's extradition to the PRC, Lai was in fact deported back to China in 2011 and sentenced to life in prison.

China also revealed the catch for approving the ADS: It wanted a consulate in Montreal. The joint statement was published on December 3. After introductory comments about the importance of Canada–China relations, the document set out ways of putting policy into effect, with future meetings to take place on trade and investment. Article 5 of the statement concerned Taiwan. It was a reiteration that Canada would abide by the PRC's One China policy.

Prior to Harper's trip, his government openly supported Taiwan engaging in activities normally reserved for sovereign nation-states, such as participating in the World Health Assembly. Some Conservative MPs openly supported Taiwanese independence. The Harper trip gave the PRC the chance to clamp down on this viewpoint and have Canada publicly assert that, almost four decades later, the old Trudeau policy still held. Article 6 watered down Canada's stance that human rights were universal (remarkable given Canada's role in the creation of the Universal Declaration of Human Rights following the Second World War). Now, according to the joint statement, "Both sides recognized that each country and its people have the right to choose their own path," and this included recognizing that the differences between nations and their respective histories could result in "distinct points of view on issues such as human rights." Human rights, then, could be whatever a country wanted them to be.

Articles 7 and 8 dealt with expanding opportunities for trade and creating the ADS. The remainder of the document concerned supporting denuclearization efforts as well as fighting climate change and celebrating the Canada–China relationship.[6]

It's difficult to find the "wins" for Canada in the trip or the joint statement, released before the Canadians departed. Canada had conceded that it would not promote the universality of human rights with China, effectively making those rights no longer human rights if a sizable portion of the global population did not have a universal right to them. Canada won tourism revenue from the ADS agreement, but at the cost of another consulate. Would this provide the PRC with more opportunity to control the Chinese community in Canada in another major population centre? Further, the agreement silenced any new support for Taiwanese independence, yet another major concession to the PRC. Arguably the worst takeaway of the joint statement was the message it implied: The only real principle Canadian governments would defend in dealing with the PRC was trade.

On December 4, the delegation flew to Shanghai for a celebration, the Canada–China Business Centennial Gala, with five hundred Chinese and Canadian business leaders in attendance. Representatives of major Canadian and Chinese multinational firms were there, and Harper praised the prosperity of China in a speech claiming that "China is truly awake—awake, and set to shape the future of the entire world!" He lauded the level of

Canada–China trade, and even threw in some praise of Norman Bethune for good measure.

The trip was viewed positively, though some, like Liberal party leader Michael Ignatieff, believed that more needed to be done to repair Canada's relationship with China. Ignatieff stated that Canada's relationship with China was the "most important relationship for the economic future of the country—the most important." Apparently, for Ignatieff, it was even more important than Canada's relationship with the United States.[7]

With all the new repairing of relations, the public was also beginning to become aware of other issues in the relationship that were continually at work behind the scenes. Before Harper returned to China in 2012, CSIS would alert the public that China was targeting and trying to control diaspora communities.

> Either by sending people here, or by using their embassies, they try to exercise some control over these communities . . . [R]epresentatives of these countries will sometimes just grab people by the scruff of the neck and send them back home so they can't continue their studies. We think that's a real interference with our sovereignty so we try to monitor this and stop it when we can.

CSIS director Richard Fadden took a drumming for these comments and for suggesting some politicians were getting too close to China. Olivia Chow, for instance, then an NDP member of Parliament, claimed in June 2010 that Fadden's suggestion that members of government might be influenced by agents of the PRC were "baseless spy stories." But Fadden's claims didn't seem like fiction, at least insofar as the general patterns and trends he was describing reflected many people's real experience, even if h s statement was opaque and the details behind it unknown.

In Ottawa, those types of experiences tended to be a litt e more hands-off. But the PRC's efforts to influence politicians were already known within political circles; my interview subjects in th∍ previous chapter told me as much. And it was witnessed openly, ıs Sears told me, when people were out campaigning. The outrage expressed towards Fadden appeared to be political theatre. While politicians were expressing shock at Fadden's comments, and the thought of the PRC attempting to influence them, the PRC was throwing weekly parties for politicians at the Chinese embassy in Otawa.[8]

Former journalist Mark Bourrie told me it was well known among Ottawa's political classes and press that during the Harper years, the PRC embassy would host weekly drop-ins. Politicians were known to stop by after work for a drink with pe∍rs and embassy staff. "If you were a politician or a staffer, you can eat and drink in Ottawa for free," he said. "You could hit something" almost every night, as there were events and gatherings held at several different locations on a regular basis, and the Chinese embassy "was a big stop" for people on these circuits. "These guys, a lot of them were senators, backbench MPs ... Any time I was there [at the embassy], they were eating and drinking ... it was very open ... a lot of backbenchers ... and not necessarily heavy Chinese ridings, but people looking for that scene ... and the Chinese wanted them, they were very welcome." According to Bourrie, this activity went on for years.

The Canadian government's naivety around China continued into the early years of the Justin Trudeau government. Bourrie thought there was a belief in government and Canadian business

circles that this type of engagement with China could be "normalized." These activities were not without consequence, however. In
one instance, Conservative MP Bob Dechert was caught professing
his "love" for Xinhua reporter Shi Rong in a string of flirtatious
emails. Dechert was the parliamentary secretary for then–foreign
affairs minister John Baird.[9]

———

Brian Shields was a senior adviser on systems security at Nortel,
and later part of a five-person team assembled to investigate hacks.
This was in the mid-1990s, and hacking, viruses and cyberattacks
were all pretty new to the public, outside of the movies. In the early
1990s Nortel had been just getting into creating firewalls and the
world of cyber investigations. Shields attended a regular gathering called the Network Security Information Exchange (NSIE), a
major industry event at which major telecom companies could get
up to speed on developments in internet and telecom security. As
luck or foresight would have it, the NSIE was held alongside US
defence and intelligence conferences. The timing and proximity
enabled the security sector to meet with and share updates with
the telcos and telecom manufacturers. Nortel was able to attend
the NSIE as an equipment manufacturer. It was at these events that
Shields became aware of the threat the PRC was posing to North
American companies and digital networks. He was beginning to
learn and understand the methodology of their attacks. "I gained
so much insight," he recalled in an interview with me. "This gave
me the insights of what to look for because I heard of attacks against
other companies and defence." But in terms of Nortel's prepared-
ness for attacks? "We were clueless," he said.

The major event that would come to define Nortel's failure to fend off China-based cyber intrusions was referred to by Shields as "the hack." In 2004, CEO Frank Dunn's account was recorded downloading troves of information. When IT asked Dunn why he was doing so, given they could just send him what he wanted, he replied that it was not him. Nortel's security realized that the company had been hacked. Shields, his boss and his team were tasked with determining who had stolen the CEO's credentials. What Shields found was that it was not just the CEO who had been compromised; other Nortel executives had been hacked too. To make matters worse, Shields examined logs of activity that had been kept for at least four years. They showed that Nortel had been compromised throughout that time, and Shields estimated that the hack might actually have happened a decade earlier and been ongoing ever since, mounds of company secrets going out the cyber door for years. "Where do you begin?" Shields lamented as he recalled trying to figure out how to combat this. "We have over 100,000 devices on the network, we knew almost nothing, we didn't know what was being stolen. How are they breaking these accounts?" It was mass confusion. But Shields drew on his knowledge from the NSIE events and quickly recognized PRC cyber-tradecraft. He put together reports and distributed them internally.[10]

The hackers were targeting what were known as domain controllers. These were areas that controlled essentially everything in a Windows operating environment. They were also the place where almost all account information was stored. What the hackers were after, Shields noted, was the "masterhash" file, because it would give them access to administrator accounts. "Once they get those main admin accounts, you are toast," Shields told me. Then they would install their malware. "You have 100,000 devices on your network, and they put their malware on, and some of it isn't operational." The malware would remain dormant until activated, sometimes months after the initial intrusion. The sophistication of the attack required a serious response. "When you have that level of being compromised, you have to shut it all down, disconnect from the internet and reboot everything over a weekend. But nobody was doing that. They tried to patch and fix what they could, but they didn't know if they got everything." Nortel would not shut down to protect its systems. Instead, it patched what it could find, but otherwise the infection simply continued quietly in the background as it had been doing for years. According to Shields, Nortel would not devote more resources to the hacks. Though its internal security sought out RCMP advice, Shields had a contact with the FBI from the NSIE conferences and asked his bosses if he could take the case to the FBI. His superiors quashed that idea because the hack had occurred in Canada. When he pressed his superiors on what was being done by the RCMP, the response was always the same: Nortel's team had heard nothing. Shields felt that if Nortel were taking things seriously, he should have been facing pressure to get results. Instead, his bosses wanted Shields to travel to Europe to train new employees. He questioned whether Nortel's executives had even been told about the hack, or how grave it was. But former CSIS analyst Michel Juneau-Katsuya has claimed that CSIS had warned Nortel's executives in the mid-nineties that they were being targeted by the PRC and that they should take precautions.[11]

The fact that the PRC was engaging in digital corporate espionage was not entirely a surprise to Shields. He had learned from his bosses that they believed the PRC was intercepting fax communications in the early 1990s when Nortel was trying to set up operations in China. In 1999, Shields visited Nortel's PRC site to conduct a security audit. He was told by Nortel staff running the operations that when the company first arrived, the PRC government told Nortel specifically who to hire while in the country. Shields asked his co-worker, "So what you're telling me is one out of every twenty is a spy working for the Chinese government and has physical access to our equipment?" Despite Shields's concerns, business carried on as usual.

Of the ongoing cyber intrusions, Shields told me, "We knew the Chinese attack model." He brought that information to people running the domain controllers, to warn them and to see what they were doing to protect them. Shields asked managers whether important files were being monitored to see if they were being downloaded, or if logs were being checked for suspicious activity. The answer was no, to all his queries. Even worse, Nortel was using old Microsoft software to store passwords. Security experts told Shields that passwords stored with the version of the software Nortel was using could be cracked in seconds using a desktop PC. When Shields asked why Nortel had not upgraded, he was told it was because the staff servicing the controllers did not want to deal with different software versions, and that the company did not have the staff to install new versions in the companies Nortel acquired. This was in 2007, and Nortel was using software from 1999. To make matters worse, even though Nortel was instrumental in developing two-factor security authentication, its own use of the security system was being phased out. The company wanted to save money on maintenance.

Shields learned from industry contacts about new software being used in the US that could scan memory for signs of malware, but when Shields went to Nortel's antivirus division to see if they could purchase the new software, they were prohibited from buying it because of the $2,000 price tag. A multinational corporation could not spend $2,000 to help protect itself from major attacks being traced to China. Shields was told bluntly by the antivirus division staff that Nortel's antivirus division was the "antithesis of security."[12]

Thanks to their involvement with the NSIE, Shields and Nortel were hearing of PRC-based cyberattacks on other companies. In 2004, Shields became concerned after hearing from British Telecom and government reps at an NSIE event that Huawei was aggressively underbidding British companies. In 2008, Telus and Bell were looking to upgrade their networks, and Huawei won the contract because, just as it had done in the UK, it significantly underbid competitors, including Nortel. Shields said that at industry meetings, people expressed suspicion that Huawei was being subsidized by the Chinese government and potentially benefited from information gained through major telecom hacks.[13]

Was there anything behind those suspicions? In the 2000s, Huawei did receive US$10.6 billion in credit from the Export-Import Bank of China and the China Development Bank, both of which are controlled by the PRC government. Over the next ten years, Huawei would receive credit worth US$100 billion. Huawei became a PRC "national champion," a designation that meant telecom operators and carriers were offered longer terms and cheaper loans from PRC banks so that they could purchase Huawei's products. The state's involvement in Huawei extended to the company's international deals, such as when, in 2005, the China Development Bank provided a loan in the amount of US$200 million to the Nigerian government so that it could buy

Huawei products for its national wireless network. That loan came at the extremely low interest rate of 1 percent at a time when the benchmark was 6 percent.

———

In 2019, the Trump administration added Huawei to the US Department of Commerce's Entity List, which restricted the exporting of goods to Huawei unless a licence was acquired from the US government. US and Canadian intelligence were already warning of the potential for espionage, given Huawei's connections to the CCP. Back in 2012, Michelle K. Van Cleave, former head of US counter-intelligence under the Bush administration, had warned of potential "back doors" with Huawei equipment, and she did not mince her words: "China is a totalitarian government, and Huawei operates at the sufferance of the government, and those relationships are there. Even if Huawei management wished them away, they would still be there." In 2011, Canada's Public Safety branch warned the government that foreign companies posed a risk in the telecom sector. Van Cleave ranked the PRC as the number one security risk to the US at the time. Since 2006, the US and Australian intelligence communities have *publicly* warned companies and governments about doing business with Huawei. Huawei went on to help Wind Mobile build its Canadian wireless network, helped fund a new research centre at Carleton University in Ottawa and integrated itself into the networks of both Telus and Bell, with Stephen Harper's government claiming it was "honoured" to witness the signing of the deals that made it all possible. One of Telus's main clients was the Canadian military.[14]

Within the PRC, the divisions between private companies and the government are not as clear-cut as they are in the West. As Jude Blanchette of the Centre for Strategic and International Studies argues, the corporate and government ecosystem can be considered 'CCP Inc." because state-owned enterprises (SOEs), private corporations, state financing institutions, state regulators and Communist party members are "connected through an increasingly complex web of direct and transitional, financial, strategic, operational and political relationships." Huawei is part of this ecosystem. Within it, the PRC government has a large degree of influence, which can be explicit or covert. PRC companies acknowledge that they will be supported by the government when the corporation's aims align with PRC national interests and curtailed when they do not. Companies do compete within the system, but they are "incentivized" to co-operate when doing so is in the PRC's interests. This complex arrangement benefits the CCP, which can then claim companies are structured legally as independent entities. It gives Beijing control while masking that control, and it is a system that is implicitly understood in the PRC. One PRC business community member summed up the situation: "Foreigners ... think companies are not related to the government. But in China, businesses are always related to the government."

Since Huawei's creation in 1987 by former PLA engineer Ren Zhengfei, who had previously run an SOE in China and was known as a "red capitalist," the telecom giant's aims have often aligned with the CCP's strategic and national interests. For example, in 2020 Huawei divested itself of its Honor brand of smartphones. It did this when Huawei was placed on the US Entity List, which restricted Huawei's access to US technology such as semiconductors, which are essential for its business. Huawei portrayed the sale of Honor as a "market-based transaction jointly initiated by Honor's private distributors." But Scott Livingston, a fellow at the Center for Strategic and International Studies in Washington, DC, demonstrated how the sale was arranged with "state-backed investors" alongside private ones, and was designed to save Honor from the US sanctions against its parent company. The sale allowed Honor to maintain the same supply lines now denied to Huawei and kept Honor in line with PRC national priorities, such as access to foreign technology and partnerships. Huawei's founder, Ren, called on Honor to now work to "cooperate boldly and firmly with outstanding American technology companies." The speech sounded like a passing of the torch to Honor, and for Livingston Ren's statement "in fact . . . suggests a clear recognition that Huawei and Honor are both team players on CCP Inc., working together to further the CCP's technological objectives."[15] Livingston notes that this kind of co-operation with Western companies was the main source of Huawei's rise in technology transfer that shot the company up to a leadership role in the sector.

———

Brian Shields was desperate to find out what was happening in his company. By 2008, he was engaged in memory forensics to find previous and ongoing intrusions. The software he was using was able to detect intrusions that Nortel's antivirus software could not. Nortel was looking to sell a business unit to stay afloat, and Shields felt the current CEO was likely still being monitored alongside other executives. Shields just didn't have confidence in the company's ability to effectively flush its systems. Any ongoing monitoring could help companies looking to buy the unit currently for sale. One of the companies interested was Huawei, which was, at the time, Shields said, trying to get into the US market.

Shields asked his superiors for access to the CEO's machine to see if it was still infected. Before approving his request, his superiors checked with their superiors at IT security. Shields was told there was no evidence to warrant access. He sat in his office, frustrated. And then it hit him: Shields had access to the internet activity of everyone at Nortel, so he checked the CEO's web logs. "Bam, there it was. I had activity that went to China in the middle of when he was doing some Yahoo stuff that didn't belong there at all. It should not have been there—this was a burst of activity, and he has a problem on his computer."

Shields went back to his IT security superiors and presented his evidence that this recurring burst of information bound for China was not being sent by the CEO, and it had been recurring over the past two months. He said he will never forget the response he received: "Mike Z. [Zafirovski] is a very busy man. We're not going to bother him with this." Shields pleaded that a memory dump of the CEO's machine would take minutes, and Zafirovski would not even know. But he was refused again.[16]

Shields was determined to identify and trace the source of Nortel's constant intrusions. After the original hack, he and his team had reset six passwords. In 2009, he found that, to his credit, the hackers did not know that he and his teammates were on to them. He acquired software from another industry expert who was providing services to US government agencies, and Shields managed to figure out the hackers' "beacon," in essence a way to identify them through their reuse of infrastructure. Shields watched for activity on firewall logs after resetting passwords and noticed that the activity on hacked machines stopped. Six months passed before the activity began again. Shields recalled that at NSIE meetings, industry and intelligence experts explained that whenever PRC hackers suspected you were on to them, they would shut everything down to prevent you from identifying them. Their standard waiting period before they resumed? Six months. Like clockwork, after six months, Shields noted, "Bam, you get some traffic. Every month it would change; different computers were doing it."

He learned from these same US industry peers that the hackers were using a virtual remote connection linked to a server farm located in China with fourteen servers in it. This also connected to a bulletin board site at a school in Beijing. The school was Tsinghua University.[17]

———

Tsinghua University was China's top engineering school. Cyber-attacks against the Tibetan community in India, the Alaskan state government and even the German carmaker Daimler had all been traced back to this computer science hotbed. Research wings of Tsinghua University were also connected to PRC bodies that had a history of stealing American technology. Tsinghua University's Office of Scientific Research and Development met in May 2018 with PRC investment company China International Trust and Investment Company (CITIC) and CCP members. This meeting centred on the co-operation between research and industry in China in the interests of the country's advancement. Going back to 1999, the Select Committee on US National Security and Military/Commercial Concerns with the PRC (what was known as the "Cox Report") determined that CITIC was connected to PLA secret operations and the stealing of sensitive US technology. The report noted that CITIC "reported directly to the highest level of the PRC government."

The chairman at the time, Wang Jun, was also president of Polytechnologies Corporation, an arms trading company whose most profitable section was owned by the PLA. Wang was known publicly in the US for his role in an indictment of Polytechnologies connected to a 1996 attempt to smuggle two thousand AK-47s into the United States.

Tsinghua's Institute of Information Systems and Engineering is also connected to China's National 863 and 973 programs. These programs centre on boosting China's key technology industries in order to obtain global superiority. They also made it easier for the PRC to covertly steal intellectual property so the programs could meet their targets. André Desmarais of Canada's Power Corp joined the board of CITIC Pacific in December 1997 and, according to the company's 1999 annual report, was also a board member in 1999.[18]

Shields's industry contacts shared a report they put together in 2011 about "the hack" for Bloomberg LP, which was subsequently shared with me. It connected the hacker not only to Tsinghua but also to the Mitzuki Community, a site frequented by current and former students of the university. The report even mentions that the "attacker" read a message from a colleague while Shields's contact was tracking them at the time. The "attacker's" colleague was a woman who was working for a PRC state-owned company, and while she was making a lot of money, she was also spending a lot and in debt, and wanted to go to graduate school. To the extent that the "attacker" was in a similar situation, it could mean they were a young professional, well-connected but also possibly in need of money and engaging in hacking as a source of income. What's more, the report noted that the Nortel machine that contained the software connected to the "attacker" was not exactly hidden, and that the user of it should be investigated for the possibility that the Nortel hack was an "inside job." After all, Nortel sought the kind of grads Tsinghua produced, and directly advertised to them.[19]

The connections between Tsinghua and Nortel did not stop at advertising to grads or even the hack. Going back to 2001, Nortel was engaged in a research partnership with the university. Their joint research focused on speech recognition technology, the same technology that ended up being used to conduct automated surveillance over telephones. It also provided fibre-optic networks that would be used in the surveillance of PRC citizens. Nortel had partnered with a PRC university where the technology would be used for PRC state surveillance, and students at this same university were quite likely assisting the PRC in surveilling Nortel and stealing its technology.

Not all of Nortel's intrusions were linked to Tsinghua. In 2013, the cybersecurity firm Mandiant identified that Unit 61398, a well-known cyber hacking unit that works for the PLA to target Japanese and American corporations, had also attacked Nortel.

After Shields found the PRC "beacon," he asked his IT superiors to set up a type of "sniffer" to monitor the suspicious data going out the door. He was again refused. Nortel had a general policy against surveilling staff communications, and it would not change it.[20]

Nortel was facing more than cyberattacks. In the early 2000s, around the same time as "the hack," Shields and other Nortel corporate security members he spoke with recalled an incident they could not forget. A piece of networking equipment, valued at approximately $60,000, was delivered to a Nortel repair and return facility in Raleigh, North Carolina. The staff handling the return promptly notified Nortel security investigators because they could see that the equipment had been taken apart and reassembled, a clear indicator that someone had been studying it for purposes of reverse engineering. Nortel fraud and security investigators believed the company returning the equipment was a front company working on behalf of a PRC telecom company and reverse-engineering Nortel products. To add insult to injury, the company demanded a refund, claiming the equipment did not work (after they'd disassembled it), even though the company hadn't even paid for the equipment, which was purchased on credit.[21]

Similar incidents were alleged to be happening overseas. *The Wall Street Journal* (*WSJ*) reported that Huawei set up an office in Sweden across the street from rival Ericsson and operated there for four years, but under the name "Atelier" to hide its presence. Robert Reid, a former contract engineer who worked in the Swedish office from 2002 to 2003, told the *WSJ* that Huawei "spent all their resources stealing technology, you'd steal a motherboard, bring it back and they'd reverse engineer it."

In 2003, Huawei was sued by Cisco. Cisco maintained that Huawei had even stolen product manuals, which were reproduced right down to spelling errors that had appeared in Cisco's original manuals. Chad Reynolds, a former Huawei HR manager, said in the court filing for the Cisco suit that "Huawei couldn't release its routers for shipment until it fixed a substantial number of the common Cisco bugs contained in the Huawei routers"; otherwise, it would reveal its exact duplication of the Cisco technology.

Huawei settled its lawsuit with Cisco in 2004 after admitting it copied some of Cisco's router software.

In 2009, Huawei was accused of stealing antenna technology critical in 5G from wireless company Quintel, who sued and then settled in 2018. In 2010, Motorola sued Huawei after finding that employees were sending documents to the Chinese tech giant One of these employees was arrested at O'Hare International Airport in Chicago with a thousand documents. She had purchased a one-way ticket to Beijing. Motorola dropped its lawsuit in 2012. T-Mobile won a lawsuit against Huawei in 2017 after Huawei stole a robot T-Mobile used to test mobile phones. In July 2013, Huawei had tried to argue that rogue employees were responsible for that theft, but the indictment documented it was company policy, and that "no employees would be punished for taking actions in accordance to the policy." In response to all these allegations, Huawei told the *WSJ* that it "doesn't spy for any government" and that no evidence of espionage was ever presented by anyone. They told the news outlet that "we respect the integrity of intellectual property rights—for our own business, as well as peer, partner and competitor companies."[22]

———

In the late 2000s, Nortel's prospects for survival looked bleak. Shields was party to a proposal for a merger with Huawei birthed by company lawyers. The rationale, as the lawyers explained to Shields, was "it was better to be in bed with the devil than out of business." But Huawei would ultimately rebuff the Canadians. Experts have maintained that Nortel's poor management was the major contributor to its downfall, and there's little doubt this was a major factor. A University of Ottawa study that investigated Nortel's demise put the blame largely on the shoulders of Nortel management. The study claimed it found no evidence of hacking or espionage. But a history of hacking and intrusions is undeniable, and Shields contended that the study authors never even spoke to him, one of the central people tasked with investigating the hacks. Perhaps the same poor management that experts believe sank the company extends to management's failure to take Nortel's security seriously. In retrospect, it seems unfathomable that a tech giant would not take care to safeguard its intellectual property (IP) against digital intrusion and theft. The loss of trade secrets and IP in today's advanced economies means a loss of hundreds of billions of dollars, enough to noticeably affect the GDP of a country like Canada. Documents stolen from Nortel had titles such as "Road-Map Values and Challenges to Nortel," "Value Chain Dynamics & Industry Structure," "Photonic Crystals and Large Scale Integration," "Switching and Tuning Highly Integrated Optical Circuits" and "Speed Data over Universal Mobile Telecommunications Service." These were road maps to communications technology that would form future 3G, 4G and 5G networks. Shields recalled that these documents represented the "crown jewels of Nortel R&D. It was the future. And the only entity that could benefit from those kinds of documents being stolen is a competitor." Huawei has repeatedly said that it "strongly denies benefitting from the hacking of Nortel" and has told Global News that it has never "been accused of wrongdoing," complies with all laws and will not spy on Canadians.[23]

———

The failure to take cybersecurity seriously helped destroy one of Canada's most successful companies. But that same failure to recognize intrusion and interference when it was plainly occurring was hardly exclusive to private enterprise and ambitious politicians. Years after Nortel's doors closed, and as the company's campus in Ottawa sat abandoned, Canada's Department of National Defence (DND) made a variation of the same mistake.

Looking to acquire a new facility, DND considered Nortel's abandoned campus and figured it would be a good fit. The deal was struck, and DND prepared to move in. But the *Ottawa Citizen* noted that while getting the former Nortel campus ready, DND staff had discovered eavesdropping devices. A spokesperson for the defence minister refuted the claim, but the *Citizen* found that government documents from a year earlier were already sounding the alarm about security at the site, noting that because people were aware of DND's impending move, securing the facility would now be more difficult. Defence Minister Peter McKay was told that "this not only raises the level of difficulty of verifying appropriate security safeguards in the future, it will probably dramatically increase security costs and cause delays to reach full operational capability." In press briefings, DND staff again maintained that no bugs were found, but added the caveat that DND had performed only limited sweeps and could not speak to what other security agencies might have found. In 2016, Vice-Admiral Mark Norman, vice chief of the defence staff, said about the Nortel site and bugs, "Anything that was there was legacy to what I would characterize as industrial activity and we are completely satisfied now that this is a site we are able to move into and it meets all of our security requirements. I am assured anything that was there is no longer there . . . It was all legacy, old-school stuff associated with the previous occupant."

DND staff told the *Citizen* off the record that Norman's convoluted statement was a veiled admission that bugs had been found but they were no longer operational.

Keith Murphy, CEO of the information security company Defence Intelligence, said in 2013 that the former Nortel site was "not a suitable home for DND." He said it "seems an odd choice to choose to move an organization of that nature into a site that you know was compromised and a victim of espionage." A billion dollars was allotted for the move. Retired Lieutenant General Andrew Leslie said in 2013 that "spending $1 billion on a new headquarters, even if it's state-of-the-art—and of course, it isn't—is a really bad idea." So, after it appeared that bugs had been found at the Nortel site and the publicizing of the move created security risks for the new headquarters, DND moved in.[24]

I asked Shields if he saw any similarities between the Canadian government's lack of attention to and action on PRC foreign interference and espionage and Nortel's failure to safeguard and protect the company when it had the chance. "One hundred percent," he said. The whole incident at Nortel left him feeling "sick." This failure bears more than a little resemblance to Canada's failure more generally to protect itself against the PRC's covert intrusions. As Michel Juneau-Katsuya, the former CSIS analyst, said when Huawei made its deals with Telus and Bell, "Unfortunately, the PMO is very nonchalant when it comes to security. They have an agenda, a political agenda ... and they disregard some of the warnings coming from the official agencies."

What had started with the Harper government's attempt to get tougher with the PRC had, within a few years, devolved into more of the same acquiescence in exchange for opportunities for Canadian business. China received a new consulate in Canada and had Canada recommit to its One China policy. In dealing with China, Canada had lost again.

Warnings of foreign interference were starting to find their way to the public, and politicians responded with faux outrage at the idea that anyone in their ranks could be influenced or corrupted by Beijing. But with Canada hell-bent on securing PRC business, and politicians' willingness to be wined and dined by the same country that was secretly tearing its multinational tech giant to bits, it was becoming impossible to believe that interference wasn't real.

Throughout the 2000s, Canada would face not only cyberattacks being conducted by the PRC but espionage attempts with people offering their services directly to the Chinese mission in Canada. Examples of this emerged through the rise of PRC hostage diplomacy—years before the Meng affair—and still Canada was not taking a more serious stance on China. I'll give the final word to Shields, whose description of Nortel's failure to protect itself could easily be applied to the Canadian government's lack of action: "We were our own worst enemies."[25]

FOUR

COUNTING THE SU BINS

Research Espionage

IN SEPTEMBER 2008, Shishir Nagaraja and Greg Walton entered the offices of the Dalai Lama in India. They had been sent by Rafal Rohozinski of SecDev, a digital security firm, to investigate a mysterious computer problem. UK-based SecDev was part of the Information Warfare Monitor, which also included founder Ron Deibert and other researchers from the University of Toronto's Citizen Lab. The staff at SecDev believed the Dalai Lama's computers might be infected with some type of worm or malware. SecDev had worked with Tibet's government-in-exile before, and Nagaraja and Walton convinced the Dalai Lama's staff to let them run a program called WireShark on their network to seek out malware. "We knew there was malware . . . but we had no idea what it could do or what it was actually doing," Nagaraja recalled. With the help of Toronto researchers, they would soon find that this malware spanned computers across the globe, including in Canada, and was linked back to China.

Canada was about to get a glimpse of just how pervasive the PRC's cyberattacks were, which makes what was allowed to occur at Nortel even more difficult to fathom. SecDev and Citizen Lab would slowly uncover this web of infected machines linked by malicious code they dubbed GhostNet. Identifying this code provided them with just a sampling of the hacking coming out of China. This chapter and the two that follow will delve into the multifaceted ways China has targeted Canada for interference and espionage—through the cyber realm and through HUMINT (using human intelligence, that is, sources working for the PRC)—as well as the ways China began utilizing hostage diplomacy.

In 2009, Canada endured repeated attacks by PRC hackers, presumably working for the CCP, given what and who the targets were. These occurred while the Harper government was trying to improve relations with China in order to secure business deals, even accepting pandas from China in 2013 as a gesture of goodwill. How much had China been stealing? In 2012, National Security Agency (NSA) director Keith Alexander called China's incessant theft of technology "the greatest transfer of wealth in human history." Even James Dyson publicly stated that the PRC stole designs for his pricey vacuums. Paint manufacturer Dupont noted the PRC had stolen the trade secrets for the colour white.[1] Cyber intrusions were just one method of attack, as the PRC continued with traditional espionage using collectors and sources (people offering their services to a foreign state to spy) as well as non-traditional methods, such as researchers looking for fame and recognition in the PRC by bringing back highly valued Western research—up to and including sensitive information about some of the world's deadliest viruses.

———

When Nagaraja and Watson arrived to investigate, the staff at the Dalai Lama's offices were reluctant to provide them with much access. "I am local," Nagaraja said to reassure them. "I can speak the language and chat people up and they let their guard down."

Eventually the pair were allowed to run their WireShark software. Similar to what Shields would later use at Nortel, it scanned the traffic coming and going from the Dalai Lama's computers without actually looking at the documents themselves. The pair worked intensively for three fourteen-hour days while being closely watched by staff. The intensive scrutiny was impairing Nagaraja's ability to do his job, but just as he was getting really tired of being supervised, he and Watson made a discovery.

Nagaraja watched as someone remotely ordered the infected code to retrieve a particular file from the Dalai Lama's computers. Nagaraja informed his hosts and wanted to know what was so special about this specific file. They did not want to discuss it, but finally conceded that it was "classified information about building contracts for schools in Tibet." With more study, the pair learned the malware was spreading to other computers by latching onto Word documents and PDF files. They named it GhostRat and were now able to identify the code. They returned to the UK and kept studying it.

Watson learned just how versatile GhostRat was. It could see what a user was looking at on their monitor, log keystrokes, download files, turn webcams on to covertly record conversations and even control a computer from a remote location. But none of this made GhostRat unique. Unlike other malware on the internet at the time, it was not just copying large amounts of data, it was able to look for specific files and bits of information according to what its controllers wanted. The data that Watson and Nagaraja studied contained links to other pro-Tibet groups around the world, and sure enough they now found GhostRat in London.

In February 2009, Watson met with Ron Deibert and the Citizen Lab team at the University of Toronto's Munk Centre for

International Studies. At this point Watson and Nagaraja had "lots of data, tons of data" for Citizen Lab researchers to analyze and use to track down GhostRat's handlers. Things were not going well, however, until researcher Nick Villeneuve tried something different. He had made a list of sites from the data and "one of [the site names] looked really funny to me." The URL was strangely long, and he decided to google it. "A control server came back. Something matched this twenty-two-character, fairly unique string of text. I was able to start identifying the network." He found a server in the US where stolen material was being stashed. From there, he realized the hackers had not password-protected their control servers. He found three more, and these were in China. The researchers could now see every infected machine reporting in, sending thousands of files. They eventually located six control servers in all: the one in the US where information was being dumped, and five others, all in China. They also had a name for the network— GhostNet. The team notified the Canadian government, which passed on the information to infected parties.

Many of the infected machines were in embassies around the world, other international government offices, the Asian Development Bank, Tibetan and Taiwanese groups, even one NATO computer—all targets of interest to the PRC government. Naturally, China denied involvement; but if the PRC were serious about stopping hackers operating from within China, it could have investigated them, as Rohozinski had suggested. The intrusions fit the mould for cyberattacks supported by the PRC, which is known to outsource to firms for cyber intrusions. For instance, the Chinese company I-Soon suffered a leak that exposed it as part of the PRC's hacking-for-hire operations. Targets included the UK government and NATO. Other hacking outfits were exposed, such as Chengdu

404, whose hackers faced indictment by the US government for their attacks on US companies and pro-democracy activists.

The nature of the outsourced hacking varied according to what services were sought by PRC officials. In one case, a public security bureau of Shandong province paid approximately $55,000 for one year's worth of access to the inboxes of ten targets. I-Soon boasted of its ability to hack X (formerly Twitter) and Facebook accounts. In some cases, it looked as though the PRC was just grabbing everything in sight. Alan Woodward at the University of Surrey claimed, "The Chinese state is basically hoovering up as much information as they can in case it proves useful." He added, "Some of it could be interpreted as laying the groundwork for being disruptive at a later stage." I-Soon also claimed it could assist the PRC government with "anti-terrorism" in the Xinjiang region and monitoring the local Uyghur population.[2]

GhostNet was uncovered in 2009. Nonetheless, Nortel was plagued with cyber intrusions, and further attacks kept hitting Canada. In 2008, a CSIS report obtained by the *National Post* claimed that Canada needed to better protect itself against cyberattacks. The warning was quite clear. And yet, when Defence Minister Peter MacKay was warning in 2011 that cybersecurity was a top priority because of the "hostile behaviour" of a foreign state, he refused to name China—this in spite of PRC hackers being engaged in attacks against the US, as well as Canada's Treasury Board, Department of Defence and Department of Finance. The attacks against Canadian government institutions in 2011 were conducted in the same manner as the GhostNet intrusions discovered two years prior. But the attacks kept coming.

In September 2013, Telvent Canada, a company that contributes to managing 60 percent of all oil and gas pipelines in the western hemisphere, was hit with a cyberattack that came from the PRC, specifically from a hacking organization called the Comment Group. One of the items stolen was technology to help mesh older electrical grid with newer smart technologies. Despite all this, Canada was still considering a PRC company, Huawei, to provide it with a 5G network for communications.[3]

When stealing classified information wasn't an option, it could simply be purchased. That happened when Canada sold the PRC the technology for its first attack helicopter. Aircraft engine manufacturer Pratt & Whitney Canada pled guilty in 2012 to two counts of violating US export permit laws for providing China with technology in the late 2000s that enabled it to produce its first such helicopter. The Quebec company also faced a partial freeze on export licences, imposed by the US because it viewed China acquiring this military technology as a threat to its security.

Pascal Girard of Public Works Canada said at the time that the conviction would not affect the company's ability to bid on Canadian government contracts, even though as early as 2007 China's Z-10 Zhisheng attack helicopters were being powered on Pratt & Whitney engines. Besides, the company claimed, there was no harm done, despite the conviction. Why? Because the sale had been approved by the Canadian government. The company was in the news again in 2014 because it was asking for approval to sell engines to China—again. This was during the Harper years, when the government signed the Foreign Investment Protection Agreement (FIPA) with China, designed to reduce trade barriers and encourage and protect Chinese investment in Canada.[4]

———

The frequency of China's spying on Canada seemed to be increasing through the turn of the millennium.

In April 2000, Yong Jie Qu's Canadian permanent residency application was denied under a section of the Immigration Act that prevented people from staying in or entering the country if there were reasonable grounds to believe they would engage in acts of espionage or subversion against democratic government, institutions or processes. CSIS claimed that while Qu was a student at Concordia University in Montreal, he was informing Chinese embassy officials about student dissidents and using embassy money to influence their politics. The judge assessing the case agreed that Qu had been engaged in espionage and subversion while in Canada, but decided it was not directed against democratic institutions, so he could remain in the country.[5]

The PRC was targeting students for recruitment, some willing and others not. In the late nineties, Yang Wang was an international student at Seneca College and then York University, where he became friends with Max Zenj, a Taiwanese student who offered him $3,000 for information on China. Wang agreed and gave him information he collected off the internet. When Wang went back to China in 2006, he was confronted by the MSS and told he had given information to a Taiwanese spy. He was now to go back to Canada and collect information for the MSS on the Falun Gong religious group. Wang gave them information on friends and acquaintances but refused to join Canada–China community organizations, as the MSS had requested. He had no further contact with the MSS after 2010. He made Canada his home after his studies were complete and started a family. He voluntarily shared his story with the Canada Border Services Agency (CBSA) in 2014, which then turned around and deemed him inadmissible to Canada and subject to deportation, which would mean leaving his family behind. The Immigration and Refugee Board overturned CBSA's ruling and he was permitted to stay.[6]

According to two PRC defectors in 2005, one of whom was involved in PRC intelligence, one thousand spies were then at work in Canada. The two claimed that wherever there were large overseas Chinese populations, as in Canada and the US, the PRC would run operations—with Canada having proportionally the larger number of spies. This is not to say there were one thousand MSS intelligence officers working in Canada; if true, the majority of the one thousand referenced were likely paid informants or people co-opted by PRC intelligence. "Co-opted" meaning someone who has been persuaded to work for an intelligence service. That work could be a single task or ongoing. As Wang's case highlighted, people could be forced into intelligence collection by the MSS.[7] In some cases, however, individuals appeared to seek out PRC officials and offer their services.

In December 2013, Qing Quentin Huang was charged with violating the Security of Information Act for allegedly attempting to communicate details about Canada's national shipbuilding procurement strategy. Huang had come to Canada in 2001 and worked as a marine engineer at Lloyd's Register Canada, a subcontractor for Irving Shipbuilding involved in the design of Canada's Arctic patrol ships. Huang had apparently called the PRC embassy and offered his services over the phone. The press reported that CSIS had been monitoring the call and notified the RCMP that Huang had "offered to provide Canadian military secrets" to the PRC. Afraid that he might actually carry out this plan to hand over documents, police posed as Chinese agents looking to acquire the information, and Huang was arrested shortly thereafter.

The sensitive information he was allegedly seeking to hand over related to a 2010 government program that would have new ships built for the Royal Canadian Navy and Canadian Coast Guard. No information was passed to the PRC. Huang claimed he was innocent of the charges. While on its face the case seemed to be a straightforward violation of the Security of Information Act, it never went to trial. In 2021 the case was stayed, with the judge citing an unreasonable delay in it being brought to trial—eight years and counting, to be precise. The delay was caused by the inability of the government to enter the intelligence collected as evidence and share it with Huang's lawyers. Huang's legal team argued that, with documents being kept secret, he could not defend himself against the charges. His lawyer had no comment on the case when approached by media.[8]

Other cases emerged and had international implications. In the summer of 2012, FBI supervisory agent Justin Vallese received a dump of emails between three Chinese operatives. "From day one, we knew it was bad," Vallese told *Wired*. "The contents of those emails are pretty explosive." One message was about the C-17 reconnaissance transport aircraft, which at the time was the US military's third most expensive aircraft ever produced, at over $30 billion of research and development costs spanning two decades. Why was this craft so valuable? It was one of the main ways the US delivered troops and vehicles into war zones and even transported US presidential armoured limousines. US intelligence knew China had problems developing their own aircraft for this same purpose, but now China was just stealing Boeing's design. With the detailed

emails before them, the FBI had enough evidence to act, but two
of the hacking operatives were members of the PLA in China safely
out of reach. The third, a man named Su Bin, was not. He was in
North America. Specifically, he was in BC.

———

Su, who went by Stephen in Canada, was featured in a *Wall Street
Journal* article about wealthy Chinese businessmen leaving for
North America. He had apparently made millions in aerospace, was
married to a doctor and had two Canadian-born kids. One of his
children attended college in Switzerland. He enjoyed doing business in Canada, he claimed, because it was "less restrictive" than in
China, where one had "to do a lot of illegal things."

The FBI knew the hacking had started in 2009 and that Bin's
efforts were connected to his business. Luke Dembosky, the pros-
ecutor in the case, explained Bin's role: "Su Bin was what we'd call
a spotter—someone who would tee up targets for a nation-state."
Su's company, Lode-Tech, gave him many contacts in the industry,
and the hacker team depended on his knowledge. Bin would direct
the hackers towards their targets, such as engineers. Once the hackers knew who they were going after, they set to work using phishing
emails to enter targeted networks. But once in, what would they
look for? Again, Bin could help. From safely within Canada, he
would receive a file listing from the hackers, and then help the
hackers identify which files were important and which were not.
These were not small listings. Sometimes Bin would get as many
as fifteen hundred pages of material. He would go through them
and highlight what was potentially of value for China. In a six-
thousand-page file listing he found twenty-two folders that seemed

valuable. The FBI later said those folders included two thousand pages about the C-17 aircraft, of which the trio netted 630,000 files, roughly sixty-five gigabytes of data.

To hide the hackers' tracks, files were moved between multiple countries, not unlike money launderers trying to pass funds through multiple businesses and jurisdictions. The files eventually found their way to mainland China after arriving at machines on the out-skirts of Hong Kong. This final leg of the journey was handled in person, in order to obscure the ultimate destination should digital trackers have somehow managed to follow the data trail.

The team noted of their achievement, "We safely, smoothly accomplished the entrusted mission in one year, making important contributions to our national defence scientific research develop-ment and receiving unanimous favorable comments." But they didn't stop with the C-17. They also scored 220 megabytes of data on the F-22 Raptor fighter jet, and files on the F-35 as well. Bin also worked as a translator for these documents. The cost to develop military equipment like this is tens of billions of dollars, and now Beijing had stolen research to assist its efforts in copying them.

The price tag for the Su Bin operation was roughly one million dollars, but he proved an invaluable component to this team. He knew the language of the industry, in both Mandarin and English, in addition to knowing what and whom to hack. And he was doing this safely from Canada for years. The returns on investment for Beijing were enormous.

As massive a leak as Su Bin was, however, Vallese expressed his greater concern: "I don't know how many Su Bins there are."

In 2014, the FBI approached Canada for assistance in appre-hending Su Bin while he was still in the country. Canadian authorities agreed, having been rocked by multiple hacks of government websites, particularly in 2011. Five years of espionage against the US assisted by an individual in Canada, and nothing was done until the US came knocking. Vallese's concerns seem valid. How many Bins were there, and why could Canada not identify or stop them until the Americans made an issue of it?

The US released Wanted posters for the two PLA hackers, and the PRC knew their major operation was blown. But it was Bin's arrest that would shape how China would deal with the incident. Bin still had to be extradited from Canada to the United States, which would take time. In response, the PRC decided to send Canada a message for its role in arresting him. The MSS invited two Canadians living in the city of Dandong over for dinner.

———

Kevin and Julia Garratt were devoted Christians who had been living in China for many years. They had arrived as English teachers in the 1980s and raised four kids while travelling across the country. They settled in Dandong, on the border with North Korea. When they first arrived in China, it was largely rural and still getting over the Cultural Revolution. For example, Shenzhen, which is today a major tech centre, had only two hundred thousand people, and Shanghai was the only city allowing foreign investment. The Garratts would witness China's explosive growth across so many sectors and industries and watch the country change dramatically over the years.

By 2014, the Garratts were in their fifties and running a coffee shop in Dandong called Peter's Coffee House. It was a popular destination among expats, with good coffee and Western food. They volunteered in the city, helped at a local orphanage and even donated aid to North Koreans. They had established deep roots in the community. On August 4, they were invited out to dinner by a friend of a friend who was looking to send their child to school in Canada and wanted some advice. The invitation seemed harmless enough.

D nner at the restaurant felt off. Kevin recalled that "it didn't seem genuine, and the daughter never came." After dinner, the couple took an elevator down to the lobby of the building. When the doors opened, bright lights shone all around them and video cameras were pressed in their faces. They thought maybe they had accidentally crashed some kind of party. But then the Garratts were grabbed and pulled apart. They were forced into separate black sedans and driven away. They thought this had to be a mistake. Julia recalled the shock of it all. "This is going to be my last night," she thought. "I don't think I've ever felt that level of fear and panic before. And also just sad for my family and my children, because there was no warning, there would be no chance to say goodbye."

The couple were imprisoned separately, and though physically unharmed, they were under constant surveillance. "You want a drink of water, they have to get it for you. Brush your teeth, they get it for you. It's really meant to frighten and control you," Kevin recalled. He remembered the size of the cell he had to share with fourteen others: "about twelve paces by five and a half." After a few days in her cell, Julia tried to cover her eyes with a blanket, but a guard came and yanked it off. "I thought: 'That's a rule. I can't cover my face to sleep in the dark, they need the lights shining in my face.' They had a very strict protocol." The couple faced daily interrogations for six hours, with nothing to confess. Their captors knew all about their time in China, and the Garratts were asked over and over to detail everything they had been doing. "They would ask the same questions two months later and compare the answers," Julia said. "It's very, very gruelling."

The couple hired American lawyer James Zimmerman, who learned that the PRC was planning on charging the Garratts with stealing PRC intelligence "about Chinese military targets and important national defence research projects, and engaging in activities threatening to Chinese national security." The charges were ludicrous. They were almost a mirror of the US charges against Bin. What was the "evidence" against Kevin? He liked to take bland photographs of public places, like at Tiananmen Square, where soldiers marched around and raised the PRC flag. Guy Saint-Jacques was the Canadian ambassador to China at the time and noted that the Garratts' case "was the first case where we saw a clear retaliation for something that had happened in Canada." While the PRC would not admit it, it was obvious they wanted a swap for Bin. Saint-Jacques noted that while "they never said directly 'Let's do a swap,' it was clear what they wanted."

If anyone wanted proof of what China had stolen courtesy of Bin and his accomplices, China provided it in November of that same year. At an air show in Zhuhai, the PRC showed off the new Xian Y-20. The cargo plane was parked only metres from a US C-17. The similarities between the two were lost on no one. The entire incident, along with the past decade of cyber hacks, led the Obama administration to announce in 2015 that the US and China had come to an agreement on cyber intrusions: The two countries were to work together on cyberspace issues and abstain from conducting or supporting the theft of intellectual property through hacking. The deal showcased how badly the US misunderstood Xi Jinping and his goals for China. Xi wanted China to supplant the US, not work with it.

China's hostage diplomacy with the Garratts ended not because of any agreement but because, on March 22, 2016, Bin pleaded guilty and did not contest his extradition. China's bargaining position disintegrated, and Julia was released in May 2016 and Kevin in September.[9]

The case of the Garratts should have been seen as a warning, a precursor to how China would behave when another high-profile arrest occurred a mere two years after Bin entered his plea. Canadians Michael Spavor and Michael Kovrig would be detained in China in 2018 after the arrest of Huawei CFO Meng Wanzhou in Vancouver (which I will discuss in chapter 7). Canada seemed wholly unprepared.

———

Given all the media attention, FBI warnings and congressional hearings about Huawei, you might think Canada would have taken notice sooner when another major tech company—operating in North America but headquartered in the PRC—aroused espionage suspicions, but it didn't. The company was TikTok, the popular video streaming social media app. TikTok took North American youth by storm, but very quickly, cracks emerged in its playful veneer.

The company had been founded in March 2012 by ByteDance in Beijing. In China, the app kept its original Chinese name, Douyin, but it was branded as TikTok for overseas markets in 2017. In 2019, *The Washington Post* reported that TikTok might have been involved in censoring Hong Kong protesters. *The Guardian* reported from leaked documents that TikTok was censoring videos deemed offensive by the CCP. US lawmakers called for investigations into

TikTok, and they were launched in the fall of 2019. Before the year ended, the US military issued a call for all personnel to delete the app from their phones. US authorities wanted ByteDance to divest its interests so it would no longer have a role in the operation of the app in the United States. In 2022, BuzzFeed published a report that showed US TikTok user data was repeatedly accessed by ByteDance employees in China, raising fresh concerns about who has access to US user data. The US Senate passed a bill in April 2024 forcing TikTok to be banned and deleted from US app stores unless ByteDance divested.

While the Americans were bringing this intense level of scrutiny to the app, Canadian politicians remained users of it, most notably NDP leader Jagmeet Singh, who had nearly a million followers. The Canadian government finally banned the app from Canadian government devices in February 2023. But even after that ban and the US decision, in April 2024, Singh was publicly musing about how he could get back onto TikTok and resume making videos. Immediately following the election of Donald Trump to the White House in 2024, the Canadian government suddenly announced, on November 6, that TikTok's offices would be closed in Canada, with the government citing "national security risks." The media called it a "ban" on TikTok operations. Except—not really. TikTok's Canadian offices were ordered to close, but Canadians were still permitted to download and install the app and develop and upload content. The "ban" did nothing to address what happened to the data harvested by the app and whether the CCP could access it. What's more, the government still permitted government departments to purchase advertising on the app. Singh returned to TikTok in January 2025. It was the same month that the US Supreme Court upheld the US government's right to ban TikTok. The ban went into effect on January 19, 2025. TikTok's parent company has continually denied the government's allegations about the security of the app's user data or that it engaged in content censorship. President Trump signed an executive order to delay the ban to see if an American buyer for the app could be found.[10]

Had China stopped its cyberattacks after Xi's agreement with Obama? Not at all. In fact, in 2024, Canadian parliamentarians learned that they had been targets of Chinese hackers in 2021. But it wasn't the Canadian government that informed them—it was the FBI. MPs who were part of the global organization of the Inter-Parliamentary Alliance on China were notified they had been targeted by a PRC cyberattack. The FBI had shared this information with foreign governments in 2022.

The PRC group APT31 was behind the 2021 hacks. The group made headlines for its sweeping attack on US officials, corporations, journalists and others. Many in the UK were also hit, but the Canadian government said nothing when the news broke. The Communications Security Establishment (CSE) is the federal government agency charged with collecting foreign signals intelligence, basically electronic communications, and mitigating foreign cyber threats against Canada. All CSE would say at the time was that "we have seen malicious activity by the same threat actor targeting Canada." According to media reports, Canadian intelligence was told of the intrusions in 2021, the year they occurred, and notified House of Commons security but not the MPs themselves. CSIS claimed they thought the MPs would be notified. Everyone presumed someone else would notify the actual targets of the hack, or so they claimed. Once again, the US was doing Canada's security work.[11]

This wasn't even the worst of it. The worst may truly never be known. In November 2024, US authorities claimed China-linked hackers had broken into an undisclosed number of major American telecom companies and intercepted information intended for law enforcement. The hackers could listen to phone calls and read texts. They even targeted the phones of President Trump and Vice President Vance when they were candidates. The chairman of the Senate Intelligence Committee told *The Washington Post* that "the barn door is still wide open, or mostly open." How much the PRC was able to collect is unknown, but the major breach of telecommunication companies was especially serious given they intercepted information intended for law enforcement, such as warrants. The theft could compromise an untold number of investigations, to say nothing of how much intelligence and information China could have collected about individuals and networks. It has been dubbed by the US press the "worst" hack in the nation's history. Was Canada exposed? If it was, or if something similar happened in Canada, Canadian authorities haven't said (or worse, don't know), but it is doubtful Canadian telecoms weren't just as vulnerable as their US counterparts.[12]

Canada would continue to fail to recognize the PRC threat until incidents at a Winnipeg lab in 2019 finally brought national attention to just how bad things had become.

———

Xiangguo Qiu was a medical doctor and biologist. She and her husband were born in China. They moved to Canada in the 1990s and became naturalized Canadians. She joined the National Microbiology Laboratory (NML) in Winnipeg in 2003. The lab was run by the Public Health Agency of Canada (PHAC). The NML wasn't an ordinary medical lab. It was a biosafety level 4 (P4) lab, a high-security facility that housed and researched some of the most dangerous viruses in the world. It was the only such lab in Canada. If the pathogen samples and research in this lab fell into the wrong hands, the results could be catastrophic.

Qiu's work focused on the Ebola virus. Her goal was to find a way to treat the virus with monoclonal antibodies. Aggressive viruses are difficult to treat because of how quickly they can overwhelm an infected host's immune system. If the treatment worked, it could be applied to treating other diseases, including coronaviruses. Her husband, Keding Cheng, also worked at the lab and assisted her with her project.

In 2005, Qiu started publishing her work, which was still in the theoretical stages. As possible budget cuts to the lab were threatening to bring Qiu's work to an end, she managed a breakthrough. By applying multiple monoclonal antibodies to the host, she witnessed infected monkeys with Ebola who were near death make complete recoveries. The mixture was called ZMab.

The lab patented ZMab and then licensed it to a Canadian company. In 2014, West Africa was hit by an Ebola outbreak. ZMab was given to infected people, and it cured them. Despite the success, Canada subcontracted further work on ZMab to an American company, Regeneron, which produced the antibodies, and new ones, to treat Ebola and later COVID-19. Qiu was recognized for her work and received a Governor General's Award in 2018. And yet, in 2019, she was quietly escorted out of her lab.

Her dismissal and that of her husband made international headlines and caused havoc and outrage in Ottawa. Parliamentary committees were assembled and documents were demanded by opposition parties, with the government refusing to hand them over and even attempting to take the Speaker of the House of

Commons to court to stop the release of pertinent documents before the country was eventually plunged into an election. So how did this successful research that helped save lives in one of the world's deadliest crisis zones reduce a celebrated scientist's career to infamy and cause upheaval in the corridors of the Canadian Parliament?

China had taken notice of Qiu's work. The PRC had just finished constructing its first P4 lab, the Wuhan Institute of Virology. Canada had no qualms about working more closely with China. Science was supposed to be different from politics. Everyone was supposed to be working towards common goals of advancing research, the growth of knowledge and the betterment of humanity. Canada's National Research Council (which had been hit with cyber thefts by China just a few years prior) willingly shared patented cell lines so Chinese scientists could create a new vaccine, which they ended up doing for Ebola in 2018. The manufacturer was named CanSino Biologics.

Qiu continued to work with scientists at a lab in China while employed by the NML in Winnipeg. A colleague of hers told *Maclean's* magazine that Qiu thought her "identity" might cause her problems in a facility where people required security clearances from csis. Instead, problems arose when Qiu's name suddenly appeared on patents filed with China's National Intellectual Property Administration for work on treating Ebola. She told her NML supervisors this was not correct and had been done without her knowledge. But why would anyone include her name if they were, presumably, trying to copy her work? What reason could there be to give her credit for the research and the patent? This was just a sign of Qiu's success, she maintained.

The staff at the NML wondered whether the growing scrutiny of Qiu might be stemming from recent shifts in attitudes towards China following the Meng Wanzhou arrest in BC and a new focus on countries retaining intellectual property. When she was finally relieved of her position at the lab, they understood her dismissal to be related to Qiu's mishandling of an Ebola shipment that ran afoul of the lab's rules on intellectual property.

Qiu had asked her bosses about sending an Ebola sample, as well as a Nipah virus sample, to the lab in Wuhan; a fellow scientist there was asking her for samples. She didn't think sending them would require a Material Transfer Agreement (MTA), a document that confirms and controls the ownership of intellectual property and stipulates what can be done with it. Qiu said the samples had been collected during an outbreak and felt no one owned them. Colleagues and supervisors had expressed no concerns about sending them to China; if anything, some were excited. Maybe China would send Canada some viruses in return?

David Safronetz, who worked with Qiu, told his bosses in March 2019 that all the necessary papers would be completed before the samples were sent to Wuhan, but that never did happen, and the samples went without the papers. The former head of the NML, Ian Stewart, told a parliamentary committee that an MTA wasn't actually required. Stewart said it wasn't the details around the transfer that led to Qiu and her husband's removal; nonetheless, just four months after the samples were sent, the couple were out of the lab.[13]

As it turns out, Qiu and her husband were not fired because of paperwork slip-ups or even because of her "identity," as she'd feared. Qiu and her husband were working with labs and people connected to the PLA and were lying about it to Canadian authorities in their security clearance interviews. The government refused to release documents about these connections and interviews, citing national security concerns. But the refusal to release information may have been dictated by a different imperative. Former justices who examined the documents prior to their eventual release in February 2024 noted the case would prove embarrassing for the government. Qiu was collaborating with PRC institutions and programs linked to the PLA and hiding it from PHAC, while her husband assisted in facilitating access to the highly secure Winnipeg lab for PRC researchers who also had ties to the PLA. Qiu had been doing this for years and lied about it when confronted.

A CSIS investigation into Qiu and her husband, released to the public in 2024, finally revealed what the pair had been up to. In March 2017, Qiu had presented a paper at the Wuhan Institute of Virology (the same lab that US authorities would years later theorize may have been behind the global COVID-19 pandemic). Qiu had been approved by PHAC to travel to a conference in Beijing. The visit and presentation at Wuhan—over a thousand kilometres south of the Chinese capital—weren't disclosed to PHAC, and the Wuhan conference didn't mention her appearance in promotional materials. The CSIS report stated that the "service [CSIS] is not aware of any PHAC approved travel for Ms. Qiu to Wuhan during this period."

CSIS also found several partially completed applications for PRC talent recruitment programs that use large funding grants to attract researchers and patents to China. Qiu's Canadian supervisors knew nothing of these applications. CSIS found evidence of a conversation with the Wuhan lab about her talent form application in which the lab claimed it was "very important for our future development." She was slotted to receive a million dollars in research grants for putting in two months of work a year at the Wuhan lab for three years. According to the CSIS documents, Qiu was of interest to China's new P4 lab because she was the "only highly experienced Chinese expert available internationally who is still fighting on the front lines in a P4 laboratory." She was an active scientist working in a P4 lab, and she was Chinese. Both were traits that the PRC not only desired but could leverage.

Wuhan was a new lab, and as with other new technologies or ventures, China appeared to want to fast-track its development by acquiring pre-existing technology and know-how from elsewhere. The CSIS documents detail that in partnering with the Wuhan lab, Qiu would be responsible for constructing the PRC's "biosecurity platform for new and potent infectious disease research," which would allow the lab to have "leading status internationally in the area of BSL4 research." Any of Qiu's research success would become the property of the Wuhan lab. In 2018, she notified the Wuhan lab that her application was essentially ready to go. And yet, during a security screening interview, when CSIS confronted her with the talent application forms filled out in her name, she denied any knowledge of them.[14]

China has maintained that the COVID-19 virus originated spontaneously at a Huanan wholesale seafood market, but concerns about the Wuhan lab and a potential coronavirus outbreak predate the pandemic. A *Vanity Fair* investigation detailed these concerns. For starters, the P4 lab in Wuhan was new, and in 2017, American health officials received a tour because the US was funding the lab's coronavirus research. As Asha George, executive director of the Bipartisan Commission on Biodefense, put it, "If you want to know what's going on in a closed country . . . give them grant money." But the lab was having trouble finding staff with expertise. The visiting health officials were alarmed by some of the lab's activities. For instance, the lab wanted to study Ebola but didn't have any samples (until Qiu sent them), so researchers were going to use reverse genetics to make Ebola in the lab.

The US Department of Energy oversees many labs and has strong intelligence collection ability. In mid-2019, after its scientists reviewed classified information from Wuhan, the department began warning officials in the US government that research from the new lab could be used for military purposes, and it expressed concern about collaborations with China, and about the security at the Wuhan lab. In June 2023, the Office of the Director of National Intelligence issued a declassified report concerning the origins of the pandemic. The report details how the Department of Energy and the FBI believed that COVID-19 likely originated with a lab leak. For instance, in October 2020, Department of Energy scientists located evidence that suggested COVID-19 had originated at the Wuhan lab. By 2023, their assessment of the likelihood of a lab leak went from "undecided" to "assessing," albeit with "low confidence" that the virus emerged from a lab. The CIA maintained there was not enough evidence to be conclusive about the virus's origins. But in January 2025 the CIA concluded work on a report about COVID-19's origins that was initiated by the Biden administration. It now assessed with low confidence that COVID-19 likely began after a lab leak.

What was driving this change of status for the Department of Energy was evidence of a coronavirus variant having been studied at the Wuhan lab. Author Elaine Dewar has documented how scientist Shi Zhengli (nicknamed the "bat woman" for her work on the SARS virus) was working with the Wuhan lab (and later with

Qiu) when in 2013 she discovered SARS-like viruses that resembled COVID-19. That same year, she discovered how to make a new virus that, if it got out, could easily infect humans and cause a pandemic. In 2015, Shi's lab collaborated with a virologist in North Carolina, using this strain for research. The goal was to create a virus before nature did, so we could learn in advance how to guard against it. But the strategy—called gain of function (GOF) research—was dangerous. In theory, it fortified humanity against future plagues; in practice, it risked accidentally unleashing those plagues before they had occurred in nature (*if* they ever occurred), and possibly before we were ready to cope with them.

An article in *The Lancet* from January 2020 with twenty co-authors noted how a novel coronavirus had been infecting patients in Wuhan during the fall of 2019, and 44 percent of these patients had had no contact with the market where China claims the virus started. As Dewar notes, these early scientific papers were suggesting human-to-human transmission with this virus from its earliest cases. Further, COVID-19 was well adapted to attack human hosts, which would be unusual for a virus that had just recently appeared in an animal. Dewar noticed what started to look like deception emerging in scientific studies on the virus coming out of China in January 2020; it seemed as if a narrative was being constructed to direct suspicions away from the Wuhan lab. China has taken steps to block investigations into the origins of the virus, such as ordering the destruction of COVID-19 samples from January 2020 that were housed in several PRC labs. The government claimed the elimination of the samples would "reduce biosafety risks."[15]

As all hell was breaking loose in Wuhan and the virus was about to drive people around the world into isolation for months on end, CSIS's investigation of Qiu found more applications on her computer for other talent programs. She didn't tell PHAC that she had collaborated on research with Major General Chen Wei. Chen was a high-ranking PLA officer who helped develop China's COVID-19 vaccine for CanSino Biologics, the PRC company backed by China's military that had developed an Ebola vaccine using cell lines provided by Canada's National Research Council. Qiu also claimed not to know Chen was working in biological weapons research. Qiu had listed the collaborations with Chinese institutes on her PRC CV but removed them from her Canadian CV. Qiu and her husband were also listed as co-authors on a paper alongside people connected to the Academy of Military Medical Sciences (AMMS) in China. The AMMS engages in high-level research for chemical and biological weapons. The AMMS even nominated her for an award. It was for "international cooperation" for using "Canada's Level 4 Biosecurity Laboratory as a base to assist China to improve its capability to fight highly-pathogenic pathogens . . . and [Qiu] achieved brilliant results."

While Qiu was secretly working on these partnerships, what was her husband, Keding Cheng, up to? According to CSIS documents, he was helping restricted visitors obtain access to NML research and materials. Restricted visitors were given access to the Winnipeg lab and left to wander about. Cheng even provided passwords to one of them so they could work and download material in the lab. Some tried to smuggle out vials of pathogens. In one instance, one of those restricted visitors was "connected to the People's Liberation Army." *A person connected to China's military was allowed to roam freely through, and have access to, a highly restricted Canadian laboratory where scientists could work only with a CSIS-level security clearance and that houses some of the most dangerous viruses in the world.* Allow that to sink in.

Both Qiu and her husband were also using Gmail addresses, which was in violation of PHAC policy since those addresses were non-government and so were not monitored for security. In the end, CSIS concluded that Qiu "developed deep, cooperative relationships with a variety of People's Republic of China institutions and has intentionally transferred scientific knowledge and materials to China in order to benefit the PRC government." The pair were assessed as having been engaged in "activities that constitute a threat to the security of Canada" and as being likely to do so again if they remained employed.

Today, Qiu and her husband are back in China. Living under an alias, she is still engaged in research and collaboration with institutes connected to China's military and patenting research.[16]

One last notable element of this saga is Qiu's work with the Wuhan lab. According to the released CSIS documents, in the spring of 2019, Qiu and other Chinese researchers in the Wuhan lab were approved by a PRC evaluation committee to conduct a project at the lab, with Qiu in charge of "overall planning." Another individual was charged with the "Project Design" and another with "animal infection." The project was to "assess cross species infection" through the creation of synthetic virus strains. The experiments were part of more GOF research—the very risky development of viruses in a lab before they develop in nature. One of these researchers, whose name is redacted in the documents without explanation, worked on bat viruses similar to SARS, and these experiments would be looking at the pathogenic risks of "bat filoviruses." We know that the "bat woman" worked in this lab as well and had done similar experiments in 2015. Just a few months after Qiu's new research project was approved, COVID started circulating in Wuhan. And where did Canada turn to first for a COVID vaccine? China. Specifically, the Canadian government struck a deal with CanSino for vaccines, a deal that ultimately collapsed when China refused to send samples to Canada. Months were wasted, which was valuable time in the middle of a pandemic. The founders of CanSino had also worked in Canada, at the pharmaceutical company Sanofi Pasteur.[17]

Let's put all this together and consider the implications. Qiu secretly works with the Wuhan lab overseeing a GOF project about bat filoviruses, and months later COVID-19 is unleashed on the world, with this lab being at the centre of the lab-leak theory. Canada then partners for a vaccine with CanSino—a company connected to the PLA, one of the officials of which Qiu had secretly worked with on vaccine research. If the lab-leak theory is ever confirmed, one has to ask: Did a Canadian researcher who was secretly assisting China have a role in the creation and breakout of COVID-19, and then did the Canadian government try to buy a vaccine from a PRC company that the same researcher had assisted and that has connections to China's military? You can't make this stuff up.

Were Qiu and her husband "spies"? Unlikely. The terms "spy" and "agent" might conjure up glamorized images of Jason Bourne or Jack Ryan, but the reality is that these terms are rarely used within intelligence circles. The better question is whether Qiu was an intelligence officer working for an intelligence service like China's MSS. This is also unlikely. As former CSIS director Richard Fadden put it, Qiu and her husband are "more likely examples of any number of Chinese citizens who, broadly speaking, agree with the views of China's [government, and] whenever they can acquire information that is of use to China, they are going to do that." There is no evidence the couple had training in intelligence collection or were working directly for the MSS.[18]

While Fadden's assessment seems plausible, it's even more likely that the pair were out for money and recognition. Qiu had strong views about how her collaborative scientific efforts were being stymied by PHAC and the Winnipeg lab's security policy, and the lab was facing budget cuts that would affect her research. The fact that Qiu had filled out multiple talent program applications that promised big funds is a strong sign that she was motivated to find funding to continue her research and to do so while making a good living. The PRC was offering that as well as playing on her heritage, in that Qiu would be helping her homeland fight diseases and deadly pathogens. It is entirely possible she viewed all those security measures as getting in the way of her doing good science and collaboration, and that the lack of government funding in Winnipeg convinced her Canada wasn't serious about doing research. If that was her thinking, Qiu and her husband would have been easy targets to be co-opted by the PRC. They may have been lured with incentives, and may have fallen for a romanticized view that science and collaborative research somehow take place outside politics. Sadly, that is an impossibility in a world of nation-states with militaries constantly seeking to gain an edge over their rivals.

The media that reported on this saga have not been able to reach Qiu and her husband for comment since they left Canada. They appear to have changed their names. At the time of this writing, my attempts to contact her were also unsuccessful.

———

People who are willing to offer up technology or intellectual property to China exist in a number of industries, not just scientific research.

On March 20, 2024, Klaus Pflugbeil, a Canadian who had been living in China, arrived in Long Island, New York, looking to make a sale. The two men he was meeting had previously met his business partner, Yilong Shao, a Chinese citizen, at a trade show in Las Vegas. The two men were interested in buying some secret information; specifically, they wanted battery technology for electric vehicles. They approached Shao because Shao and Pflugbeil had worked for a company called Hibar Systems in Ontario. Hibar was a Canadian company that sold technology for battery manufacturing. Tesla had bought Hibar in 2019.

The US Department of Justice (DOJ) alleged that after the Hibar acquisition, Pflugbeil and Shao had held on to Tesla proprietary information about battery manufacturing, such as technical drawings, that could allow someone to copy the battery technology. Between October and November 2019, the duo discussed their plans to open a rival company in China and use Tesla's technology to get it going. Pflugbeil told Shao he had "a lot of original documents" and he would get more. According to the DOJ indictment, Shao would later confirm that "we have all of the original assembly drawings by PDF." The next summer they started up their own company in China with offices in Canada, Brazil and Germany. Their business depended on Tesla's battery manufacturing secrets. When their company, which was not named by the DOJ indictment, needed parts built for its plants, they allegedly sent Tesla's drawings to suppliers and manufacturers, changed the company name and dates, and wrote the drawing ID number in the reverse order of Tesla's original. They told the manufacturers to "please keep the attached information confidential."

At the Las Vegas trade show in September 2023, Pflugbeil and Shao had found someone willing to buy the technology that had been acquired by Tesla, along with the rest of Hibar, in 2019. The Las Vegas buyers were planning on opening some sort of manufacturing plant on Long Island. Pflugbeil emailed his buyers a sixty-six-page PDF that he stated contained "proprietary information" from his business that had to be kept secret; in reality, it was Tesla's information. Pflugbeil then went to New York to finalize the sale. But instead of receiving an offer, Pflugbeil got handcuffs. The buyers were undercover officers. They were part of an interagency strike force set up to protect supply chains and prevent technology from being acquired by hostile nation-states and authoritarian regimes—though in this case, it is likely the information is already in the hands of the PRC, given Shao and Pflugbeil had created their company in the PRC and Shao was not arrested. Shao has never commented publicly on the charges, and I could not locate him. Pflugbeil pleaded guilty to the charges in June 2024, while Shao remains at large.[19]

An obvious question regarding this case remains: Where was Canada? The pair had set up a company that had operations in Canada after allegedly stealing Tesla's information. Just as in the Su Bin case, it appears the United States was seeking to protect itself and its technologies from individuals who were assisting (and alleged to be assisting) the PRC for profit. These are the well-documented cases. I can't help but think back to the FBI agent Vallese's comments in the Su Bin case: "I don't know how many Su Bins there are."

The cases here also highlight another important question: Do they demonstrate PRC espionage or foreign interference? In some cases, people willingly agreed to help PRC espionage and intelligence collection efforts, even though they were not trained intelligence officers; in other cases, there are no indications that

PRC intelligence services like the MSS were ever involved. Even in cyberattacks, the PRC was known to use private contractors and sometimes student groups to engage in hacking. All of this illustrates that, for the PRC and its intelligence collection, the boundaries between traditional espionage and foreign interference are fluid. The activities resist being categorized and contained by the old paradigms.

Covert influence attempts are also early forms of interference. Take the case of Qiu. The attempts to influence her were deliberately kept secret and resemble efforts where the goal is to establish a relationship with a target individual that can grow to a point where the target begins engaging in interference or espionage for the benefit of the hostile state. Influence that is covert is covert for a reason. Laws meant to target traditional forms of espionage have no effect in deterring some of this activity. As of 2024, Canada now has legislation that can target this interference, but it remains to be seen whether its laws will stand up in court.

Difficulties in prosecuting alone don't explain why Canada is so often left waiting for countries like the US to act on threats that exist in or emanate from Canadian soil. The boundaries of espionage collection and foreign interference continue to blur, and the following chapters will show how Canada has failed to deal with the PRC's relentless collection efforts. The question is not just how many Su Bins are in Canada, but how many researchers and academics who think like Qiu are comfortably giving up Canadian research.

FIVE

RED CARPETS
AND PYROTECHNICS

Interference and Academia

BENJAMIN FUNG RECEIVED an email with nothing in it. There was no message, no attachment, and it had come from an anonymous sender. But the McGill University professor knew enough to look closer. The email wasn't completely empty. It contained a one-kilobyte graphical file. The file was so small that anyone could be forgiven for missing it. It would be like opening a paper envelope with nothing inside but a speck of dust. The file wasn't a virus, and it wasn't an attempt by anyone to hack Fung's device, at least not yet.

Fung's expertise is in AI and data science, with a cybersecurity and privacy focus. He did some investigative work on this little file and discovered it was a type of scout. Its purpose was to collect information on the device Fung was using, such as the brand, the operating system and what version it was, and other pertinent details. It would then send that information back to the email's sender, likely so that the person could devise something to attack Fung's specific device. Where was the information being sent? Who was the sender? Fung doesn't know who sent it. But he knows where it originated: Shanghai.

Why was Fung targeted by the PRC? Well, for two reasons. One, as an expert in AI and data science, he was an academic working in fields that China was interested in. Two, he was involved in Hong

Kong pro-democracy activism and had refused to work for the PRC. Fung had been approached by China to receive grant money under its Thousand Talents Plan (TTP). This program was designed by the PRC as an attempt to cultivate international researchers involved in areas of interest to China, such as AI, quantum computing and other sensitive technologies, all priority areas outlined in China's latest Five-Year Plan, its list of social and economic national goals released by the CCP every five years since 1953. This attempt to recruit academics abroad has helped China develop its knowledge and research bases in these fields by essentially buying them.

As this chapter will show, China's attempt to influence academia isn't limited to acquiring IP. China also targets students and student groups. Its activities on university campuses attempt to control what is said and taught about the PRC. The strategy is twofold: Controlling the messaging about China on campus also helps attract more researchers. By co-opting the principles of academic freedom and international partnerships, the PRC has been able to advance its interests with the help of Western academics.

I met Ben Fung when he and I participated in a university round table I organized about PRC interference in the Five Eyes intelligence community countries. The participants were experts and scholars from the nations involved: the UK, the US, Australia, New Zealand and Canada. In our interview for this book, he told me that he immigrated to Canada from Hong Kong with his parents in the 1990s, settling in Vancouver. He studied at Simon Fraser University and eventually landed at McGill, in 2013. Fung first experienced foreign influence when he started working as an academic. He explained how the PRC had pitched its Thousand Talents recruitment program to him. "It is an attractive program," he said. Typically, people are offered a million RMB (approximately US$138,000) "just to get started, and the idea is that you can still be a professor in Canada . . . You spend three months in China, or even half of a summer semester in China, doing research or teaching some short courses, and that will satisfy their requirements. So on the one hand you can receive a salary from a Canadian university, and on the other hand they offer the same amount of salary, basically, but we don't have to be there. So it's like free money. That's the approach they take." China makes the deal sound very enticing, but as Fung added, "As a Hong Konger, we understand there's no free lunch. After you rely on them, then they will start asking for different things, different unreasonable requests after one or two years."[1]

A devil's advocate might say these programs are about academic freedom, academic exchanges and the funding of research. But they're not. CSIS's interpretation of them was released along with the Winnipeg lab documents in 2024. The documents detail how China's TTP was the most prominent of its kind, though others also exist. The objective was to recruit ethnically Chinese scientists and researchers from Western universities, research centres and private companies to bolster the PRC's science and technology programs. The goal was to make China a leader in innovation. For a Western researcher with no funding, dealing with government underfunding of universities and colleges, the TTP and other programs like it tug at the desire to get their work funded and published. What the PRC does not disclose about programs like the TTP is that they weren't ended. Instead, they were absorbed into the new National High-End Foreign Experts Recruitment Plan (NHFERP) in 2019. This program became the successor to the TTP and is handled directly by China's Ministry of Science and Technology.

The PRC is still running talent programs—just under a new name.

CSIS documents released to the public about the Winnipeg lab incident outline the aims of the TTP: to "serve major national [PRC] strategic needs," mainly through acquiring foreign researcher support in "cultivating and developing strategic emerging industries." The PRC's Ministry of Science and Technology stated that its main priority was to recruit foreign experts working in new sensitive research fields, such as those outlined in the PRC's thirteenth Five-Year Plan and the Made in China 2025 plan. The goal with these is for China to increase its role in the global supply chain and to expand R&D and patents in areas like biotechnology, next-generation IT, robotics and aerospace industries, among others. The 2025 plan is a policy initiative that seeks to make China a leader in high-tech industry.[2]

The West was slow to recognize the PRC's aims, given the TTP had existed since 2008, but in 2018 US authorities, such as the FBI, began delivering more significant warnings to the public about the threat of the PRC acquiring intellectual property for its military and strategic aims. It wasn't until two years later that warnings about the PRC's Thousand Talents Plan started to appear in Canadian media. This was months after Qiu and her husband finally had their security clearances revoked in 2019. Public warnings about the TTP could have been made by Canada as early as 2018, but the government said nothing until well after the serious breach in Winnipeg. The PRC's aims were hardly unknown to the government, given the investigation into the NML. But by the time official warnings had been issued in the media, *The Globe and Mail*, for instance, had found fifteen Canadian academics who had participated in the TTP program. They were involved in quantum computing, engineering, vaccines and AI. These individuals defended the program as "mutually beneficial." But given what we now know about the TTP, this characterization seems doubtful.

In 2019, a US Senate report outlined the threat the TTP posed by its acquisition of advanced technology research for the PRC and the Chinese military. The report revealed that Western academics were required to sign contracts that prevented them from disclosing that Chinese institutions would have the rights to a portion of the intellectual property they created when involved in the program. In the US, some professors faced charges under the DOJ's China Initiative for not disclosing funding links to China, while others were pressured to retire early or resign on their own. The China Initiative program was meant to discourage these partnerships from happening, but it was discontinued in 2022. Still, the point and concerns remain: The PRC wanted to secretly target and fund Western academics. And it incentivized lying. One Canadian professor told *The Globe and Mail* that in the PRC "they treat you like a star. In my case, I have had red carpets. I have had . . . pyrotechnics," and, at some functions, "people clapping and wanting to take pictures with you." Beijing knows the power of flattery.[3]

Fung explained to me how the program spots and approaches academic targets. "Usually they start from a friend. We always have some friends of Hong Kong or Chinese origin." Fung said it was friends like these—some of whom had returned to work in China—who approached him. Other academics had been approached by non-professional friends. The simple point was, "It's not a cold call." When he was offered the chance to enter the TTP in 2014, the Canada–China diplomatic relationship was calm; there was only "friendship," as he put it. Nonetheless, he declined. He felt the program violated ethics because he was employed by Concordia University; to join the TTP would mean agreeing to a competing claim of ownership to any research he undertook at the Montreal school. Fung no doubt made the ethical decision, but that didn't necessarily mean universities or governments would follow his lead.

Even after the Winnipeg scandal, China continued seeking out research gains for its military. Despite warnings from security services, Canada's federal research funding councils do not presently screen applicants to determine whether they are connected to PRC talent programs. This means that researchers could already owe their results to the TTP and yet still apply for, and receive, Canadian federal research dollars. In replying to media questions about this, three research funding councils released identical statements:

> Canada's research ecosystem must be as open as possible and as secure as necessary as researchers need to collaborate with reliable and trusted partners to drive innovation ... [W]hile the federal granting agencies do not collect data regarding participation in foreign talent recruitment programs, such as China's Thousand Talents program, they do provide advice and guidance on how researchers can mitigate their research security risks.

The Canadian research funding bodies could be unwittingly financing research whose results will be laid claim to by PRC programs, which means in essence Canada is funding research that is contracted to benefit the PRC.[4]

In 2017, Fung had a year of sabbatical leave and spent it in Hong Kong teaching a digital privacy course and visiting family. While there, he was approached by a friend working at a leading PRC telecommunications corporation. The friend asked Fung to give a talk at the company. Fung agreed; he had given the same talk numerous times at other institutions. "At the end, I find that this is not a talk. This is actually a job interview!" he recalled, laughing. "Then several directors came to me and said, 'Hey, you interested in staying in China, in Hong Kong, for another year to two years?' and I told them it's the end of my sabbatical leave, I can't stay longer. They said you can take a no-pay leave and we can pay your salary, salary is not a problem. They wanted me to participate in the AI team." He said they didn't specify the salary, just that it was a very good salary. They would offer him a car, a place to live, all the amenities.

It wasn't what they said about compensation that Fung found surprising, but what would be expected of him in getting ideas to market. The director told him that whatever idea he had, from idea to product, the time frame would be six months. Fung recalled them telling him, "Let's say you have three possible solutions to solve a problem. We will allocate three development teams to implement all three solutions so we don't have to worry about which solution is the best. We try all of them, and we see which one is the best and we put the best one on the market, and the time frame is six months." This sounded like a dream, because a professor in Canada could need a year to secure a funding grant, another year to get students who will do the research, and as much as four years to see a product emerge from all that work. This accelerated time frame was the most attractive element of the company's offer.

But Fung had one concern. "As an AI guy, we always ask the same question: Where do we get the data? We always need the data, and the response was something like, 'You don't have to worry about the data, we can get whatever data you want, we have the phones, we have the network, whatever data you want, we can get it for you.'"

"Okay," I said to Fung uneasily.

As he told me this, Fung let out a nervous laugh, and we both paused, each of us contemplating and coming to the same conclusion. Fung guessed that the directors of the company meant that all the data would come from within China, so he shouldn't worry about the ethics of its collection. Fung didn't agree. Privacy in cybersecurity is the essence of his work. He told them he was going back to his job, a graceful way to say no, as he put it to me. Despite the money, a dream lab and ample research resources, Fung knows right from wrong when it comes to the privacy rights of people, be they Chinese or Canadian or from anywhere else.

———

There was nothing uncommon about Chinese companies publicly partnering with Canadian universities. Nearly two decades into the twenty-first century, it was happening around the country, despite concerns appearing in the media about some PRC companies acquiring Western IP and being directly connected to the CCP.

In 2018, the University of Toronto and Huawei agreed to extend an existing partnership by five years. Ali Sheikholeslami, a professor at the University of Toronto in electrical and computer engineering, claimed in a press release that it was "important to partner with companies that share the vision we hold as a university of addressing significant challenges of our society over the longer term."[5] But it wasn't just the University of Toronto engaging in partnerships with Huawei. The University of Waterloo had established a similar partnership in 2016. The president and vice-chancellor of Waterloo were welcomed at Huawei's headquarters in Shenzhen, China. Huawei was even given a research and development office in the university's David Johnston Research and Technology Park.

But Huawei wasn't just providing funding and partnering with the University of Toronto and the University of Waterloo. The University of British Columbia also signed a research collaboration agreement in 2017, covering next-generation communications and data analytics. And it wasn't just the universities of Toronto, Waterloo and BC. McGill University had also received research dollars from Huawei.

A trend begins to emerge.

By 2019, Huawei was funding about $50 million in academic research in Canada. This is the same company that was accused of being a Trojan horse for the CCP, and that was eventually banned from the 5G network infrastructure in Five Eyes countries. While all this funding was flowing into Canada, Huawei spent nearly zero in the US because the company had been flagged there as a security concern for so long. Yet for the Americans' supposed closest ally ("closest" perhaps only by geography), the brakes on Huawei's funding of university research were applied only years later. It wasn't only Canada's allies, either, that had been warning about China's acquisition of IP through research partnerships. In 2018, CSIS had engaged in presentations to academics about China exploiting a "culture of openness" to acquire knowledge and technology. China was named in these presentations, but not publicly. Much like other government agencies in Canada, and the government itself, Canada's intelligence community appeared to have a hard time calling out China's tactics in a way all Canadians could hear.

Patent lawyer Jim Hinton put it this way when discussing the way Canada willingly allows IP to fly out the door: "Canada is creating the technology and will pay to use the technology we created. We're missing out on that middle piece—the commercialization of innovation. That's where the money is . . . As it currently stands in the technology space, Canada is an employee and consumer state—we work for pennies to harvest the land, then pay our foreign masters dollars to eat what we had harvested." Thirteen of Canada's leading research universities signed deals like the ones I mentioned above, and yet it was Huawei that used the Canadian research to file its own patents.[6]

But these were not the only research collaborations that seemed to betray Canada's investment in them. Researchers at fifty different Canadian universities—*fifty*, including all the major research institutions mentioned above—conducted research with, and published papers between 2005 and 2022 with, scientists who had ties to the PLA. For nearly twenty years this situation was permitted to continue unabated. *The Globe and Mail* reported that from 2018 through 2023, researchers at Canada's ten leading research universities published more than 240 papers on topics the government considers sensitive, such as "quantum cryptography, photonics and space science," with PLA scientists at the National University of Defense Technology (NUDT). Some of the Chinese scientists are experts in missile systems and autonomous surveillance. The NUDT was, as *The Globe and Mail* put it, "blacklisted" by the United States in 2015 and subjected to US export controls during the Obama administration because the Americans believed it "is involved, or poses a significant risk of being or becoming involved[,] in activities that are contrary to the national-security or foreign-policy interests of the United States." Indeed, PRC president Xi Jinping praised the NUDT, claiming it was a "highland for training high-quality new military personnel and for independent innovation in national defence technology." The NUDT also informs the CCP's Central Military Commission.

Canada's main trading partner, the ally with which it has the most military and defence agreements and that it depends on for intelligence and security, blacklisted this institution in 2015. Despite that, Canadian researchers partnered with researchers from NUDT on sensitive research projects and published hundreds of papers with them. In short, Canadians were helping researchers at a PRC institution that is very likely intended to undermine and challenge US national security—and, by extension, Canada's. If this wasn't bad enough, even Canada's National Sciences and Engineering Research Council, which is the federal government's funder of scientific research across the country, contributed to this research with PLA scientists.[7]

———

China's aggressive attempts to recruit Fung continued. When he returned to Canada, the company approached him again and told him they understood he wanted to be a professor, but maybe he could just be a consultant for the company? They offered him triple his McGill salary, and he asked what he needed to do in return. They said he just had to answer their emails if they had questions. These would be questions about AI research, and the company would give money to McGill for his research team. Fung declined again.

The corporation approached him yet again at the precise time Fung was eligible to take a sabbatical. "I don't know how they calculated this," Fung told me, "but . . . two to three years later, they contacted me at the exact time I was eligible to have sabbatical leave. They said, 'We know you are eligible to have a leave again. Would you consider being a consultant for us?'" Fung again turned them down. At this point, "they started to get the message I wasn't going to join them, so they started to approach my students." Fung said they approached his post-doctoral students who had just graduated, and he figured they were trying to access his research through them.

Fung shared some of his experiences with a Quebec journalist in 2023, and on the day a story ran about these recruitment attempts, the company contacted him again, and again representatives asked if he would join as a consultant. The company now said it was interested in malware analysis, the same work Fung's students were currently doing. Fung refused.

Fung outlined how, in the past, PRC companies would approach Canadian researchers and ask for a partnership with the professor and to jointly apply for a Canadian federal funding grant. By 2021, the government had finally tightened the rules around receiving federal funds when partnering with foreign companies on sensitive research if the foreign partner could pose a national security risk. Applications could now face a national security review, although the process for that review was unclear. And even if this funding corridor was closed, the PRC could still poach Canadian academics and their research, because Canada's top ten research universities still would not bar academics from working with institutions like the NUDT. The universities claimed it's the federal government's job to tell them *definitively* whether a partnership is off limits; until then, the partnerships would continue.

In 2024, the government finally introduced a list of organizations with connections to foreign militaries, and NUDT was one of them. While the public release of this list is a positive step, it doesn't solve the problems of the partnerships. For instance, photonics is on the list of sensitive technologies that require a national security review for funding, but a Huawei rep is on the board of the "research consortium Photonics Canada" even though, in addition to the many other concerns about Huawei, it has worked with the PLA.[8]

Partnering for federal research money isn't the only way these partnerships were taking place. PRC companies and researchers with military ties also approach professors directly with research contracts. If the company goes directly to the university and a professor without seeking to partner for federal money, the professor can sign a contract with the company. This is outside government control, and whether these contracts happen depends entirely on the effectiveness of the university's research security offices in flagging potential security issues. Fung witnessed these kinds of partnerships take place, in which professors who worked for top North American tech companies in sensitive areas were approached by PRC competitors; the professors then "switch to the other side," move to the PRC and take their research with them to China. Chinese companies can also hire a professor as a consultant, as the company pursuing Fung kept trying to do, or they can reach Canadian researchers through the China Scholarship Council (CSC).

Many CSC-sponsored students come to Canada every year. They are top-quality students, but they are supported by the CCP and are compelled to sign an agreement that prevents them from doing anything to shame or embarrass the PRC government, Fung has testified to Parliament, and their families must sign this agreement as well. At the very least, these students would be barred from engaging in protests against the CCP. But because China controls their funding and ability to study abroad, they could also be forced into intelligence collection. If they resisted pressure to engage in this work for the PRC, their families could pay a price. The CSC can serve as a means to weaponize student scholarships in service of the state.

One of the PRC's most recent attempts to get at Fung was the cyberattack I mentioned at the beginning of this chapter. But what provoked it? In 2019, he joined a Facebook page about Hong Kong's pro-democracy protests, and he gave a speech online about the protests. The next day, he told me, "I received a completely blank email, an HTML-format email. It was weird to receive a blank email. So I looked into the code, there's a PNG in there, a picture file, a zero-pixel image. So it's a PNG file with no pixels in there. At that time there was a PNG vulnerability, a specific PNG vulnerability, so if your phone was using that PNG library, you would be subject to that vulnerability." But Fung said the email's targeting of the weak spot in his digital security wasn't an attack, at least not yet. He thought the email had been sent as a test. "This wasn't an attack yet. It was probing to see what type of device I was using, including the screen size, whether I'm using an Android or IOS, and that PNG file linked to an IP address. I used a geolocator to find the address is in China, in Shanghai." The likelihood of it being a state actor is high. Fung believed this was a more sophisticated kind of attack, one where the attacker would quietly seek to gather information about Fung, his contacts and possibly even his work.[9]

Graduate studies offices and international university offices, which work to build partnerships with universities abroad and to attract students, often take pride in setting up international partnerships, including with China. This causes friction between them and research security offices. Targeted academics I have spoken to maintain that these academic offices do not consider the security implications when arranging partnerships. Furthermore, they resist scrutiny from the security office. Professors concerned about research security told me that even when seminars on research security are made available to faculty, they are poorly attended by professors involved in sensitive research.[10]

———

The PRC's attempts to target Canadian researchers do not stop with efforts to acquire IP; they extend to influencing the perception of China within the university, and by extension within Canadian society. Beijing has long been aware that to engage in research partnerships, it needs to improve its image.

In the early 2000s, the PRC settled on invoking the ancient scholar Confucius to project an image of China that academics and the West could find agreeable. It created a series of international schools called Confucius Institutes (CI). But Confucius was just the symbol—a marketing strategy. What was actually being taught was the CCP version of China, complete with its views on Taiwan, Falun Gong, Tibet, Uyghurs and Hong Kong. The choice of Confucius for the name of the schools, as author Jonathan Manthorpe has noted, was "ironic" given that the Cultural Revolution that raged through China and was led by Mao centred on the destruction of China's traditional cultures. But selling "Mao Institutes" to the West would probably have been a struggle.

The CIs ran as an integrated system within institutions across multiple countries. Colleges, universities and even public school boards could host an institute. Chinese teachers would give classes in Chinese culture and language, and the money to pay for the institutes and teachers would come from the PRC. Drawing students from the local Chinese community at little expense presented a means for schools to boost their enrolment, which made CIs an attractive option. The PRC sold these as a means of culture promotion, no different from what European countries had engaged in over the years with the Goethe Institut or Alliance française, except this wasn't about sharing Chinese culture and language. It was CCP propaganda.

The first CI appeared in 2004 in Tashkent, Uzbekistan. This was no random test site. Uzbekistan has a large Chinese expat population, and it wants PRC investment and immigration. Its government courts foreign investment and specifically needs capital. The economy grew 6 percent in 2018 and has maintained that level of growth to the present, thanks in part to the country's young population and rapid industrialization. As a gateway to central Asia, it plays a central role in China's Belt and Road Initiative (BRI). The BRI is China's plan to create a new "silk road," investing in infrastructure projects across the globe until all trading roads lead back to Beijing. The investments create a situation in which China can wield influence over indebted countries. It has poured investments and loans into Uzbekistan, and having the country host the first CI helps Uzbekistan continue to see China in the way China wants to be seen, and ensures that PRC expats and their families maintain a link to the PRC, never venturing too far ideologically.[11]

Essential to the BRI is the Asian Infrastructure Investment Bank (AIIB). China created the bank in 2016, and the US immediately viewed it as a means for China to advance its foreign policy agenda, including the financing of BRI initiatives. The US discouraged allies from joining. Canada joined in 2018, though in 2023 it opted to freeze its ties with the bank after Bob Pickard, the bank's Canadian global communications director, fled China. Pickard publicly announced the bank was under the control of the CCP. When we spoke, he told me that party people "would run amok at the bank." Canadian government officials who participated in meetings asked too few questions, in his view, because out of Canada's $1 billion investment in the AIIB, he never saw in his tenure "a single benefit to Canada or Canadian taxpayers"—no investment in Canadian enterprise or foreign investment opportunities for Canadians. Canada was "getting nothing in return," and he could not understand why Canada was putting its reputation on the line by investing in this bank.

In Pickard's previous business dealings, the business environment in China had been one where people got things done and didn't "stand on ceremony." Things changed when Xi took power and the business community faced uncertainty about how he would govern. When Pickard joined the AIIB, he thought China benefited from the bank but didn't control it, and he expected it would serve as a new rival to the World Bank. As an apparently multilateral organization, it even had other Western powers as members. His optimism about the bank was quickly tested when he learned that in order to get resources for his job, be it new hires or office funding, he had to go through CCP members who worked with him.

In Pickard's view, the bank functioned as the "PR arm of the Belt and Road Initiative." It would finance BRI projects in countries where it could play hero to locals for getting projects done. It didn't matter that the bank was "multilateral," he was told by a CCP member; you needed "two wings to fly." One wing was the BRI and the other was the AIIB. The bank operated "basically like a Chinese bank." People were appointed to work in senior executive offices, but no one knew what the appointees did, other than being party members. Locks were installed on the president's office so foreigners working there didn't have easy access to it. The picture Pickard was painting for me was of a bank that maintained a benevolent multilateral veneer but was being controlled within by individuals tied to the party whose sole function was to monitor others. Suspicion was cast on any Westerners who worked there.

Pickard became uncomfortable when he was ordered to post condolences on the AIIB's website regarding the death of a former PRC state official. He protested the order because he didn't think a multilateral organization should do this. The AIIB hadn't posted condolences when Queen Elizabeth II died, for instance, so why do it for a PRC official? He realized he hadn't really been hired to be the global director of communications; instead, "they wanted my job to be Director General of Propaganda." He also learned that an assistant assigned to him was a party member tasked with reporting on his activities. In 2023, less than two years after accepting his position, Pickard's values compelled him to resign, which he did once in Japan and safely out of China.

As of this writing, Canada has frozen its involvement with the AIIB but remains a member.[12]

———

By 2018, 511 CIs were operating around the world. Twelve were in Canadian universities and colleges, and thirty-five were in Canadian high schools. Well before most of them were established, there was already plenty of reason to believe these were propaganda outlets for the CCP. In 2009, in *The Economist*, Li Changchun, a senior member of the PRC's Politburo Standing Committee, stated that the CIs were "an important part of China's overseas propaganda set-up." In 2019, the CI's governing council was chaired by Liu Yandong, who was the former head of China's United Front Work

Department (UFWD), the CCP's main body for engaging in over-seas influence.

The first CI in Canada was set up in 2006 at the British Columbia Institute of Technology (BCIT). It drew hardly any students, though BCIT's vice-president lauded the opportunity to "build bridges" between countries. What did those bridges look like? The CI agreements with Canadian schools had secrecy clauses that gave the CIs complete control over what political topics could and could not be taught in them. You read that correctly: Beijing decided what topics were off limits in CIs hosted in Canadian universities, colleges and high schools. Here's a look at that secrecy clause:

The two parties to the agreement will regard this agreement as a secret document, and without written approval from the other party, no party shall ever publicize, reveal, or make public, or allow other persons to publicize, reveal or make public materials or information obtained or learned concerning the other party, except if publicizing, revealing or making it public is necessary for one party to the agreement to carry out its duties under the agreement.

Have you come across a school in Canada that engages in this kind of secrecy about what it teaches? Article 5 of the agreement states the CIs must follow the customs, laws and regulations of China, as well as those of the hosting nation. You might reasonably question how following both simultaneously can even be possible in a democratic country.

Cracks in the CI veneer began to emerge with warnings from CSIS of the soft-power purpose of the institutes. In 2011, Sonia Zhao,

a teacher at McMaster University's CI, filed a human rights complaint with the province because she'd needed to hide her Falun
Gong beliefs in order to teach. McMaster didn't renew the cor tract
with their CI and it lapsed, leading to its closure in 2013. That year,
the Canadian Association of University Teachers demandec that
all CIs in Canadian universities and colleges be closed, and that they
cut ties with the Beijing office overseeing them. The group declared
the CIs were "essentially political arms of the Chinese government.
They restrict the free discussion of topics Chinese authorities deem
controversial and should have no place on our campuses."

The resolution had little effect on the overall status and adoption of CIs within Canadian schools. In some cases, the desire for
new CIs led to very public and contested battles. The Toronto
District School Board (TDSB) in 2014 opted to host a CI The
main proponent of the deal was the board chair, Chris Bolton. The
TDSB would have established the largest CI in the world. Protests
erupted between parents protesting the CI and supporters of it.
They squared off outside TDSB board meetings and ahead of votes.
Bolton was forced to resign from the board because he was found
to have steered school donations to his own charity before he joined
the board. He established a school in Vietnam shortly afterwards.
In the end, the TDSB voted against the CI because of its ties to
the CCP and the censorship in its curriculum.[13]

At the time of writing, eight Confucius Institutes are still oper-
ating in Canada. This includes one in the BC Coquitlam Public
School District, though in 2022 that CI was renamed the Chinese
Language and Culture Institute and is now supported by South
China Normal University (a rebranding I'll return to shortly).
China's Ministry of Education was clearly sensitive to what was
being exposed about the CIs, and so in 2020 it made an adjustment

and changed the name of the CI headquarters in China from Hanban to the Centre for Language Education and Cooperation. The centre is affiliated with the PRC's Ministry of Education and claims it is "committed to providing quality services for people from all over the world to learn Chinese and understand China."

Within Canada, CIs made the news in 2019 when New Brunswick opted not to renew its contract with a CI. Within CIs, no discussion of the Tiananmen Square massacre or the Cultural Revolution was ever permitted, nor was discussion of China's annexation of Tibet. Dominic Cardy, the former education minister of New Brunswick, has stated that when he supported the closing of the CI in 2019, the PRC consul general of the Montreal consulate came to his office unannounced and threatened New Brunswick lobster exports if Cardy didn't back down. The consulate denied Cardy's account, but he added that the consulate next reached out to the premier in 2021 as a last-ditch effort to keep the CIs open.[14]

———

Fung called it "feed, trap and kill."

In his view, the Confucius Institutes employed the same strategy to insinuate themselves into education systems as the PRC used to target academics. Where the talent programs targeted academics with funding offers, the CIs targeted the schools themselves. "They know when it's the right moment," he said. In 2010, for instance, the CIs were very actively approaching schools following a series of funding cuts. The CIs were a very enticing offer of value for students, communities and cash-strapped educators. This is the "feed" stage, as Fung described it in his parliamentary testimony. The "trap" stage occurs next, when a researcher or school becomes dependent on the money they are receiving and is thus compelled to go along with whatever is asked of them. The "kill" stage comes when the target is deemed to be no longer useful and is discarded or discredited. In the case of a researcher targeted with this strategy, it could mean the PRC spreads lies about them. Organizers of the CI events were the same group of people organizing other pro-PRC events in the community. The overlap in personnel indicated for Fung that the CIs were sponsored and promoted by the UFWD and the Chinese consulates.[15]

Were there more warnings about CIs? Of course, and they came from the United States. In 2019, the US Department of Defense made an announcement that it would not provide funding for any universities that hosted CIs. On August 13, 2020, the State Department labelled the Confucius Institute US Center, the CI's headquarters for its American locations, a "foreign mission of the People's Republic of China." The designation underlined "the opacity of this organization and its state-directed nature." It also meant that the organization had to report to the US government about its funding and personnel, as well as what it teaches and its activities within the United States. Canada had no laws that would allow it to demand the same.

As of this writing, Seneca College and Carleton University still have Confucius Institutes. Even after the designation in the US, the CI spokesperson at Carleton, Steven Reid, told *The Globe and Mail* that "at this time [2020], there is no evidence that anything prejudicial has been or is being promoted by the institute. The institute's activities and programs follow their stated purpose of sharing traditional Chinese cultures and languages."[16]

Rebranding of the CIs began in 2020, not surprisingly coinciding with the American designation of the US Center as a "foreign mission." Rachelle Peterson is a senior fellow at the National Association of Scholars in the US and co-authored a report on CIs. While she said that the closing of CIs was a success, she added,

> Its also a story of warning because right now the Chinese government is trying to sidestep those policies. In military terms, this would be called an outflanking maneuver. The Chinese government is betting that if it takes away the name, Confucius Institute, and tweaks the structure of a program, no one will realize the Chinese government influence remains alive and well in American higher education.

On July 1, 2021, a day after the CI at the College of William and Mary in Williamsburg, Virginia, shut its doors, a new "collaborative partnership with Beijing's Normal University" was announced. This PRC university was the former provider of CI programs to the college. The only thing that appeared to change, then, was the removal of the name "Confucius Institute." US representatives also claimed the CIs, and their new rebranded iterations, had ties to the CCP's international influencing organization, the UFWD. US representative Jim Banks said, "If you are in a Confucius Institute and create some programs with CCP money, would you host a memorial event for the Tiananmen Square Massacre? Of course not. Are there written rules that stop you? No. Did someone above tell you? No. It's self-censorship, it's psychological." According to Banks, people conducting PRC influence operations abroad don't need to be told what to do. The PRC's interests become their own.[17]

Why did China become so concerned about what was taught in schools? As scholars on the subject have documented, universities in China served as a gateway to the West for many years. But after the Tiananmen Square massacre, China modified its curricula and upped its level of supervision. After June 4, party secretaries were inserted into university administrations with the purpose of purging education of "all tendencies towards bourgeois liberalization," which the party saw as the cause of the student protest movement. Each department chair in the humanities had to review all their programs and courses and remove anything that contained a hint of Western ideals. Academic journals and student publications also came under review for "errors" made by faculty or students.

The State Education Commission led the charge in producing new program guidelines, with one of its top objectives being devotion to the political system. The Vice-Commissioner for Education, Teng Teng, stipulated in 1991 that the goal of humanities education was to create new heirs for socialism, not democracy. Electives should be Marxist in orientation because the university should not be interpreted as a "free market-place of ideas." These restrictions formed the basis for all PRC education after Tiananmen, in that the social sciences were to be subservient to the party, and all faculty were tasked with exposing the evils of Western ideas and democracy.

The PRC promoted "scientific socialism" instead of "democratic socialism." With science elevated to the highest level, little to no space remained for the kind of critical thinking and adoption of Western ideas that the party claimed led to Tiananmen. The type of individualism that was allowed to blossom in China in the 1990s would be tolerated only if it could be justified in the language of Marxism. The university became the hall monitor for the whole of the PRC's education system, ensuring any whiff of Western liberalism was expunged once detected. Ironically, the curriculum resembled the type of education changes made by the Nationalists in the 1930s, who feared challenges to the political order and sought to promote allegiance to that order through the education system.[18]

Xi Jinping has intensified the political messaging within the PRC. While past messaging that decried Western liberalism sought to emphasize the collective "us" within the PRC, Xi's revisions centred on the "evil of others." His message has been about restoring China to hegemonic power. The education system is supposed to produce classes of young patriots who express hostility to anything that could be perceived as acquiescence to the West or an insult to China. Xi's portrayal of the "China Dream"—his vision of an ascendant China articulated upon his assuming leadership of the party—was in essence about *making China great again*, so to speak. It combined bitterness over past abuses by foreign states with cautions about their current intentions and continual mention of China's past glory and great future. A strong military is central to Xi's vision, hence the acquisition of Western technology and IP. There is also no distinguishing between love of the state and reverence for the leadership of the CCP, and so criticism of the party is interpreted as unpatriotic and, if done by non-Chinese, as racist. The nation is depicted as rising to its rightful place, and its problems are blamed on "hostile foreign forces." The Umbrella Protest movement in Hong Kong, which challenged Xi's attempts to control Hong Kong's democratic system by essentially screening candidates for public office, was blamed on "external forces." Outside meddling was again blamed for the 2019 Hong Kong resistance movement against the creation of the fugitive amendment bill on extradition, with the PRC bypassing Hong Kong's legislature and creating the 2020 National Security Law, which made any critique of the CCP illegal and required Hong Kong lawmakers to prove their loyalty to Beijing. Foreign forces were also blamed for China's White Paper

Revolution of 2022, during which street protests erupted over China's failed zero-COVID restrictions.[19]

What are the ramifications, then, of China's, and more recently Xi's, nationalist push in education? It indoctrinates Chinese youth into the belief system of the party, one that masks the brutality inflicted on that same demographic decades ago at Tiananmen Square and more recently in Hong Kong. Professors of Chinese origin working in Canada told me of situations in which they published videos and statements critical of the PRC government's actions in Hong Kong only to have their graduate students from the PRC turn hostile towards them. One professor of Chinese descent told me they had taken on a grad student from the PRC who "was very polite and very respectful," but after an incident in which the professor criticized the PRC, the student had "suddenly become very rude." When the professor asked why the sudden change, the student told the professor they had seen the public remarks the professor made that were critical of China and they made the student very angry. The professor told me the student "thought that I betrayed my motherland, my mother nation, and then refused to collaborate on anything." International students from the PRC were also utilized to protest Hong Kong pro-democracy gatherings throughout Canada.

———

Academics of Chinese descent spoke to me chillingly about the Chinese Students and Scholars Associations (CSSAs). These are groups housed within universities around the world. They are organized for the benefit of international students and focus on three key issues: studying, accommodations and lunch (social meetings).

The associations encourage communication between members by the use of WeChat groups that focus on aspects of student life. That sounds delightful, but of course, for those unfamiliar with WeChat, it is the PRC-based social networking app that the CCP utilizes to monitor user activities and promote censorship. Tencent, the company that owns WeChat, said that it "operates in a complex regulatory environment, both in China and elsewhere," but a "core" tenet of the company "is that we comply with local laws and regulations in the markets where we operate." The CSSAs also arrange for airport pickup of new students, which means, as the academics noted, "from day one, you're with them."

I was told that individuals with pro-CCP views who run for municipal elections will reach out to groups like the CSSAs for supporters and volunteers. CSSAs have been accused of controlling the views and actions of visiting Chinese students, ensuring they are in line with the PRC government. Is there any reason to believe this? According to the US Department of State, there is certainly cause for concern.

When the PRC first began to allow its students to attend universities in the West, during the late 1970s, the Communist Party created scholar associations to monitor the actions of students and rally them in support of party activity. Since their creation over forty years ago, the US State Department has claimed, the CCP directives that compel the associations have not changed. Directing these associations is China's UFWD, the international foreign interference and influence arm of the Communist Party. It is a network whose specific aims are to control and influence local elites and community groups. Within the US, the bulk of CSSAs prohibit membership to non-Chinese citizens, which is a violation of university policy that student groups must not discriminate based on nationality for membership. In addition, the State Department notes that PRC missions (consulates and embassies) provide funding and direction to association chapters and have ordered them to disrupt events or talks that are critical of Communist Party ideology.

I asked the Australian PRC defector Yonglin Chen how PRC missions influence students and CSSAs. Chen believed that the PRC consulate and embassy operations in every country follow the same formula because "that's their goal, to promote the China mission and message abroad." Chen said that Chinese students must register with the consulate or embassy, and when they graduate, they need their degree to be authenticated by the PRC mission, which gives China a large degree of control over students. The CSSAs, Chen said, send reports to the PRC missions' educational office, and the mission will direct the associations to lodge complaints about other student clubs with the hosting university if the mission perceives other clubs to be hostile to the PRC. They would also try to ban student organizations they do not agree with, such as those linked to Hong Kong pro-democracy groups. China's nationalistic education system has also created "personality cults" around Xi Jinping, Chen claimed. The result is that PRC students who once needed to be formally directed to engage in counter-protests against opponents of Beijing now do so voluntarily.

The US still regards the CSSAs as an integral part of China's influence and interference network. In 2018, the US–China Commission formed by Congress reported that CSSAs "frequently attempt to conceal" their connections to the CCP and "are active in carrying out overseas Chinese work consistent with Beijing's United Front strategy." The Chinese embassy has dismissed claims that CSSAs are used to advance China's political objectives or harass students and said these allegations were "a sheer smear and vilification."[20]

———

In sum, Fung's "feed, trap and kill" formula seems to be at work in Western universities—starting with the "feed" stage, approaching a target by fulfilling a need. When timed correctly, the offer of financial support, be it to an individual professor or a university, can seem as if the PRC company or PRC university has just come along at a fortunate time. Recall the case with Fung, in which the offers came via a trusted friend and just happened to arrive when he was going on sabbatical. In the case of universities, partnership offers suddenly emerged when schools were reeling from budget cuts. This suggests that PRC officials are actively watching their influence targets. Faced with such a strategic approach, it is easy to see how institutions or individuals find themselves trapped by financial arrangements they cannot easily do without. Consider how colleges and universities can become dependent on the income generated from international students and CIs, or how a professor's research becomes dependent on foreign investment. Once that dependency sets in, it can be difficult to remove oneself from it without suffering serious financial costs. The "kill" stage that Fung identified occurs once that IP is stolen, the research value has been acquired, and the deals end. Vulnerable professors who speak out may now be smeared by the PRC with disinformation and see their careers ruined. Given that it is only very recently that Canada has begun to get more serious about protecting its IP, it is staggering to contemplate just how many patents, how much IP, how much economic value Canada has forfeited through these arrangements. The dollar figure would be impossible to calculate. Even the US, which has taken a much tougher stance over the years towards the PRC's attempts to acquire American IP, still finds itself fighting these battles.

Huawei was essentially blacklisted from funding research in the US, but it secretly managed to continue funding researchers at several American universities, including Harvard. Huawei turned out to be the sole funder of a research competition that had given out millions in the United States since 2022 and received proposals from top researchers, including at universities that were banned from engaging in research partnerships with Huawei. The Optica Foundation Challenge was run by a part of the non-profit society Optica. The society's members participate in sensitive research areas such as biomedical and laser research. Bloomberg reviewed a document intended to remain confidential between Optica and Huawei that stated the Optica Foundation "shall not be required to designate Huawei as the funding source or program sponsor" and that "the existence and content of this Agreement and the relationship between the Parties shall also be considered Confidential Information." In essence, the foundation would secretly allow Huawei to provide funding for the competition but then keep the company's role hidden from the participants. This strategy appeared to be one way Huawei circumvented US restrictions on its research funding.

Applicants and university officials notified of this situation by the press said they hadn't known Huawei was involved, with many thinking the funding came directly from the foundation. On Optica's website, other competitions funded by other corporate donors list their funders, but the competition funded by Huawei, which was twenty times richer than the next-richest funding award, did not. Huawei claimed it sought to hide its name to prevent the competition from being interpreted as "promotional." This type of funding arrangement would likely manage to skirt the US Commerce Department's regulations that prevent the sharing of technology with Huawei. It's not clear from Optica's public statements if it is commonplace for it to accept money from donors that want to be anonymous and are also under restrictions from the US Commerce Department.

These competitions are seeking science that is supposed to be published—and therefore shared with the public. Kevin Wolf, a specialist in export controls, explained that this loophole most likely enables the arrangement to be legal. Huawei isn't vacuuming up America's closely guarded IP if the research is being published. But the legality of Huawei's involvement is only one element. Appearances matter. The arrangement looks like an attempt to circumvent the rules. James Mulvenon, who co-authored a book on PRC espionage, told Bloomberg that "it's a bad look for a prestigious research foundation to be anonymously accepting money from a Chinese company that raises so many national security concerns for the US government." Optics aside, Jeff Stoff from the Center for Research Security and Integrity said the funding lets Huawei have a say in "what research projects it would like to see without having to contract directly with academic institutions." It could also give the company a chance to recruit researchers by funding individuals it's interested in through third-party organizations and then securing the IP from their research.

Regardless of the bad optics, professors were taking the bait. One researcher who applied to Optica's competition came from the Massachusetts Institute of Technology, which had announced in 2019 that it would halt new deals with Huawei. Universities were required to accept the money on behalf of the winners of the competition. Those universities included Harvard and the University of Southern California, as well as Canadian schools such as the University of British Columbia (UBC) and Wilfrid Laurier. UBC claimed its relationship was with Optica, and it was not aware of the third-party funding. A Huawei optical expert became a member of the foundation's parent organization in 2021, and Huawei had an executive on the selection committee for the foundation's next competition.

The Bloomberg story caught the attention of Congress. Lawmakers said the funding arrangement with Huawei helped foreign adversaries fund research. "By masking the source of the Optica Foundation Challenge funding, your organization has compromised the ability of US research institutions to comply with the law," the unnamed lawmakers stated. Following Bloomberg's reporting on this, the CEO of Optica resigned and the head of the foundation also left. In addition, Optica has severed all ties with Huawei, and the funding it received from Huawei since 2022 will be returned.[21]

The situation demonstrates how pervasive and persistent PRC companies are in their attempts to continue funding academic research. The hiding of Huawei's relationship to the competition bears similarities to the Confucius Institute's attempts to keep its arrangements with schools out of the public eye. The recent rebranding of the CIs suggests that little has changed. The PRC wants to continue its operations on university campuses, even if it is becoming more and more difficult to find ways to hide them.

Universities are one means of influencing Canadians, but China's ability to engage in any foreign interference and influence operations in Canada must begin with its ability to exercise its will over the communities China targets. These are the same communities the Canadian government had promised to protect against interference when it originally recognized the PRC in 1970. As the next chapter will so painfully demonstrate, these were promises that were unequivocally broken.

SIX

"YOUR EXISTENCE
BECOMES POLITICAL"

Transnational Repression in Canada

CHEUK KWAN CAME to Canada in the 1970s then returned to Hong Kong in the 1980s before participating in the student protest movements in 1989. When we spoke, he recalled a march in Hong Kong in the spring of 1989 and the feeling of being enlightened and so alive. I could hear the remnants of that optimism in his voice when we talked, nearly thirty-five years later. But his tone switched to one of dismay when he described how he and his friends had to leave Hong Kong after the Tiananmen Square massacre brought intense scrutiny on protesters, even in the British territory. Three years later, he became chair of the Toronto Association for Democracy in China. The group advocated for democratic reform, held memorials on June 4 and worked to expose human rights violations by China. He had personal experiences of PRC interference in Hong Kong and witnessed how these tactics were imported into Canada, where Hong Kong expats and Chinese Canadians have been battling them for decades since.[1] Kwan and other activists within the community shared their stories with me.

Despite China's attempts to portray the Chinese-Canadian community as a homogeneous whole, the most frequent targets of CPP interference within the community are what China has referred to as the "five poisons." These consist of pro-democracy movements, as well as support for Taiwanese independence, Tibetan independence, the Uyghurs in the Xinjiang region and the Falun Gong religious group. Spearheading this interference is the UFWD, the importance of which has grown during Xi Jinping's time as leader of the PRC.

This chapter will focus on the targets of PRC interference within the Chinese-Canadian community and other ethnic communities, and how people have resisted the interference that has continued ever since Canada recognized China in 1970. They have had little choice but to resist, as their calls for help often fell on deaf ears. As I have already demonstrated, even while China continued to meddle in Canadian communities, Ottawa, the business community and academia courted Chinese investment. As Ottawa turned a blind eye to what were often regarded as internal community battles, it made a crucial error, one the CCP has capitalized on for half a century.

The CCP exercises a transnational form of sovereignty that extends to wherever its citizens or former citizens live. It does not recognize other forms of citizenship and seeks to retain its control over its diaspora, or ones it claims ownership of, wherever they live. In doing so, China disregards the sovereignty of other nations as it applies to their Chinese diasporas, expatriates and descendants, irrespective of the laws and customs by which they now abide.

PRC interference of any kind has only ever been possible because the Canadian government ignored this transnational conception of sovereignty and the harassment it has facilitated within Canadian communities. With this extension of power allowed to take root there, it could spread to all of Canada.

Western intelligence is poorly equipped to deal with the kind of widespread threat the UFWD poses. As Australian academic and author Clive Hamilton has pointed out, this has led to its function and organization being largely misunderstood. So it is helpful to see how researchers believe it fits within the larger context of PRC interference operations.

The UFWD is an organization within the party and functions differently from China's intelligence service, the MSS. The UFWD is not an intelligence arm of the PRC state, though it can certainly collect intelligence—but of course, in the PRC, so can anyone. The "united front" is a reference to the melding together of the interests of the Communist Party with the state, and the UFWD is the principal organization that puts this means of enforcing party ideology into practice. It is a strategy that dates back to Vladimir Lenin, and a tactic he articulated in his pamphlet "Left Wing Communism: An Infantile Disorder":

> The more powerful enemy can be vanquished only by exerting the utmost effort, and *without fail*, most thoroughly, carefully attentively and skillfully using every, even the smallest, "rift" among the enemies, of every antagonism of interest among the bourgeoisie of the various countries . . . and also taking advantage of every, even the smallest, opportunity of gaining a mass ally, even though this ally be temporary, vacillating, unstable, unreliable, and conditional.

Domestically or abroad, this strategy involves finding allies who can be influential, control messaging and promote propaganda, and, if possible, collect intelligence. As Anne-Marie Brady, a political science professor at the University of Canterbury, New Zealand, has noted, in the midst of the Cold War, China relied on patriotic overseas Chinese to assist it with technological development, investment and helping get the PRC government recognized. When the united front supported Communist movements during the Mao years, Brady points out, it did so by "using civil actors to promote political ends." The party sought relationships with influential foreigners and overseas Chinese to influence but also, if necessary, "bypass" their home governments to support the CCP's global interests.

Following the Tiananmen Square massacre, united front work took on a renewed importance. The PRC had become isolated. Gaining support among overseas Chinese could help break that isolation and recover China's standing internationally. As Brady explains, the CCP's aim was to turn overseas Chinese groups "into propaganda bases for China." Through 1989, the State Council Overseas Chinese Affairs Office (OCAO) grew immensely in size and in its importance to the Communist Party. This office conducted and organized united front work among overseas Chinese communities to steer them towards supporting China's policies and away from the five poisons. The OCAO became subsumed formally under the control of the UFWD in 2018. UFWD personnel, as Yonglin Chen and Anne-Marie Brady have noted, often operate within the PRC missions abroad through China's Ministry of Foreign Affairs. Once posted in a mission, UFWD personnel court politicians or high-profile community members and support PRC media and cultural events. Embassies and consulates provide guidance to community groups, and high-ranking OCAO and UFWD officials meet with their leaders, some of whom are sent to conferences in China to keep them up to date on policy changes. The CCP tries to avoid giving the impression it is ordering or directing groups and individuals. Instead, Brady outlines how the party tries to present itself as a "guide," with overseas Chinese community leaders engaging with the UFWD as a "form of service, serving the Chinese Motherland, the Chinese race, and the ethnic Chinese population within the countries where they live." The party presents this as being good for community development and good for China. Groups that try to avoid "guidance," such as groups that fall into the category of the five poisons, become targets of united front work, with other groups mobilizing to operate against them.

In some cases, united front work moves beyond China's foreign policy aims and is used as a means of cover for intelligence operatives. The Ministry of State Security, Ministry of Public Security, PLA Joint Staff Headquarters' Third Department, Xinhua News Service, and International Liaison Department have all been utilized by the PRC for intelligence collection and have been put in service of the UFWD. Other bodies also participate in the united front strategy, like the All-Chinese Federation of Returned Overseas Chinese and the Chinese People's Political Consultative Conference (CPPCC), which is a major political conference that takes place in the same weeks as the National People's Congress—China's legislative body—holds its annual session. Both the Federation and the Consultative Conference participate in the united front strategy, but they don't fall under the direct control of the UFWD—in the same way that China's military can participate in the united front without being controlled by the UFWD.[2]

How, then do things play out in the community?

———

Cheuk Kwan was among the original founders of the Chinese Canadian National Council (CCNC) in 1980. The group advocated for human rights in China, supported anti-racism policies and promoted pro-democracy initiatives. It also connected with and supported Chinese immigrants across Canada.

Post–Tiananmen Square, in the early 1990s, Kwan noticed the appearance of a new advocacy group, the National Congress of Chinese Canadians (NCCC). Kwan regarded it as an "astroturfing" organization that gave the impression of community leadership. Just consider the similarity in initials—CCNC and NCCC. The emergence of this group was a significant play for influence, because when "the [Canadian] government comes calling," wanting to speak to leaders within the Chinese-Canadian community, the NCCC and other groups he claimed were pro-Beijing, step up to answer. Most Canadians would never notice the distinctions between these groups.

After 1989, much as Brady describes in her landmark paper "Magic Weapons: China's Political Influence Activities Under Xi Jinping," Kwan believes that China sought to improve its image and bolster support for the PRC regime abroad. It used groups like the NCCC to promote the policies of Beijing through apparently community-based voices. Kwan noticed that many of these organizations share the same leaders, and they are loyal to the Chinese consulates. This isn't hidden, Kwan pointed out. The support these "astroturfing" organizations give the PRC is reciprocated with visits from consular officials at public events, further cementing the impression of the organizations' legitimacy as voices of the community. As a 2024 article from *The Economist* highlighted, in some cases overseas Chinese genuinely support the CCP because doing so can lead to business opportunities in China or ensure the safety of family still there. The NCCC denies it has a pro-Beijing stance and states that its position is politically neutral.

One of the first issues where Kwan claims his group clashed with new pro-Beijing groups was Chinese head tax redress—acknowledgement that Canada's punitive tax on Chinese immigrants from 1885 through 1923 remained a stain on Canada's past and an unsettled source of grievance within the community. His group advocated for the Canadian government to apologize and settle the issue, but then the NCCC joined this discussion to negotiate with the government, with the support of a government minister. The NCCC did not support an apology, only a financial settlement. The result was a persistent deadlock on the issue. Kwan claims the NCCC was promoting a counter-narrative to the idea that Chinese immigrants had been unfairly targeted as undesirable to Canada in favour of one in which strong Chinese workers had come to Canada to build the Canadian Pacific Railway but were unfairly compensated. Kwan claims that the people promoting the counter-narratives have no connection to descendants of the head tax and no vested interest in cultural redress. Another counter-narrative initiative emerged during debate with the TDSB over the implementation of the Confucius Institute into the curriculum. Kwan's group opposed bringing CIs into Canada, but he stated that the same groups emerged to promote a counter-narrative in support of the CIs as a form of valuable cultural exchange. He recognized these counter-narrative tactics he was seeing in Canada as the same united front tactics he'd witnessed in Hong Kong.

I asked the PRC defector Yonglin Chen if he knew anything about the groups Kwan had mentioned to me, like the NCCC. Chen claimed he was labelled as a traitor to the PRC by the NCCC when he visited Canada after his defection. He believed the NCCC, and other organizations structured like it, were aligned

with the UFWD because they operated in a near-identical way to
Australian community organizations he knew to be connected
to the UFWD, such as the Australian Council for the Promotion
of the Peaceful Reunification of China. PRC methods for domi-
nating community groups, he believed, are the same everywhere.
UFWD-aligned groups "have a hierarchy structure because it
makes it easy to command" member groups under the umbrella
of the organization. The PRC mission ultimately controls them,
though they do compete with each other for support and recognition. Some are created with an initial grant from the PRC
consulates or embassies, usually two thousand dollars, Chen said.
If the organization is a "top one," one that controls other groups,
it has usually been created by China for the purposes of control
of the community and will only "operate at the will of Chinese
officials," he explained. This type of "superstructure" encompass-
ing multiple organizations then draws other existing groups who
reach out to join. The NCCC has repeatedly stated that it is
politically neutral and denies that it has a pro-Beijing stance and
is controlled by the PRC mission or CCP.

While I learned much from the first generation of activists, I
also connected with newer ones. Cherie Wong is among the new
activists who joined movements after the PRC undertook repression against her community. She grew up in post-handover Hong
Kong and moved to Canada as a teen. While in Canada, she
watched from afar as the PRC attempted to crush pro-democracy
protesters in Hong Kong. She felt compelled to do something
about it. Though open and friendly, Wong's fierceness comes out
when she talks about China's attempt to control people.

For Hong Kongers back home or abroad, Wong explained,

surveillance is something people live with daily, and it manifests even in the comfort of their own homes. "You're having dinner and someone brought up something sensitive, and you're told, 'Shussh . . . the neighbours could be listening.'" In the more distant past, family members who had taken issue with the CCP found themselves in labour camps. When she was growing up, however, there wasn't much that couldn't be said, though one never directly attacked or criticized the party. Wong remembers how this started to change in Hong Kong in 2003 with the creation of Article 23, a law targeting sedition and subversion against the CCP. She remembers going to protests against it with her family, before they left for Canada. The opposition wasn't hidden then. By 2014, this had begun to change, and people were masking at protests. Then overseas, Wong founded a new organization, Alliance Canada Hong Kong. She and her group members had witnessed surveillance against activists in Hong Kong through monitoring of their transit records, geolocating on phones and using cameras to identify their movements in real time. Now that targeting was about to be directed her way—in Canada.

In 2019, Wong began to receive so many death and rape threats online that her phone would not stop alerting her, and by October of that year she was feeling threatened in person. She attended a protest on Parliament Hill that occurred on the PRC National Day of October 1. She and fellow protesters were "kettled," basically surrounded and held in place. This is a known tactic used by police to intimidate defiant protesters. But it wasn't police holding the protesters in place, it was pro-CCP demonstrators. Prior to the COVID pandemic, masks were not permitted on the Hill. Cherie Wong was easily identified amidst the crowd. Following this protest, as well as her public speeches in support of Hong Kong and against foreign interference, "I was told by people on chat groups that my name, my information, neighbourhoods that I visited, was being massively shared on chat groups. One day I was waiting at a bus stop . . . minding my own business . . . scrolling on my phone, feeling weird . . ." She looked up and saw two people of Asian descent staring at her. One of the pair "had their phone in my face recording me . . . and the other guy is on his phone texting . . . This was really strange. I tried to approach them and they turned and ran across the street . . . Since then, things like that do happen to me on a seemingly regular basis."

Wong participated in a protest outside the Chinese embassy and afterwards noticed a car following her. On another day, she was walking her dog after a media story had appeared about the kinds of harassment she was experiencing. As she was entering her apartment building, she made eye contact with a man watching her from across the street. He then "just booked across the street, so I start booking it into my apartment building and I pulled the door shut and he started banging on the glass door, screaming profanities at me."

As Wong related these events to me, I could hear the frustration in her voice and could feel how this upset her as she described it. She reported these incidents to police, only to be told "you're not in danger" and no threat could be observed, even though she warned police this could be transnational repression.

Wong and her fellow group members started hearing about foreign interference from the community, too. But it wasn't until 2021, when they came out with their "In Plain Sight" report on foreign interference, that more media and politicians started taking notice of community concerns. She continued:

What [community members] worry about is, if I attended a Hong Kong protest, will they [the CCP] bully me for it? As an international student, will my scholarship get revoked if the embassy or the consulate finds out about it? For those that are established and working and are Canadian citizens, they worry about job promotions. If you work for someone who does business with China, they are certainly not going to promote you if you are seen as anti-China because you now piss off the person who your business is collaborating with. Professors who will not get funding if they don't smile and nod at funders who also happen to do business in China. There are so many layers of cost-benefit analysis in a diaspora's life, on a social basis—"Will my friend hate me? Will my friend's family hate me? Will my husband's family hate me? Will my own family hate me for doing this [speaking out against the CCP]?" Friends who will cut ties with you, who will happily call the police on you, which is not unheard of, people would actually tell, "Oh, my little niece is doing this, and you should know about it, and this is information I can give you about her."

Wong didn't see this behaviour as necessarily malicious, but done out of self-interest and even self-preservation, a way for people to protect themselves from CCP suspicion. In Hong Kong, a call like this would be made to a hotline for reporting suspicious behaviour; in Canada, there are other means of reporting people to the PRC. International students can go to the CSSA, who can in turn contact the PRC mission. "In the diaspora," Wong told me, "you don't need to 'report' but rather whisper and gossip" about someone, which would then lead to the community gossiping and coming out to isolate the person. The PRC mission then doesn't need to devote much in the way of resources to monitoring communities abroad. "They can just watch what's happening on WeChat channels, on discussion forums," Wong told me. The community has internalized the surveillance it has been subjected to and now polices itself. Actively reporting others to the PRC mission remains the exception, not the norm, she said, and those who do it are most likely leaders in community groups and people with financial interests in China—people tend to know who they are. But it is the threat of surveillance and monitoring that is most effective, keeping community members in a condition of not knowing whether their case is a "bad one" that warrants the attention of the state.

Katherine Leung of the group Hong Kong Watch told me other stories of community members in Canada facing harassment and threats. In one case, a woman I'll call Anna, to protect her identity, participated in the 2019 pro-democracy marches in Hong Kong. She fled to Canada in 2020 and claimed asylum. Anna continued her advocacy but began receiving threatening messages via the social media app Telegram. Some of these included graphic images of a woman with blunt force trauma to her head, and the sender had details about Anna's life such as her work address, the name of her boyfriend and photos of her friend. She reported the incidents to police, but she doesn't know whether they investigated.

In another case, a pro-democracy activist in Canada was planning on travelling to Japan when they were messaged anonymously by someone on Telegram that they should "take care" of their daughter during the trip. The activist hadn't told anyone about the upcoming travel with their daughter. Someone had found out and was now making threats about the daughter's safety were she to stay behind in Canada.

Lawsuits are another mechanism by which the CCP and its supporters use democratic institutions to harass and intimidate the diaspora. Sheng Xue, who shared with me her story of the night of June 3 to 4 at Tiananmen Square, told me how she was subjected to a lawsuit from an individual who repeatedly and wrongfully accused her of being a spy for China. For months, the individual would stand on Parliament Hill holding signs that defamed her, and despite Xue's repeated attempts to stop this behaviour by notifying police, nothing was ever done. Instead, the individual sued her. By the time the suit was tossed out for lacking merit, she had spent months agonizing about it and paying for legal advice. Xue believes it was another attempt by the PRC to silence her pro-democracy activism.

In another case Leung mentioned, a member of a Calgary pro-democracy group was sent a video of an ISIS beheading and told he and others in the group would meet the same fate. The video was sent alongside images of the activist participating in a rally outside the PRC consulate in Calgary. In the Toronto area, a car painted to look like a Chinese police vehicle was spotted on the road. It is hard to imagine this as anything but another attempt to remind the community who the real authorities are.

Activists often face surveillance and threats of violence at protests. Activists told me Hong Kong protesters were regularly photographed in Canada by individuals sitting at a distance, especially when the protest was outside a PRC consulate. They found a way of resisting these surveillance attempts: by photographing the people taking the pictures and drawing attention to them.

The community also fights back by compiling reports on foreign interference against activists, making these surveillance and intimidation tactics known to the broader Canadian public. This exposes

AN ACTIVIST CONFRONTING A PERSON PHOTOGRAPHING A PROTEST IN CANADA.

the individuals in the community engaging in foreign interference on behalf of the PRC to public scrutiny; in the absence of sufficient laws in Canada against the activity, public shaming is one of the few methods the community can use to fight back. Activists infiltrated pro-CCP groups on WeChat to monitor their activities, mirroring the surveillance done to them. One activist shared with me a screenshot of a pro-CCP WeChat group discussion in which people in the group were watching a pro-democracy protest from a high-rise building in Hong Kong. People in the chat were calling for others to throw chairs and other things down on the protesters from above, which if done from the height seen in the photos would have seriously injured if not killed someone. I was told that in other forums, pro-CCP WeChat groups called for pork oil to be thrown at Uyghur protesters as an insult to their religious beliefs.

———

Another "poison" in the eyes of the PRC is the Falun Gong religious organization, also known as Falun Dafa. Falun Gong focuses on meditation and the transcendence of the soul, and its adherents believe in reincarnation. The group is also anti-CCP and anti-revolutionary, which led to it being banned in China in 1999, despite having an estimated 70 million followers in the country. Over the years, international human rights organizations like Amnesty International and Human Rights Watch have reported on the persecution Falun Gong has experienced, including arbitrary beatings of practitioners and their families, along with detentions and abductions.

In Canada, Falun Gong members' fear of PRC targeting is immense. While a few people connected to the group agreed to speak to me, none would agree to be identified. A media outlet connected to Falun Gong in Canada, *The Epoch Times*, has been actively documenting suspected cases of PRC interference in Canada. I was told by supporters how pro-CCP actors would try to smear the reputation of the group. This included emailing politicians en masse, labelling and accusing the group of being "a cult." Discrediting the organization as a cult spreads through word of mouth within the community, and the defamation becomes widely accepted as fact. It wasn't long before I got a taste of what Falun Gong members put up with as a fact of life.

When I spoke to a Canadian individual connected to the group, we met in a public place, a coffee shop in a largely Chinese community. We sat, just the two of us, at a high table with seating for four. Plenty of other seats were available in the café. After I had conversed with my interview subject for about forty minutes, a man approached our table and sat right beside me, pulled out his phone and began using it. He said nothing, just sat with us in an otherwise half-empty café. It was immediately clear to me this was an unsubtle attempt to silence our conversation. In retrospect, I am mindful of the gap in culture and experience between my interview subject and me. While I stared at this man and would have had no qualms with calling out his blatant intrusion in public, I refrained. I refrained because I considered suddenly all that was at stake in this moment for my interviewee. We moved our conversation outside, and the table we sat at soon attracted others interfering as brazenly as the man inside had done.

I was struck profoundly by the realization that we were being deliberately silenced from speaking in a public place—in Canada—by people acting on behalf of a foreign government. This was something I had never experienced. I gave serious thought to whether this was just a case of someone being rude. If it really was someone acting in support of the CCP, what did they know of me or my interviewee despite the precautions we had taken? But I supposed that was the effect the PRC was aiming for. Maintaining uncertainty in a target's mind is a means of exerting control through their unease and paranoia. At the same time, I wondered if disregarding the intimidation tactic and speaking anyway was an effective means of fighting back. Possibly, but it is admittedly easier to consider doing that when you don't have to work, eat and sleep in the targeted community.[3]

———

As I sought to meet others who had been targeted, I took even greater steps to ensure their protection, such as being far more selective about where we met. I turned my attention to another community regarded as one of the "five poisons," the Uyghurs, and spoke with Mehmet Tohti. Tohti has been an activist for decades and has lived a life of exile since 1991. He has isolated himself completely from his siblings and family while pushing to make the plight of the Uyghurs in China part of a national conversation in Canada. Disputes emerged early in the establishment of the PRC between Uyghurs and the CCP. The Uyghurs have claimed ancestry in the western Xinjiang region for centuries. CCP policies over the years have included promoting Han Chinese migration into Xinjiang and suppressing expressions of Uyghur identity. In response, public unrest and terrorist attacks occurred throughout the 2000s. In 2014, the PRC launched a new crackdown on the region that included widespread surveillance of the civilian population and even incarcerations without trial, forced labour and internment camps.

In February 2021, Canada's Parliament voted 266–0 in favour of declaring what was happening to the Uyghurs in Xinjiang a "genocide," though the prime minister and most of the cabinet abstained from the vote. The United States passed legislation in 2021 to halt the import of goods manufactured through forced Uyghur labour, but at the time I spoke to Tohti, Canada was still lagging on the issue.

Tohti recounted the kind of transnational repression he and others in his community face and recalled that, for him, it began in 2007. Neighbours made him aware of two SUVs that appeared to be watching him day and night, and that came and went when he did. Tohti reported these incidents to authorities, but it was always "in one ear and out the other." The targeting tends to be carefully timed. Threatening phone calls often arrive when major public events highlighting the Uyghur plight are about to occur. This prompted Tohti to point out that "someone follows the schedule." Oftentimes, he claimed, the PRC would try to manipulate him with disinformation, such as telling him his uncle was in hospital when really, Tohti believed, his uncle had been jailed. In another instance, in 2023, as Tohti was leaving a summit in Quebec on the plight of the Uyghurs that had government departments such as Global Affairs in attendance, two cars started following him. One had a covered licence plate. Tohti believed all this was done to make him aware he was under watch "all the time." It is a type of psychological torture. He said it has become "routine" to be monitored openly in Canada by a foreign government, and to see his reports of the incidents to local police or RCMP disappear because he cannot link these occurrences to confirmed PRC agents. Tohti said the PRC twists the raising of awareness of this repression into accusations of "racism," and that ultimately the harassment continues because of political parties' unwillingness to "lose the vote" in Chinese-Canadian communities.

———

I next turned to the Tibetan-Canadian community and spoke with Chemi Lhamo, an activist who had been targeted by the PRC while she was a student at the University of Toronto. Our meeting was arranged through an intermediary. Although Lhamo maintains she is a public activist and takes it upon herself to speak publicly on these issues, it was becoming clear to me that precautions were still necessary, and I took what care I could to ensure we met safely. What weighed on me again was that this was Canada. Taking precautions to meet a fellow Canadian in public, in Canada—this was now required? It was incredible to me, yet here I was.

We exchanged pleasantries and sat down for coffee. Almost immediately, Lhamo set the tone, helping me understand her situation and that of her community. Tibetans abroad are a stateless community. She had arrived in Canada from India at the age of eleven. Lhamo told me that often Tibetan refugees have no passports and are unable to identify as citizens of any state. It's one more thing most Canadians take for granted. What happens to your existence without those documents that prove your birth when your country is gone? The majority of Tibetans now live in India and Nepal. Lhamo put it best: When you are stateless, "your existence becomes political."

I sat with that phrase for a moment, trying to relate. I could only scratch the surface of understanding, having been through nothing comparable. For Tibetans, their existence as a stateless people, not accepting the annexation of their homeland by the PRC, automatically puts them in a political space. How can most Canadians possibly relate to being caught in that liminal space where your identity and existence are now a political liability and inconvenience for a powerful nation?

Lhamo had a calmness about her, as if she had been forced to age quickly and well beyond her years. She spoke with a note of deep introspection. It was clear to me that she spent time ruminating on the predicament faced by Tibetans, in addition to fighting against it. Our conversation turned to more recent history, when Lhamo became a target of the CCP. She was already involved in anti-racism and Free Tibet campaigns on the University of Toronto Scarborough campus when she was elected to the student union.

As vice-president, she had been working with Chinese international students to support their rights as part of her portfolio, which made what happened next all the more surprising. Someone had leaked her intention to run for president, and she immediately became a target. Petitions amassing thousands of signatures protested her candidacy. She was threatened with death and violence on WeChat and told she couldn't be president because of her separatist thoughts. As she said to me of taking a public stand against the PRC's repression in Tibet, "you are reminded by the world" about who you are.

Along with the barrage of threats, lies were circulated claiming she didn't support students. Security at the university told her they "didn't have time" to deal with something of this magnitude, but it was becoming abundantly clear this was about more than bullying. She approached the police, and among the tens of thousands of messages directed her way, it was clear some were legitimate threats. She opted not to pursue charges that could be levied against her fellow students, though she continued to be harassed and followed on campus, even into washrooms. Hong Kong students had to cover their faces and hide their identities just to speak to her, as their newly elected student union president. "They had to risk so much," Lhamo said—just to talk. University students in Canada had to hide their identities to speak to a student union leader on campus. How on earth could this be tolerated in Canada?

Lhamo's situation attracted media exposure, which led to the threats against her dying down. Months of isolation during the pandemic actually helped her stay physically safe. But life has not been the same since for Lhamo. She has spoken with journalists and Non-Governmental Organizations (NGOs) and met parliamentarians. But the bigger purpose of helping the stateless remains. She can't afford to say no to their cause, but it has meant asking her family to disconnect from her for their own safety. Sadly, it is a sacrifice I have heard too many say they have had to make.

I asked Lhamo how all this has made her feel. She said she had to feel optimism, though she admitted it was mixed with frustration and disappointment, as she felt her community's plight was ignored by Canada. But Lhamo believed she and her fellow activists would keep fighting until Canadians understood what was happening in their own country. She had no choice, she said, because "I don't have any other Canada."[4]

———

Examples of transnational repression targeting individuals are far too numerous to mention them all, even just the ones that happened in Canada. Where there are individuals from one of the "five poisons" speaking out against the PRC, repression attempts quickly follow. The origins of this kind of foreign interference illuminate its current employment around the globe.

For instance, in an attempt to unify Taiwan with China under the "one country–two systems" model, the PRC launched united front tactics from groups based in Fujian province, 130 kilometres across the Taiwan Strait. The idea was to create economic links between the mainland and Taiwan so that the short-term economic linkages could help facilitate the long-term goal of unification. The strategy has been in place at least since US recognition of the PRC in 1979. To the CCP, no friends and no enemies are ever permanent. Such standing is determined by historical conditions and can change, which is why a united front strategy can be applied against anyone. As professor King-Yi Hsu explained in *Asian Affairs* in 1980,

"The united front is thus an alliance between the proletarian political party, other revolutionary classes and all forces that can be united with under certain historical conditions to fight the main enemy and carry out the current political program." This strategy is not only long embedded in China's foreign policy, it is required under the PRC's constitution.[5]

While united front work has its origins in the CCP's history and is often overseen by the UFWD, in the case of Hong Kong it has become increasingly decentralized, with both state and non-state actors participating. Pro-Beijing groups frequently have more interaction with the Special Administrative Region government in Hong Kong than with its predecessor government. This was a change from the pre-handover days, when colonial Hong Kong was targeted mainly through a centralized "statist corporatism" structure; because China did not control Hong Kong, united front work was covert. After 1997, non-state community groups became openly involved in mobilizing the electorate to support pro-Beijing groups and encourage officials to join grassroots political opposition against pro-democracy protesters. The similarities to Canada are already apparent, with pro-Beijing groups being involved in trying to connect with government officials and creating counter-narratives and protests within diaspora communities.[6]

And of course, it wasn't just Taiwan and Hong Kong that were targets. Repression and surveillance of Falun Gong practitioners and of Uyghurs in Xinjiang helped the CCP further hone its surveillance tactics. PRC companies could acquire the technology abroad to refine surveillance at home, whether this was done over social media apps or through widespread camera use and facial recognition. United front work can be subtle and established through partnerships and economic linkages, or it can be brutal and outwardly oppressive in seeking to destroy cultures, beliefs or an entire people.

United front activity can even centre on the use of ceremony. For instance, international Tibetan organizations have noted that, across Tibet, the PRC raises its flag at events celebrating China's National Day of October 1. The raising of the PRC flag in a territory whose inhabitants do not accept the PRC is regarded as the imposition of a colonizer flag, signifying an attempt to dominate. The PRC also engaged in flag raisings across Western countries, until the practice waned with the deterioration of relations with China and the COVID-19 pandemic. Raising the PRC flag in Chinese-Canadian communities can also cause division. For pro-PRC groups it is an attempt to unify diaspora communities around one identity, while for those who fled China, it is the flag of an oppressor that still seeks to dominate them in their new home and fracture their chosen loyalties.

But the question that puzzles many in the West is, why? Why would the PRC engage in transnational repression of its former citizens and diaspora? The failure to understand this is what has led Westerners to dismiss the repression as nothing more significant than community infighting. Transnational repression is as old as states and nations, and amongst researchers it has many names, such as "counter-exile strategies" and "extraterritorial security practices." Driving this repression is the fact that, for authoritarian regimes, emigration is a problem. The world saw this with the Soviet Union and Stalin's attempts to hunt down his political opponents, such as Trotskyites, Ukrainian nationalists and any Russians challenging his rule from abroad. Some were assassinated, while others were lured back to Russia. Authoritarian regimes are not confident by nature; they fear their own collapse, and so their hold on government takes precedence over everything. Exiles and émigrés can openly challenge the regime through "voice after exit" activism, or by creating an opposition government-in-exile, or by funding and supporting insurgencies within the nation.

Fearful of these possible threats, repressive governments use transnational repression tactics, several of which I have already mentioned: surveillance technology, community informants, exerting pressure on family members still in the home country, and foreign missions that spy on and help capture exiles. The American NGO Freedom House has noted that China is the "most-prolific user of transnational repression." Professor Lynette Ong at the University of Toronto has also demonstrated how China outsources state repression through what she calls non-violent brokers and violent thugs. Violent thugs are usually unemployed, often anonymous individuals, paid a daily rate, and are essentially hired muscle who are dismissed when no longer needed by the government. Brokers are community members who believe in serving the party, individuals who are deeply embedded in the community and volunteer to assist in enforcing state policies, often through persuasion. Brokers have social capital and a deep network the PRC can utilize. If we look at the examples I provided, from activists and the targets of transnational repression, of how PRC transnational repression is conducted abroad, it appears that China has exported its outsourced repressive tactics to Chinese communities around the globe.

But while a desire to clamp down on challenges to the regime from abroad might account for much of this repression, the PRC seems to take this strategy further. The targeting of Falun Gong or Ughyurs abroad isn't about arresting plots to undermine the regime; that these groups even exist is perceived as a threat.[7] China employs the same tactics it uses to conduct repression at home, and the same local united front strategies, and exports both abroad to try to enforce an overseas Chinese identity that conforms to, and is in service of, the ideology of the CCP.

This would mean that community groups or informants are called upon by the PRC to, in essence, be its enforcement arm abroad, continuing to police a One China policy and report on individuals who actively challenge Beijing's authority or even contradict it through their religious beliefs and identity. So bold are these strategies of ideological enforcement that China has created an entire program to capture what it calls "economic fugitives" who have fled the country—a program called FOXHUNT.

———

Just as the former Soviet Union was plagued by corruption within its ruling Communist Party, as are many single-party states, so too has the CCP suffered from a history of corruption within its ranks. Within the theoretically classless socialist state, there has always been the exalted class of the party official, whose life is much more comfortable than that of the average citizen. In the 1980s and '90s, the party sought more decentralization in the economy. Local governments gained more control over budgets and more power, and consequently their officials became more corrupt.

A new local tax system tied to development and land use incentivized local governments to encourage development. Urban construction and real estate projects built up local government coffers. Corruption between those governments and developers grew substantially. State-owned enterprises (SOEs) with monopolies in areas like energy, telecommunications and finance became hotbeds for bribery, as their uncontested control of these sectors of the economy allowed SOEs to reap large profits without benefiting communities. SOEs were permitted to operate, as author Yongnian Zheng describes, "like independent kingdoms with their leaders usually nominated by CCP organization departments."[8]

PRC leaders felt the need to be seen by the population as taking on government corruption. Where taking a stand against corruption had once meant purging the party of traitors, since the 1990s it has increasingly focused on China's leaders taking aim at the corruption of party officials and those who benefited from their crooked dealings. But purging China of corruption is almost a fool's errand, since it has become so ingrained in a culture where capitalism has been allowed free rein but the CCP has the final say in who wins or loses. As author James Gorrie puts it, corruption "has led to an epidemic of very bad behavior throughout all levels of society, creating great ethical challenges and a moral vacuum within Chinese society where the key to success lies not in talent or hard work, but in guanxi," that is, "access to government officials."

The concept of *guanxi* is important within Chinese society for building relations. It loosely means "social networks" or "connections." It's a way of creating bonds and social ties. Scholars have often argued that it underpins the Chinese social order. It's a way of understanding and viewing society differently from in the West. China's well-known sociologist Fei Xiaotong describes how, instead of distinct organizations and groups, guanxi allows for a society of "overlapping networks of people linked together through differentially categorized social relationships." Put more simply, within Chinese society, scholars have noted that people's understanding of the world and their place within it is based on the web of relationships they are a part of. Central to guanxi is the gift economy, which develops and reinforces these social networks. It functions through a type of gift-giving exchange between individuals or even groups. Once upon a time this gift economy strengthened ties within villages, but in modern China gifts like cash are used to strengthen ties far from home. Even gossip functions as a currency, a way of "establishing reciprocal obligation" among community members, another medium for the custom and traditions of guanxi used by party officials and business to facilitate corrupt practices.

China's military, the PLA, is yet another breeding ground for corruption. Guanxi practices became a way to buy and sell promotions within the PLA and ensure that people were sufficiently bound to their obligations that they did not feel guilt for engaging in corruption. Over the years, the PLA's focus on modernization pulled it away from party work. That shift meant less ideological leadership in the PLA, which had existed so that the party could confidently regard the military as well versed in CCP ideology. The PLA, while still loyal, had also become entangled in commercial activities, which further bred corruption in its ranks, along with the cronyism linked to promotions.[9]

In 2003, President Hu Jintao tried to focus on promoting fairness in the economy because he saw rising corruption as a threat to social stability. Unchecked corruption was also causing capital to flee the country. James Gorrie cites a wealthy writer who explained why he was considering leaving China and why others already had:

The elite exodus (from China) is a potentially troubling
development for Party leaders, many of whose relatives have
long since chosen to live or study overseas ... (W)hile the
party touts the economic success of the "Chinese model,"
many of its poster children are heading for the exits. They are

in search of things money can't buy in China: cleaner air, safer food, better education for their children. Some also express concern about government corruption and the safety of their assets.[10]

It was against this backdrop that President Xi Jinping launched a new campaign against corruption when he took power in 2012, while at the same time exerting greater controls on capital flight, particularly after a series of downturns on Chinese markets in 2015. The anti-corruption campaign led to the immediate arrests of over fifty PLA officers, and the campaign is ongoing.[11]

As part of Xi's anti-corruption effort, in 2014 he launched Operation FOXHUNT. The program was designed to repatriate individuals the PRC accused of being involved in corruption who had fled the country. In essence, they were economic fugitives. In 2018, the CCP's Central Commission for Discipline Inspection (CCDI) laid out its interpretation of article 52 of China's 2018 National Supervision Law. The CCDI is under the direct control of the CCP and is responsible for defending the party constitution and coordinating anti-corruption efforts. It spelled out how China would get the accused back.

The first way was through extradition based on existing treaties and reciprocity—asking for a host country to return a FOXHUNT target. The second was repatriation. Relying on immigration laws where the target is located, the PRC provides the country with information about illegal activity, such as the forging of passports, that could enable the fugitive's host country to deprive them of residency status and compel them to return to China. A third option was remote prosecution, which involved the PRC giving evidence to a target's country so they could be convicted of a crime locally and deported back to the PRC. Option four was persuasion. Agents might appeal to emotion or offer a chance of a lighter sentence if the target returned and was convicted. The fifth was "irregular measures." Kidnapping is one such measure. The other is luring the target to international airspace or a third country that has an extradition treaty with China so they can be arrested and extradited.

The FOXHUNT campaign is executed by China's Ministry of Public Security (MPS). The MPS is not only a law enforcement body; it is tasked with ensuring the security and stability of the CCP. Before any type of formal arrest and trial, the MPS has the authority to "disappear" a target to a covert location and prevent them from having contact with anyone, including their family and lawyers. Agents can interrogate a target for months. This practice is known as Residential Surveillance at a Designated Location, and the UN has repeatedly called on China to halt it, equating it with torture and gross human rights abuses. In 2015, FOXHUNT was folded into the much larger Operation SKY NET. This overarching operation has a much-expanded mandate that includes confiscating so-called illegal income from people who have fled China and targeting their fraudulent passports.

At first glance, the pursuit of financial criminals appears legitimate. But as some scholars have pointed out, politics would inevitably enter the definition of who is or is not an economic fugitive. Since the absorption of the OCAO into the UFWD, the PRC has now included FOXHUNT as part of united front operations and is turning to its overseas communities to assist in the hunt, willingly or not. In 2022, a Canadian federal court weighed in on how the OCAO was now functioning under the UFWD, calling it "an entity

that engages in espionage and acts 'contrary to Canada's interests.'"
The pursuit of FOXHUNT targets has often entailed the targeting of
family members in China and pressuring them to encourage the
target to return, the same strategy that is used to silence dissidents.

The PRC has issued red notices through Interpol so that other
countries can act on the notices and arrest the FOXHUNT targets.
But it quickly became evident that the PRC was abusing the red
notice system by issuing notices targeting activists from the five
poisons. This violated article 3 of Interpol's constitution, which
prohibits the organization from taking "any intervention or activities of a political, military, religious or racial character." On October
28, 2020, the FBI made it clear they would not tolerate individuals
assisting China's pursuit of fugitives in the United States and exer-
cising its transnational view of sovereignty on US soil. The FBI
charged eight individuals, three of them Chinese citizens, with
acting as "illegal agents of the People's Republic of China." They
had been acting as part of FOXHUNT. The charges stemmed from
a 2016 investigation that involved the coercion of a Chinese citizen
residing in the United States to return to China by threatening the
target's spouse and child in the US and other relatives living in
China. The FBI warned in July 2020 that FOXHUNT was now being
used to suppress dissent in Chinese communities abroad. Director
Christopher Wray said it was nothing but an attempt by President
Xi to "target nationals who he sees as threats and who live outside
China, around the world."

After the American arrests, the RCMP claimed they were aware
of FOXHUNT but hadn't laid any charges. *The Globe and Mail*
reported that Chinese government officials would arrive in Canada
and book meetings with Canadian government officials days or

even weeks apart so the visitors would have time between meetings to pursue and intimidate PRC targets. In 2018, the *Globe* reported that one individual took out full-page ads in a Canadian Chinese-language newspaper that accused a person of being a Chinese fugitive and listed their passport number and birthdate, and urged them to give themselves up. The person who took out the ads was not identified, and no charges appear to have been laid in the case. In fact, only one person appears to have been charged in relation to this activity. In 2023, a former RCMP officer named William Majcher was charged with conducting foreign interference by assisting the PRC in its FOXHUNT activities, though the charges have not been proven in court. In a CTV interview, he referred to himself as a "patriot" and not a "traitor" and said he was prepared to fight the charges. Prior to this, Canada had actually *helped* the PRC pursue foreign nationals for decades.[12]

———

Calvin Chrustie, a former RCMP operations officer in BC, told the CBC he had direction "from Ottawa at the highest level" to "assist and collaborate with" Chinese officials about a "high-profile fugitive that they were after in the Vancouver area." He refused to do so. The documentary series *The Fifth Estate* found in 2023 that Canada was continuing to assist China with FOXHUNT. China dangled incentives: trade, offers to help fight the importation of illegal drugs into Canada, the release of arbitrarily detained Canadians in China. In 2019, a Canadian intelligence review body, the National Security and Intelligence Committee of Parliamentarians (NSICOP) reported that in 2015 Global Affairs Canada took the lead in Ottawa and created "an interdepartmental working group with CSIS, the RCMP, the Department of Justice and CBSA that met regularly to discuss FOXHUNT." Years after Canada learned of FOXHUNT operations on its soil, it was still assisting them.[13]

How does the PRC maintain a presence within a target country to help it locate and confront targets it wants back? In line with the PRC's transnational view of sovereignty, one way could be through the establishment of secret police stations. On September 12 2022, the European human rights NGO Safeguard Defenders reported that two PRC Public Security Bureaus had set up at least fifty-four overseas police service centres on five continents, and that they work in co-operation with the PRC's UFWD to target individuals wanted by China. These "stations" are not outwardly identifiable. They operate under the guise of an office that provides services in association with a Chinese community organization. When host nations began investigating these offices, the PRC mission in Canada claimed that Canadian locations were just "service stations" meant to help Chinese citizens with immigration paperwork. The FBI again took the lead, in the spring of 2023, arresting two New Yorkers involved in US stations who were accused of assisting Beijing's MPS. As of this writing, no charges have been laid in Canada, and one of the community groups alleged to have been involved with the centres in Canada is suing the RCMP. Another community organization alleged to be hosting one of these stations received as much as $200,000 in funding from the Canadian federal government.[14]

Does jail await FOXHUNT targets if they are deported? Maybe, but not always. In one documented case in 2017, a Uyghur man targeted by the PRC, Huseyin Imintohti, was arrested in Istanbul. He was interrogated by Chinese agents, who gave him three options:

go free by agreeing to spy overseas for the PRC on other Uyghurs; stay in prison in Istanbul; or go to a third country. The man chose to go to Dubai. He then disappeared, suggesting that death remains a possible outcome of arrest. The FBI noted that, in one case, the Chinese government sent an emissary to the US to visit the family of a target they could not find. They left a note saying that the person could return to China or commit suicide.

In Canada, Global News reported that the RCMP was investigating the death of a man named Wei Hu, a vocal critic of Beijing found dead in July 2021 in an apparent suicide. The investigation was launched after police learned he was being harassed by Beijing. Could the PRC engage in murder and make the death appear to be a suicide? According to Cheuk Kwan, it was a well-known tactic of the CCP in Hong Kong. Hong Kongers even have a term for it—the person had been "suicided." Yonglin Chen told me that, yes, China's MSS does engage in assassinations abroad. They are rare, he said, but they do happen.[15]

Is it any wonder members of diaspora communities feel unsafe? At present, whether Canada's new laws created in 2024 to target this activity will curb harassment and repatriation efforts remains to be seen. Communities targeted by China have largely felt abandoned by successive Canadian governments, and for good reason: they were. China engages in transnational repression because it believes profoundly in its transnational conception of sovereignty. Wherever a diaspora is located, the PRC believes it has a right to control them, irrespective of the laws of the other country. How else do we explain the establishment of overseas "police stations"? Nonetheless, members of targeted communities have fought back, despite what the fight has done to their personal lives and families.

It's the failure of the Canadian government to see this foreign interference for what it is that has allowed Beijing to strengthen its surveillance and expand its foreign interference. If the PRC-targeted communities are truly a part of Canada, then interference against them is interference against all of Canada.

SEVEN

BELIEF AND SEEING

The Threat to Democracy

"CANADA IS BACK!" declared the country's new leader, and so was the Liberal Party. Justin Trudeau was elected prime minister in 2015, and his declaration of Canada's return might as well have been spoken directly to Beijing. He had campaigned on improving relations with China, making it a "top priority," according to his PMO. The next year he made an official visit to the PRC and began exploratory talks on a free trade deal with China, and—in a move that must have left Canada's pro-democracy activists in shock—even considered an extradition treaty.

Soon after, Trudeau would attend a $1,525-per-plate dinner party in Toronto with several Chinese billionaires. In the years ahead, as we will see, quite a number of guests from that night would find themselves the focus of attention in the Canadian press, and in less than ten years' time, Trudeau's desire to improve Canada–China relations would be shattered. China would engage in another act of hostage diplomacy, and decades of Canadian governments seeing only what they wanted to believe when looking at China would come home to roost with an intelligence review body publicly announcing that some Canadian MPs had possibly betrayed their country.

I had already heard that, historically, Ottawa took a juvenile view of intelligence. As discussed earlier, I was told lawmakers liked receiving it but not acting on it. Instead of using the insights provided by intelligence reports to help direct policy decisions, they created conditions for a uniquely Canadian iteration of plausible deniability. Instead of government being able to deny involvement in an important decision, the Canadian version of the concept relied on denying they even knew what was happening. Adhering to a culture like this could be disastrous in the Xi Jinping era, when the new president of the PRC is seeking to make China a hegemonic power in the world and has ramped up the country's united front efforts, along with espionage and cyber intrusions.

In this chapter, I will explore the PRC's tactics for political interference and influence, drawing on interviews from within the Chinese-Canadian community, along with former and current politicians from multiple parties as well as media reports and the work of other scholars in New Zealand and the US. Trudeau's government wanted to improve relations with China from where they had devolved under Harper, and again this clashed with what China was doing in Canada—but the costs were so much higher than during the previous government because China was now interfering in Canadian elections. Media stories from intelligence leaks culminated in four separate reviews launched by the federal government. Accusations of MPs engaging in treason swirled in the press, but in the end, the events confirmed a famous quotation from American author Michael Kinsley, that scandals are not about "what's illegal, the scandal is what's legal."

———

By the time Justin Trudeau's Liberals had assumed power, veteran members of Canada's political class were concerned about the PRC's level of influence in the country. David Mulroney, Canada's former ambassador to China, recalled to me how, in his dealings with Chinese diplomats during his tenure, he faced a growing arrogance.

"There was a certain pragmatism," he said, that existed when he'd dealt with China in the past. But by the turn of the century, everything had become "zero sum." He told me, "You begin to get this sense of a China that was infallible." This attitude became exacerbated with Xi Jinping and his consolidation of power. Mulroney noticed a tendency of business leaders to be "overwhelmed" by PRC officials, in that they seemed easily taken in and in awe of them. At Chinese New Year events in Canada, Mulroney witnessed how politicians at multiple levels "would be kissing the ring" of the Chinese official at the event and ceding political space and clout, which struck Mulroney as odd given they were in Canada.

Other former diplomats I spoke to highlighted how their biggest concerns were not so much the actions of politicians while in office, but their actions upon leaving: the acceptance of plum jobs in China, sometimes direct offers of assistance to the PRC government. Others told me how they'd witnessed during sensitive government discussions that the PRC was able to pick off members of Canada's negotiating teams and influence them against Canada's own interests.

Once elected, Trudeau immediately went to work detailing how he was going to deal with China differently than Harper had done. At the 2015 G20 meeting in Turkey, President Xi remarked that China would never forget how Trudeau Sr. had welcomed the PRC with official recognition in 1970. In 2016, the PRC and Canada celebrated forty-five years of official recognition at a gala event, one at which the PRC ambassador, Luo Zhaohui, remarked that Justin Trudeau "carries forward his father's legacy." Apparently, the Canada–China relationship was coming full circle.

Trudeau's trip to the PRC was celebrated in Chinese media with references to him as the "little potato," as the name "Trudeau" sounds much like the Mandarin word for potato. It was a term of endearment, if not exactly a compliment. Trudeau told Premier Li how pleased and "very happy" he was to be following in his father's path with China. Exploratory talks on free trade were set to begin, although the extradition treaty China wanted was not on the agenda. A 2014 document from the Canada Border Services Agency claimed the PRC wanted such a treaty so it could immediately apprehend FOXHUNT targets with little fuss. CBSA officials appeared willing to come up with an agreement that could allow people to be sent to China in the absence of an official treaty, what one official called a "blank removal cheque." Trudeau was keen to figure something out. CBSA documents from the time considered the PRC one of the main sources of "irregular migration" to Canada, with substantial fraud taking place in visa applications. A portion of this fraud could likely be attributed to organized crime working with the PRC mission, as chapter two has illustrated. Even in the absence of an extradition treaty, Canada was willing to permit Chinese police to testify at immigration hearings in Canada, and in 2016 Canada actually allowed PRC Ministry of Public Safety officers to meet with PRC targets to negotiate a "voluntary return." Despite these concessions, PRC officials also met with targets without supervision and against agreed-upon protocols, pressuring them to return.[1]

According to Global Affairs Canada documents obtained through an access to information request, the sky was the limit as Canada filled its cart with items from Beijing's shopping list. On bilateral relations,

Canada wanted annual meetings with PRC leaders, with 2016 slotted for free trade discussions. The Canadian government wanted to
expand collaboration on green mining technologies and the development of eco-cities; it was seeking memorandums of understanding
between the Canadian Institute of Health Research and the National
Natural Science Foundation of China; and it wanted to expand
cultural partnerships in the film industry and sports. Apparently
disregarding what Canada already knew about Confucius Institutes,
the government also wanted to "liaise with provinces and munici-
palities with respect to enhancing Chinese language and Asian
history curricula in Canadian schools." Global Affairs Canada even
sought to "normalize Asia-related content in Government of Canada
training"—whatever that meant—as a "long-term initiative." Then
there was the memorandum Global Affairs sought between the
RCMP and China's MPS, the details of which have yet to be revealed,
though I anticipate it's something to do with FOXHUNT.

There's more. Canada wanted to examine the potential for the
Department of Defence to allow members of China's PLA to participate in Canadian "winter training" and "in each other's military
courses." Global Affairs' wish list even included a memorandum of
understanding between the Supreme Court of Canada and the
Supreme People's Court of China, the subject of which remains
unknown. A liberal democratic country like Canada was seeking a
memorandum of understanding with the legal system of an authoritarian regime—the same regime that had engaged in hostage
diplomacy against Canadians (and soon would again) and wanted
to displace the US as the world's superpower.[2]

And then came dinner.

In November 2016, *The Globe and Mail* reported that Trudeau
had partaken in a Toronto fundraising dinner in May with a group

of Chinese billionaires, what the press was calling a "cash for access" event. At $1,525 per person, attendees included a "political adviser" to the PRC government, a man named Zhang Bin, who, along with another wealthy partner, Niu Gensheng, donated a million dollars to the Pierre Elliott Trudeau Foundation in Montreal, a funding program for doctoral students, to honour the "memory and leadership" of former PM Pierre Trudeau. The gift would be divided as follows: $200,000 to the foundation and $50,000 to build a statue of the late PM, with $750,000 to fund faculty of law scholarships at the University of Montreal. Bin was also named in the story as president of the China Cultural Industry Association.

Among the other attendees was real estate developer Ted Jiancheng Zhou; Jenny Qi, an investor and president of the Canada Confederation of Shenzhen Associations; and a wealthy businessman named Edward Gong. The dinner was hosted by Benson Wong of the China Business Chamber of Commerce. One of the people behind the event was a man named Richard Zhou, who was an organizer of such funding events for the federal Liberal Party. Another attendee was Shenglin Xian, the founder of Wealth One Bank, a Canadian financial institution that catered to Chinese clients. Xian's attendance stirred controversy, as shortly after the dinner the *Globe* reported that Wealth One Bank's application for Schedule I status had been granted, giving it the same status as any other domestic bank in its ability to accept deposits in Canada. The *Globe* reported that a key investor in Wealth One was a grocery business owner named Yuansheng Ou Yang. The bio for Ou Yang on the bank's website claimed he had served as a member of China's National People's Congress and was part of a policy conference that plays a role in the PRC's united front strategy. Representatives of the bank told the newspaper that the bio must have been a mistake, an attempt by Ou Yang to sound more impressive. Meanwhile, Xian stated to the *Globe* that he never discussed Wealth One Bank with Trudeau.

The PM defended the dinner. No ethics breaches were found, and the party claimed the fundraising complied with Elections Canada rules. Nonetheless, news of the dinner likely unsettled researchers in other Five Eyes countries and experienced China watchers. Creating opportunities for people connected to the PRC government to rub shoulders with politicians from nations China was looking to influence was a hallmark of PRC united front interference and influence operations.[3]

———

As experienced China researchers Anne-Marie Brady and Clive Hamilton have shown, community groups in service of the UFWD and united front policies writ large are also instrumental in waging interference on the political level. This interference often begins with seeking to influence important individuals in a targeted country over time before having them engage in interference on China's behalf. Some degree of influence peddling is acceptable in free societies, when it is overt and transparent. But united front work very often has a far more nefarious goal, and is covert for that reason. Some democratic states have sought to expose UFWD tactics. While introducing legislative changes, such as foreign interference laws, to counter this activity, former Australian PM Malcolm Turnbull, for instance, identified this "covert, coercive or corrupting" behaviour as "the line that separates legitimate influence from unacceptable interference." It's a simple distinction. The PRC would attempt to influence individuals and promote their mission abroad, much like any other country, but when China's influence becomes secret and sustained over time, with incentives such as gifts or blackmail, the PRC could then leverage an individual to engage in interference on their behalf. That interference is a violation of the target country's sovereignty, and the word that best describes this interference activity is *hostile*.

Cheuk Kwan told me about "astroturfing" by pro-Beijing groups, referring to their role as conduits for politicians to access the Chinese-Canadian community, and activists also informed me that politicians thus seeking inroads with a Chinese-Canadian community in order to secure its electoral support are led to believe they can only gain that access through these groups. For instance, activists shared with me WeChat images showing a sitting provincial politician courting the support of an overtly pro-CCP group in order to boost the politician's "follower" counts on social media.[4]

Within Chinese culture, Cherie Wong told me, politics is often associated with corruption. But "if you don't become a politician," she asked, "how do you gain political influence?" Buying access and becoming "friends with people in power and people of political means" is how. You build relationships with people who have political power. Within China itself, this type of influence activity led to Xi's so-called anti-corruption campaign. But the formula it was built around continued to be put to work by PRC operatives in the West, as was the most visible means of demonstrating one's influence, the photo op. Wong told me photo ops are a "favourite thing of united front folks, because photo ops is how community leaders garner power . . . They love having famous people and politically important people in these photos." When a community leader can show photographic evidence they are connected to or associated with a politician, they increase their influence. Wong said that "money" as a type of currency in Chinese culture is far more than just "cash" as it is understood in Western society. Gaining influence with political leaders is a type of "money" or currency that can pay off later.

What events a person is invited to also matters. Is it a CCP official event? "Are you at the VIP table?" Wong elaborated. "Are you in the private room?" These associations can serve as more effective signifiers of power and influence than actual business transactions. "It's what rooms you can get into, who you can associate with for that level of power . . . Can you advance me in my life?" In essence, an ambitious person looks to build influence as a type of currency or social capital that can later be used to make real money and build wealth.

Wong believed that photo ops by CCP supporters with politicians is an illustration of this practice. Many of them can be found online, and Wong points out how Westerners miss the significance of what is occurring when they agree to requests for a photo. To them, these are just pictures, souvenirs of meeting someone of status. For the Chinese community, the picture sends a message. "It is why community members don't trust politicians, because politicians do photo ops without thinking who they are 'photo-opping' with. It sends the virtual signal, 'Okay, you are photo-opping with the consulate's favourite member in the community, so you are pro-consulate.'" The PRC consulates are so active in public events, Wong said, because their involvement conveys a message of control to the community, as do photographs. The consulate taking pictures with Canadian politicians signals to the community that the PRC has influence and control over access to these political figures. In Western politicians' zeal to court the "ethnic vote" without understanding the nuances and culture within that community, they may have inadvertently strengthened the PRC's grip on the community and exposed themselves to influence attempts in the process.

Activists within the community also told me that it's not fair to interpret a politician as having been wholly co-opted on account of these photo-op appearances, not only because of the obvious lack of cultural understanding but also because they may be at the event due to the influence of staffers. One of Canada's intelligence review bodies came to similar conclusions as these activists. NSICOP reported in 2024 that "political staffers in particular are a sought after proxy for foreign actions." They claimed that "staffers can influence or exert some measure of control over a politician by influencing messaging and controlling the calendar of the elected official for whom they work to covertly support the interests of the foreign state. They have also been used to monitor their employers and report back to foreign state actors."

Informal networks run by "foreign states' officials" to conduct foreign interference consisted of "political staffers." In one PRC network cited by NSICOP, it had some contact with "13 campaign staffers, some of whom appeared to be wittingly working for the PRC." NSICOP went even further, stating that redacted information from their report included an example of "the PRC using intermediaries to provide funds likely to support candidates in the 2019 federal election," and that a "political staffer" was one of the individuals involved in "two transfers of funds."

The PRC does not need to target federal officials as researchers have demonstrated. They can instead direct efforts at different levels of government where national security is less scrutinized and less likely to generate much attention. American researchers have highlighted how trade and commercial associations within PRC society are state controlled and have long been utilized in united front work. Chinese efforts to target multiple levels of government in the West not only mirror this activity in China, they can serve to bypass any blocks to engagement set by federal lawmakers. Often these united front efforts are made by way of economic exchanges. Brady highlights the use of "sister cities" as one form of these united front efforts. They allow China to advance its economic agenda in a target country while avoiding the scrutiny of that country's national policies.[5]

More revelations about Canadian politicians rubbing shoulders with people who had PRC ties made the news before 2018 closed out. *The Globe and Mail* reported that a rich developer "with close ties to Beijing's Communist Party" had donated to politicians at multiple levels of government. Ted Jiancheng Zhou was one of the people who attended the dinner with Trudeau. He had condo developments in China and Canada and began to grow in influence in the community shortly after arriving in Canada in 2013. The *Globe* reported that he boasted of being well-connected in the CCP. In November 2018 he created ten non-profit groups designed to help the federal Conservatives get more support in the Chinese-Canadian community. But just two years earlier, Zhou was donating the maximum allowable amounts to the Liberal Party of Canada. He was also involved in assisting candidates at other levels of government. While splashing this cash around, he was reportedly a speaker invited by two organizations with UFWD connections. Zhou stated that the *Globe*'s reporting was "beginning to seem like a fishing expedition with conspiracy theories." He stated that his role in PRC organizations like the Chinese People's

Political Consultative Conference were "honorary" and he was no longer a member at the time of the reporting. He declined to comment to the *Globe* about any ties to CCP officials or political activities in Canada.[6]

———

The government pressed on with its desire to improve Canada–China relations until December 1, 2018, when even the appearance of goodwill came to a crashing halt. At the request of US authorities, the RCMP arrested Huawei CFO Meng Wanzhou, daughter of Huawei founder Ren Zhengfei, while she was transferring flights at the Vancouver International Airport. On January 28, 2019, the US announced the fraud charges and revealed that its request to arrest Meng was in response to accusations that Huawei had attempted to sell equipment to Iran and skirt American sanctions, an arrangement Meng was accused of covering up. In essence, the case was concerned with whether she misled HSBC about the relationship Huawei had with the Iranian subsidiary, Skycom, which could have put the bank at risk of violating sanctions. She denied the charges and said there was "no evidence" she had deceived HSBC. For a state that often claimed it did not control companies like Huawei, the PRC was furious and demanded her release. On December 10, nine days after Meng's arrest, Canadians Michael Spavor and Michael Kovrig were arrested in China. While the PRC denied the arrests were in retaliation for Meng's arrest, the connection between Meng's arrest and theirs was patently obvious. Once again, as with Kevin and Julia Garratt, Canada was facing hostage diplomacy at the hands of the PRC.

Enter members of the former Chrétien government, including the thrice-elected PM himself. Jean Chrétien had offered to serve as a type of envoy for the government to negotiate a release, while other members of his former government suggested that *the Canadian government* should have tipped off Meng so she could flee arrest *by Canadian law enforcement*. Media reports of the detention of the two Michaels sounded eerily similar to details of the Garratts' detention. That is, they were under constant interrogation and surveillance, with lights on at all times. Events took another strange turn when Canada's ambassador to the PRC, John McCallum, shared his thoughts with a news reporter.

McCallum held a press conference about the arrest in Markham, Ontario, for Chinese media and told reporters that the PRC and Meng had a good chance at fighting her extradition. McCallum would end up being fired by the government and losing his ambassador post as a result. At the Chinese media press conference, McCallum had, naturally, posed for pictures. Interestingly, Chen Bingding, the former head of the NCCC, the group that Yonglin Chen claimed was connected to the UFWD, was standing with McCallum, as was Yuansheng Ou Yang, the PRC-connected major shareholder of Wealth One Bank identified earlier by *The Globe and Mail*. Following this conference, Canadian media highlighted that McCallum had received $73,000 in free trips to China, with at least one trip sponsored by the Canadian Confederation of Fujian Associations (CCFA), a group that Ou Yang also headed. Perhaps also coincidentally, as the authors of *The Mosaic Effect: How the Chinese Communist Party Started a Hybrid War in America's Backyard* highlight, Ou Yang is also listed on the former website of the HuaZhu Overseas Chinese Service Centre in

Toronto as the honorary president. Long before the topic of Chinese PRC police stations became news in Canada, Matt Schrader, writing in the Jamestown Foundation's *China Brief*, identified the HuaZhu centre as being openly sponsored by the UFWD through the OCAO.[7]

McCallum's replacement as ambassador was Dominic Barton. Barton was the global managing director of the consulting firm McKinsey & Company, where he had worked for thirty-two years. McKinsey marketing materials had stated, on a now-deleted web page, that it had been an adviser for the Chinese government: "McKinsey's impact in China goes well beyond our work in the corporate sector ... [I]n the past decade alone, we've served over 20 different central, provincial and municipal government agencies on a wide range of economic planning, urban redevelopment and social sector issues." At a glance, this connection might not seem like reason for concern, but some US lawmakers felt otherwise.

McKinsey has faced calls from some US lawmakers to be barred from any contract work for the US federal government because of its inconsistent statements on its business with China. McKinsey's global managing partner stated in a congressional hearing that "we do not work, and to the best of my knowledge never have, for the Chinese Communist Party or for the central government in China." He claimed the defunct website was not part of McKinsey.com and contained an "inaccurate representation of our client service." The site was online from 2014 to 2019. Chinese state media claims the firm was commissioned as far back as 2007 to advise on health care reform. The calls to bar the company from more US consulting work stemmed from concerns that McKinsey, given its US contracts, would have knowledge of US military planning. If it was also working for China, information could leak from one country to the other.

In one infamous example of the potential for conflict between competing elements of the consultancy's work, McKinsey had paid $573 million to settle cases with forty-nine states that claimed the work the company did for opioid manufacturers had "turbo-charge[d]" drug sales during an overdose epidemic while at the same time it was advising the US Food and Drug Administration on prescription policies. The firm denied wrongdoing and said its work in the past was "lawful." McKinsey said it settled to "provide fast, meaningful support to communities," and that it improved its "risk and governance process" and fired two partners "for violating the firm's professional standards." It also expressed regret for not adequately acknowledging the "tragic consequences of the epidemic unfolding in our communities."

McKinsey was also advising in areas of US intelligence and military planning at the same time as PRC state-owned companies were seeking out McKinsey's advice. The PRC companies were blacklisted by the US in 2019 and 2020 after contracts with them were taken by McKinsey. US politicians have stated that McKinsey's work "on behalf of Chinese . . . firms, is tantamount to work on behalf of the CCP and could lead to direct or indirect support for the CCP's armed wing, the People's Liberation Army."

During Justin Trudeau's time in office, Canadian government contracts with McKinsey ballooned. During the Harper years they totalled $2.2 million, but from 2015 through 2024 McKinsey contracts swelled to a total value of $116.8 million. On appointing former McKinsey global managing director Barton as ambassador, Trudeau claimed it was Barton's years of experience in Asia that would "make him a great choice to represent Canada—and Canada's interests—in China."[8]

By 2021, Meng Wanzhou was running out of legal options to avoid extradition. At the same time, a closed hearing was held in China for Kovrig, and what Foreign Affairs Minister Marc Garneau called a "mock sham trial" was held for Spavor. This came after China had tried to pressure Canada's position on Meng with trade sanctions. The two Canadians were finally released on September 24, 2021, hours after Meng made an agreement with US prosecutors to avoid fraud charges. As part of the agreement, Meng pled not guilty to the charges, but entered into a deferred prosecution agreement that required her to admit to a series of facts in the agreement, including that she "misrepresented Huawei's relationship with Skycom to HSBC." The US dismissed the charges against her on December 1, 2022. The entire time, Beijing had tried to claim there was no link between Meng's arrest and those of the two Michaels. As Munk School China specialist Lynette Ong phrased it on CBC Radio, the connection was "totally undeniable."[9]

In spite of this hostage diplomacy, Canada was still dithering on its decision about whether Huawei would be permitted to build Canada's 5G network. That delay continued for almost a year after the Michaels' release, until the Canadian government finally banned Huawei from involvement in the new network. If that decision might suggest the Canadian government was making progress on its China position, other procurements pointed in a different direction. On October 6, 2021, the RCMP contracted with a company called Sinclair Technologies to provide radio frequency equipment. Public Services and Procurement Canada (PSPC) told Radio-Canada that security concerns with respect to Sinclair's ownership were not factors they considered when assessing bids for the contract. Perhaps they should have been. Sinclair's parent company, Norsat International, is owned by the PRC company Hytera, in which the PRC government owns a 10 percent stake.

The US Federal Communications Commission banned imports of Hytera equipment in 2022, citing national security concerns. Hytera claimed that the FCC was unfairly targeting it and it could only target products, not blacklist whole entities. It claimed Hytera vendors were suffering "greatly, losing deals, being barred from bidding for projects, being maligned." Huawei was targeted in a similar way by the FCC, and it also claimed that the FCC had no evidence it violated any rules, nor did its equipment pose a threat. Hytera was also facing twenty-one espionage-related charges in the US. The charges were against the company and seven of its employees. Hytera US claimed that the majority of their product is not covered equipment in the FCC ruling, including broadband-capable equipment that cannot transmit or receive at 200 kbps or above. The company's website stated it was actively engaging with the FCC to ensure it is in compliance with the US market. In January 2025, Hytera pled guilty to felony conspiracy charges and "admitted that it knowingly agreed to take, without authorization, Motorola solutions documents and source code related to DMR technology" that it used to develop its own products. One of the employees pled guilty, while the other six remain at large. The company was to be sentenced in November 2025.

However, in Canada, it wasn't just the RCMP disregarding the news in the US that had led to the company being banned across the border. Canada's border services, CBSA, were also using Hytera equipment. In 2017, PSPC gave a contract to Canquest to provide digital radios and radio communication infrastructure for CBSA. Hytera was supplying that equipment to Canquest and worked with Canquest to build the infrastructure. Three USA–Canada border crossings had stopped using the equipment, but the Peace Bridge between Fort Erie, Ontario, and Buffalo, New York, continued to use it until March 2023.

In general, PRC-based companies could pose significant security risks because of a suite of national security laws China has enacted since 2017. These laws can compel individuals and organizations to provide "support, assistance and cooperation" to China's intelligence institutions, as the laws make everyone responsible for state security.[10]

Three days after the Michaels' release, the PLA asked if representatives could attend an international "military sciences" conference being held at Canada's Royal Military College in Kingston. One of the sessions dealt with "China and Russia's information space attacks on democracy." The request was approved, though no officers ultimately attended. The decision was an about-face after the threat of military-oriented intelligence gathering seems to have been taken more seriously in 2019, when Canada cancelled joint military exercises with the PLA. The exercises had been called off by General Jonathan Vance, chief of the Defence Staff. Global Affairs had worried how Beijing would interpret the cancellation. A draft letter from Ian Shugart, then deputy minister of foreign affairs, to then–deputy minister Jody Thomas at the Department of Defence advised that in future the military should consult with Global Affairs before taking any action that could affect the "Canada–China relationship," which "remains important."

Joint exercises had apparently been going on for years, dating back to 2013. It took something as drastic as China seizing the two Michaels for Canada to finally get real about letting the PLA train in and travel through Canada, though Ottawa insisted on clinging to a view of China that seemed centred on belief rather than reality. Consider Canada's defence minister at the time, Harjit Sajjan, who made headlines when he stated at the 2019 Halifax International Security Forum that even though China had detained the Michaels, "we don't consider China as an adversary." His statement looked to be at odds with Halifax Security Forum president Peter Van Praagh, whose welcome speech described Beijing in adversarial terms, stating "it is no longer a secret that Xi Jinping's China is working to make the world safe for authoritarianism. It is time for a comprehensive strategy for the U.S., Canada and their allies that make[s] the world safe for democracy."[11]

During the pandemic, in 2020, York Regional Police made arrests in connection with what they alleged was an illegal casino being hosted in a mansion in Markham, Ontario. In an operation known as Project ENDGAME, police seized a cache of guns and more than $11 million in cash. Gamblers apparently had access to high-end spa treatments, dining and accommodations. As the months went on, more information on the arrests and the owners of the mansion at 5 Decourcy Court came to light—although the existence of the mansion and the character of the activities inside were no secret; hundreds had attended the casino opening in 2019.

The alleged mastermind behind this casino was a developer named Wei Wei. He had arrived in Canada from China ten years earlier and was head of Skywalk investment and a delegate of the China Cultural Industry Association, which had ties to the PRC government. He also appears to have been a Liberal party donor.

In fact, he met Prime Minister Trudeau at Liberal fundraisers in
2016, including the one mentioned earlier in this chapter. The
charges against Wei Wei were eventually withdrawn due to mishandling of evidence. Speaking through his lawyers, Wei Wei
consistently denied all the allegations against him. But the case
lived on in the press because photos of him with various politicians
raised questions about the connections Wei Wei appeared to have
with them. Years ago, a leaked draft of a joint RCMP and CSIS
report from the 1990s called Project Sidewinder made claims of
links between the PRC state and organized criminal networks (I
highlighted some of those connections between crime networks
and the PRC in chapter two). The report ended up taking a drub-
bing in the media for its lack of analytical rigour.[12] But in hindsight,
how far-fetched were its conclusions?

———

The Hogue Inquiry into foreign interference (more on this later)
revealed that the RCMP suspected that PRC organized crime in
Canada does have links to foreign interference. In fact, the inquiry
heard about how money laundering networks were being used in
support of foreign interference activity. That should hardly be
shocking. In 2023, India was accused of hiring assassins in the US
and Canada. The Russian state has widely been known to employ
the services of organized crime. That the PRC would also make
use of criminal networks just makes sense.

A ProPublica investigation detailed the arrests of Chinese
organized-crime bosses in Italy. Investigators said the bosses who
were arrested do "what the consulate doesn't do, or [do] it better."

They have "the network, power, resources." They "know the dias-pora," and the bosses are "feared and respected." American inves-tigators have reached similar conclusions. US law enforcement has monitored Chinese government operatives being tied to Chinese-American mob bosses and harassing dissidents, engaging in political interference and moving money for CCP officials. One veteran US national security official told ProPublica, "Organized crime is doing services for the Chinese government . . . [T]he government tasks them to expand influence and become eyes and ears overseas." A US intelligence official said, "China uses a range of proxies and cutouts, and organized crime is one of those proxies. We see a growing brazenness in [Chinese] malign operations." Western security officials believe this partnership is for "mutual benefit." Individuals involved in money laundering in Europe were also behind secret Chinese police stations there, ProPublica reported, and "gangsters help monitor and intimidate immigrant communities for the regime in Beijing, sometimes as leaders of cultural associations that are key players in China's political influ-ence operations and long-distance repression."

Emmanuel Jourda, a scholar on Chinese organized crime at France's Centre for Studies on Modern and Contemporary China, stated that the CCP "takes the most powerful, richest, most suc-cessful figures overseas and recognizes them as the nobility of the diaspora. And it doesn't matter how they made their money. The deal, spoken or not, is: 'You gather intelligence on the community, we let you do business. Whether legal or illegal.'" In exchange, the CCP protects the gangsters. US authorities have discovered similar trends where crime and espionage mix. US authorities tracked indi-viduals who fed the PRC intelligence in exchange for being allowed to continue engaging in criminality. For these individuals, one former US national security official said, their "currency was influence." The PRC selected criminals to work with based on their influence ability.

Drawing on this research we can boil down why a state would use organized criminal elements to do their dirty work to three factors: It allows the foreign state a level of plausible deniability, giving them a degree of separation from the activity; the crime bosses know the local area better than the foreign state does; and the local criminal gangs just do some things better.

Despite what the Hogue foreign interference inquiry found and what Canada's allies are saying, and although the government publicly named India as a nation that used crime groups to engage in criminal and interference activity in Canada, the Canadian government hasn't said anything about China.[13]

————

Shortly after the 2019 election reduced Trudeau's majority Liberal government to a minority, Canada's Parliament passed the motion presented by Conservative MP Michael Chong that recognized China's treatment of its Uyghur population as a "genocide." Despite the Liberal cabinet mostly abstaining, the unanimous vote was one sign that Canadians were finally beginning to understand that China was an adversary of the West.

Conservative Opposition leader Erin O'Toole began campaigning for the 2021 election by declaring he would take a tougher stance on China. Along this theme, a group of Opposition members, including Conservative MP Kenny Chiu, presented a bill that called for the creation of a foreign agent registry, so individuals working for Beijing would be compelled to register their work or face fines or prosecution. The bill didn't make it through Parliament, but it did serve as another sign that Canadians were losing patience with efforts to appease an evidently hostile power. The September 2021 election delivered the Liberals another minority government. Following the loss, O'Toole was forced by his party to resign. Kenny Chiu lost his seat, though it was difficult to know at the time whether his Chinese-Canadian constituents had rejected him specifically or the Conservatives' tougher stance on China.[14]

Before 2021 was over, more news emerged about connections between China, money laundering and Canadian real estate. CBSA files and investigations showed that relatives of foreign students were being used to move wealth out of China and into Canadian real estate, especially condos and high-priced houses. Canada's financial monitor, Financial Transactions and Reports Analysis Centre of Canada (FINTRAC), identified connections between Zhang Guanqun, a nineteen-year-old international student who had sent tens of millions of dollars through bank accounts, Hong Kong businessman Jiuju Wang and a third party, Xin (Richard) Zhou of Thornhill, Ontario. Zhou was working in "community outreach" at the time for Kathleen Wynne's provincial Liberal government and was one of the organizers of the Trudeau dinner mentioned earlier. He received almost $3 million in transfers from Zhang. Zhou then wired more than $6 million to Wang in Hong Kong and received $800,000 back. The transactions were flagged as suspicious because Zhou had refused to give any details on his relationship to these people or where the money came from. He later told his bank that he provided "assistance to overseas students with arranging housing needs and school applications."[15]

Another wealthy Chinese-Canadian businessman made news in 2021. *The Globe and Mail* reported that businessman Edward Gong had forfeited $60 million to the New Zealand government. Gong was another of the attendees at the Trudeau fundraising dinner. Gong's accounts in New Zealand were frozen for three years as part of an international investigation. The *Globe* reported that the assets were connected to a type of pyramid scheme in Canada and China. Gong was the sole director, officer and shareholder of the Edward Enterprise International Group, or the Edward Group. In 2021, the Edward Group pled guilty and was convicted in the Ontario Court of Justice of using forged documents and operating a pyramid scheme. Under the settlement Gong made with the Ontario Securities Commission, Gong is restricted from participating in Ontario capital markets, with some limited exceptions, and had to pay a fine and forfeit properties in the US and Canada. The proceeds-of-crime seizure set a record for New Zealand authorities. Gong maintained his innocence, despite his guilty plea on his company's behalf. He also sued the Ontario Securities Commission, claiming they were violating his Charter rights by cooperating with China on their investigation. That suit is before the courts.[16]

Shortly after the 2021 federal election, media outlets in Canada were reporting that the Conservatives believed thirteen ridings had been targeted by foreign electoral interference. No evidence was presented by the party, but senior party members and disinformation researchers believed that the Conservatives' tougher stance on China had made their party a target. The party was quick to point out that they didn't believe the election result would have been different if they had won the ridings. Party sources told the media they were briefed on foreign interference by CSIS during the election but had heard nothing since. A statement from CSIS indicated it did not detect foreign interference threats "that rose to the level of jeopardizing Canada's ability to hold a 'free and fair' election or that warranted warning the public." An independent research group named DisinfoWatch claimed it observed "Chinese government media and pro-Beijing actors publishing and promoting disinformation narratives on various platforms, including Global Times, WeChat, and local Canadian-Chinese websites."

The electoral controversy continued into 2022, with the now-former leader of the Conservative Party, Erin O'Toole, publicly blaming PRC interference for the loss of as many as nine candidates in the election. O'Toole said on a podcast, "We lost eight or nine seats to foreign interference from China." Conservative MP Michael Chong agreed that interference played a role in the results, saying, "The Communist leadership in Beijing did interfere in the last federal election by spreading disinformation through proxies on Chinese-language social media platforms that contributed to the defeat of a number of Conservative MPs." CSIS told the online newspaper *Politico* that a public notification would have occurred if leading national security officials who were part of the Security and Intelligence Threats to Elections (SITE) Task Force had determined that "an incident or a series of events has occurred that threatens Canada's ability to have a free and fair election . . . [N]o public announcement was made related to the 2021 federal election."[17]

In November 2022, more news dropped about PRC interference in elections. Global News reported that the prime minister had been warned by CSIS in January 2022 that China had been targeting Canada with a clandestine network aimed at eleven federal candidates. Global News claimed that these activities allegedly involved moving money through intermediaries to candidates who had ties to the CCP and that the activities were an attempt to gain leverage in Ottawa by corrupting officials as well as punishing any politicians speaking out against the PRC. The PMO refused to comment, but then a bizarre story emerged at the G20 summit in November. Government sources told media that Trudeau had privately discussed PRC interference at the summit with President Xi. Caught on camera the following day, Xi confronted Trudeau and chided him for making the subject of their previous conversation public. Not only was the scene of the prime minister being dressed down in public by his Chinese equivalent an embarrassment for Canada, but if the government had known of this interference for so long, why had he waited until the high visibility of the summit to confront Xi about it?[18]

More stories followed, including one that claimed Wei Chengyi, the "permanent honorary chairman" of the Chinese community association Confederation of Toronto Chinese Canadian Organizations (CTCCO), was being investigated by the RCMP for alleged ties to the PRC "police stations" in Toronto and Vancouver. RCMP investigations into the alleged police stations in Canada are ongoing as of this writing, and the RCMP has refused to comment on whether any are operating. Chengyi claimed the allegations against him were "total nonsense" and a "complete fabrication." In April 2025 the *Globe* reported that TD bank had closed CTCCO bank accounts due to concerns of suspicious transactions and possible money laundering, and that it had ties to the UFWD. Chengyi and the CTCCO have denied any wrongdoing and stated that any claims it is "Pro-Beijing" are "ideological bias" and that Global News reporting about it was "not based on facts" and false. *The Globe and Mail* reported that Trudeau was briefed in the fall of 2022 about China's consulate having targeted eleven candidates during the 2019 federal election, although no evidence of illicit funding had been found. The PM denied having been briefed in January 2022 and would not answer clearly about whether China had tried to assist eleven candidates.[19]

Reporting bombshells continued from Global News and *The Globe and Mail* into 2023, with much of it based on reported intelligence leaks. In February, the *Globe* reported that top-secret CSIS documents revealed that China employed a strategy to disrupt the 2021 election in order to back the re-election of a minority Liberal government. The *Globe* claimed the documents show that the PRC uses Canadian organizations to act on China's behalf "while obfuscating links to the People's Republic of China." The PRC reportedly wanted a Liberal minority because, a PRC mission staff member claimed, China "likes it when the parties in Parliament are fighting with each other, whereas if there is a majority, the party in power can easily implement policies that do not favour the PRC." The documents added that "the Liberal Party of Canada is becoming the only party that the PRC can support."

The *Globe* went on to report that the documents explained how cash donations to political parties were used, as well as how businesses hire international Chinese students and then "assign them to volunteer in electoral campaigns on a full-time basis." The reporting claimed a key tactic is to influence "vulnerable Chinese immigrants in Canada." A PRC official reportedly claimed that it was "easy to influence Chinese immigrants to agree with the PRC's stance." The *Globe* reporting stated that PRC officials "wanted the Liberal Party to win the 2021 election" and that they made "discreet and subtle efforts" to encourage members of Chinese-Canadian organizations to get behind the Liberals to defeat the Conservatives. Intelligence sources told the *Globe* that Kenny Chiu was also targeted for his criticism of the PRC and his private member's bill to introduce a foreign agent registry. The Chinese consulate in Vancouver rejected the allegations that it interfered in a federal election. It stated "China has always adhered to the principle of non-interference." It went on to say the claims were "smearing and discrediting China" and that the accusations about "the Consulate General and consular officials" was "false information."[20]

I spoke with Kenny Chiu as the news coming out of Canada was making headlines around the world. Chiu expressed a desire to make a difference for his community, a desire he had determined to take with him into government. He had followed politics since his days as an international student, when what he saw in Canada had stood in such contrast to politics in Hong Kong, which didn't have the same kind of political freedoms. Hong Kong, he told me, "was the mecca of capitalism," and because of that, people were not well protected from poverty and misfortune. Early on, he gravitated to the NDP and the ideas of a social safety net championed in the past by the likes of Tommy Douglas. Chiu had initially focused on his career in Hong Kong, but then the Tiananmen Square massacre, he said, "changed the trajectory of my life." He told himself, "I'm not going to live under this kind of government." He decided to make Canada his new home. He became a software engineer and was living in Richmond, BC, in the 1990s, the Chrétien years. But a rising trend of the era was leaving him disaffected about politics. He was being asked to support other community members' political runs simply because of his and their Chinese heritage, which was not reason enough for him to support a candidate. He became dismayed at seeing former members of Hong Kong pro-democracy movements abandon their ideals when they entered politics, and even start rubbing shoulders with PRC officials, including ones linked to Tiananmen.

His politics eventually led him to the Reform Party. He took up the issue of redress for the Chinese head tax and saw his and others' advocacy pay off during the Harper years with the government issuing a full apology for the tax. Once his children were grown, he entered politics in 2019 and won a seat for the Conservative Party. I had heard the excitement build in Chiu's voice when he spoke of getting involved in politics, but his tone changed to one of dismay as we turned our focus to 2021. Chiu told me of his "three deadly sins" that he felt led to the PRC targeting him. The first was his support for the translation and publication of a report on genocide in the PRC by the House of Commons subcommittee on international human rights. The second was supporting the motion his fellow MP Michael Chong put forward on genocide occurring in China. The third was the bill he put forward supporting a foreign agent registry.

As a community member, Chiu claims he witnessed the rise of foreign interference in Canada. He saw more and more celebrations of the PRC National Day of October 1, more and more associations forming to help Canadians do business in China. He said his campaign team kept him in the dark about interference attempts so they wouldn't demoralize him during his run. He recalled campaigning in the community at the tail end of the pandemic, when he was being confronted by angry Chinese-Canadian constituents who had once been his supporters. One person answering his door yelled at Chiu, who was wearing a mask, "Are you afraid of me? Pass you some germs?" At the very next house, a resident would say, "Why are you not wearing a mask? Are you crazy?" It was COVID, he figured. Masking policies exposed many divisions, and different people interpreted them differently.

But Chiu believed there was more going on than that. The biggest shock for Chiu came from campaigning at households that had once been warm to him. As soon as he knocked, the door would open and he would be told, "No, I'm not gonna support you, you're a traitor." It happened often. Other times, the door opened and the occupant was friendly until Chiu said his name. "So you're Kenny Chiu?" they'd say, and the door would slam shut, leaving him to wonder what exactly the resident had been told about Kenny Chiu—and who told them. He had never been met with such a level of hatred.

He received no coverage in Chinese-Canadian media, while his political opponent did. And then in early September, in WeChat groups, he noticed an article by the PRC outlet *Global Times* being shared around. It was criticizing O'Toole, and the WeChat groups were spreading the idea that he and the party were anti-Chinese. Most of these people on WeChat weren't readers of *The Globe and Mail* or other mainstream news; stories about foreign interference were unlikely to reach them. The CCP was now weaponizing racial suspicion to the point where people are "brainwashed to believe the Party is the state, and the state is the race." Chiu told the party leader O'Toole, "We poked the panda's eyes without defending ourselves, that was stupid of us."

Chiu's experience seems to reaffirm that politicians cannot claim to be concerned about stopping political interference while simultaneously allowing the community to be targeted by agents of the PRC. Political interference and interference in the community are both interference; the distinction is false. In the end, Chiu acknowledged he was targeted for those previous "sins" he had engaged in. They were all things that he believed were "the right thing to do." All the media stories on the 2021 election interference vindicated

Chiu to some degree, as did the independent studies he pointed me to, such as those done by DisinfoWatch and the Atlantic Council in 2021. They confirmed that there did appear to be a disinformation campaign launched against Chiu and the Conservatives, and it was designed to look as though it originated from the Toronto area.[21]

———

Michael Chan is a Toronto-area politician who was also the subject of stories from *The Globe and Mail* and Global News. A Liberal MPP and cabinet minister in 2015, Chan caught the attention of *The Globe and Mail* when the press outlet reported that their investigation led them to believe Chan was the subject of CSIS director Richard Fadden's cryptic remarks in 2010 when he stated publicly that CSIS was concerned about provincial ministers being under the influence of a foreign government but did not name the country or the ministers. The vague comments outraged politicians and forced Fadden to recant. The *Globe* reported that, privately, Fadden stood by the work of CSIS. According to the *Globe*, CSIS reportedly briefed the province—then under a different Liberal premier, Dalton McGuinty—as early as 2010, expressing their concern that the minister was too close to the Chinese consulate.

The *Globe* was highlighting Chan's position on topics in which he displayed a pro-Beijing stance, such as the presence of Confucius Institutes in Canada. In February 2023, Chan, now the deputy mayor of Markham, was the subject of more reporting. *The Globe and Mail*, citing security sources, claimed that CSIS had observed Chan meeting with two PRC consulate officials, Zhao Wei and Vice-Consul Zhuang Yaodong. The meetings were described by the *Globe* as "clandestine" in nature. The *Globe's* source described Zhao Wei as a "suspected intelligence actor." Sources also told the *Globe* that the PMO had been briefed about Chan back in 2019, with Trudeau's chief of staff, Katie Telford, being told that Chan should be "on your radar." Global News was also reporting in early 2023 that Chan had been involved in the removal of one federal Liberal candidate, Geng Tan, and his replacement by another, Han Dong, who was described as a "close friend of the Toronto Consulate." Chan has denied all the allegations against him and defended his innocence and loyalty to Canada, claiming that the reporting had caused "continued, unwarranted, and irreparable damage to my reputation and the safety of my family." In August 2024, Chan's lawsuit against *The Globe and Mail* for its 2015 story was dismissed by an Ontario court.[22] The federal government and CSIS may be able to confirm or disprove the media stories about Chan and thus clear his name once and for all. To date, neither has issued any statement that could clear the air.

I asked Australian defector Yonglin Chen to help me understand how the PRC mission and its diplomats operate in the political space. He explained that there are different branches to the consulates and embassies: an education office, a science and technology office, a cultural affairs office (connected to the OCAO and therefore under the control of the UFWD) and a political office. Each employs one staffer and one senior person to develop relationships and networks in their field. Chen referred to this process as "seeking friends." All departments in the PRC missions would be involved in some type of information gathering, at least on a rudimentary level.

According to Chen, the political office Zhao Wei was reportedly working for was tasked with political outreach and responsible for building relationships among non-Chinese elements of the host society. Because this office is involved in political research and outreach, Chen claimed it could look as though it was engaging in intelligence collection because the office handles not only bilateral outreach but "sensitive political issues" such as the five poisons. However, staffers aren't necessarily intelligence officers, nor are they all engaged in interference. Nonetheless, these mission offices can look like intelligence collection arms, even if they weren't, as much as any other nation's consulate or embassy offices. Chen allowed that in some cases the offices could be cover for MSS operations, but not often. Surprised, I asked, "Why not?" His answer shocked me. The MSS, he replied, already "has a spot in the embassy and consulates." This, I needed him to explain.

Chen shared with me something similar to what he has publicly said previously, that the MSS was given international postings years ago, back in 2006, when he was still the first secretary at the PRC embassy in Australia. It happened, he said, "because the MSS wanted it." Its reasons were surprisingly mundane. Members wanted to travel and see the world; plus, he said, "it pays more" to work abroad. I asked Chen how to recognize who was MSS in the consulate or embassy. He said that usually a PRC mission has only one deputy head or vice-consul. "If there's two," he said, "one is MSS."[23]

———

The intelligence leaks continued, and the media was having a field day. The *Globe* reported in March 2023 about a leaked CSIS report detailing how the Vancouver consulate wanted pro-Beijing candidates elected into municipal office as a way of "grooming" these politicians for a "higher office" later, from which they could more effectively advance PRC interests. As mentioned earlier, China and

the Vancouver consulate have consistently denied any interference
in Canada. In Ontario, Global News reported that a Progressive
Conservative MPP, Vincent Ke, was allegedly an intermediary in
a CCP interference "scheme" in which money originating from
the Chinese consulate in Toronto was "channeled through a series
of intermediaries." Ke denied the allegations and subsequently
resigned from the Progressive Conservative caucus.

Others faced accusations in the press as well, such as MP Han
Dong of the Ontario Liberal Party. Reports surfaced that Dong had
a call with the Toronto consul general during which Dong allegedly
stated that if the two Michaels were released, the opposition Conservatives could benefit. Dong denied making the statement and
subsequently left the Liberal party caucus.[24]

The foreign interference beat soon dragged the Pierre Elliott
Trudeau Foundation into the news. Reports emerged that CSIS had
intercepted a conversation between a billionaire named Zhang Bin
and a Chinese diplomat. You'll recall that Zhang was one of two men
responsible for the million-dollar donation to the Trudeau Foundation at the fundraising dinner with Justin Trudeau. According to
The Globe and Mail and citing unnamed sources, Zhang was reportedly instructed by the diplomat to donate the money to the Trudeau
Foundation with the understanding that the Chinese government
would reimburse him. Zhang did not reply to the *Globe*'s requests
for comment. This allegedly took place before the 2015 election that
first brought Justin Trudeau to office. Experts in Chinese politics
noted that Zhang's bio contained "many points of contact with the
United Front Work Department and potentially Chinese intelligence," such as his role in the China Cultural Industry Association.[25]

Shenglin Xian and Yuansheng Ou Yang, the major shareholders of Wealth One Bank, were also drawing fire in the press. Xian's

presence at the Trudeau fundraiser had earlier been the subject of media reporting. Finance Minister Chrystia Freeland notified the bank's founding shareholders, which included Xian and Ou Yang, that they could be susceptible to PRC government coercion. Her letter also stated that the government believed "you may have been involved in financial activities that other regulated institutions have assessed provide reasonable grounds to suspect such transactions are related to the commission of money laundering." The pair, along with shareholder and developer Morris Chen, were ordered to divest their shares. In addition, restrictions were put on the bank, including the vetting of all bank employees. The bank's Toronto head office was moved to a "new secure premises," and "sweeps of its corporate property for surveillance devices" were to take place. Further, the institution was prohibited from using the Chinese social media app WeChat for banking. These types of restrictions were unheard of for a Canadian bank. The bank was fined $676,500 by FINTRAC for failure to abide by the Proceeds of Crime (Money Laundering) and Terrorist Financing Act and associated regulations.

The bank stated this came about during a regular compliance examination and "has nothing to do with money laundering . . . and that any allegation that the bank, or anyone who works here, may be involved in money laundering is completely unfounded." Xian launched a lawsuit against the federal government. His lawyer stated he was the "victim of mass dissemination of false information that went into the public record," and that Xian has "effectively been banished from the Canadian economy following his divestiture. The three shareholders denied the claims of Finance Minister Freeland and argued they were "unfairly targeted 'due to the rise in geopolitical tensions with China'" that they claimed led to "an unwarranted challenge to their loyalty to Canada."[26]

Of all the foreign interference stories hitting the news in the 2020s, one of the most shocking was China's reported targeting of Canadian politicians, both former and current, for their outspoken positions on issues that concerned the PRC.

The *Globe* reported that another leaked CSIS report stated that the MSS "has taken specific actions to target Canadian MPs" who were linked to the February 2021 motion condemning China's actions against Uyghurs and Turkic peoples. The press named Conservative Michael Chong as the targeted MP and Zhao Wei as the diplomat involved in targeting Chong by collecting information on him. Chong claimed he knew nothing about it. It was only after he had learned from the media that he was targeted by the PRC that CSIS, the PM and his security adviser Jody Thomas filled him in. CSIS later sought meetings with former Conservative leader Erin O'Toole and NDP MP Jenny Kwan to notify them that China was also targeting them. Zhao Wei was eventually declared *persona non grata* and expelled from Canada—but again not until news of his actions became public. Zhao had reportedly been in charge of targeting Chong two years earlier, and there appeared to be no indication he would have been expelled otherwise.[27]

In my research for this book, I spoke to Michael Chong. I often found that current and former politicians didn't present themselves as partisan or engage in any attacks on their political rivals when I interviewed them. Chong exemplified this tendency, though I saw it also from Liberal MPs I spoke to on background. Chong was pressed for time, but as we began, a warm smile came to his face when reminiscing about the past.

He was a child of immigrants. His father was born in Hong Kong, his mother in the Netherlands. Both had experienced war. His father witnessed Canadians fighting to defend Hong Kong during the Second World War, and his mother's homeland was liberated by Canadian troops in their final push through western Europe. His parents would eventually meet in Canada. From the time Chong was young, his parents instilled in him a deep appreciation for their new country and the belief that a person had to "give something back" to their home. His desire to be involved in politics arrived in his early teens, though he would enter politics only after several years in the private sector.

Early in his political career (he was first elected in 2004), Chong noticed that the PRC was putting on a "full-court press to charm me and other MPs." He said these attempts were legitimate diplomatic exchanges, but they were different from how other missions approached him. The PRC, he said, was unusually interested in cultivating personal relationships. The first time he noticed what he called an "inappropriate influence" attempt on Canada occurred in the 2010s, when the PRC mission issued a strongly worded letter with threatening language to a parliamentary committee looking into issues China opposed. Chong did not specify what these issues were, but he made it clear that the PRC mission became more belligerent and aggressive in its diplomacy from that point onward.

Chong said the PRC diplomat who targeted him personally was collecting information about him and his family to pass on to the MSS. The purpose, he said, was to carry out future actions against him and them. "That, to me, was shocking," Chong said. I could hear the anger growing in his voice. "That the government knew about this consulate official . . . and either didn't inform me about it, in order to equip me with information to protect myself against this, or declare this person *persona non grata*—that to me was a shock. I expected that the PRC would be collecting information about me, I didn't expect the government of Canada [to] know about it and not disclose this to me . . . I felt very disappointed in my government and worried that our government is not capable of defending national security and not capable of protecting the safety and security of Canadians." Chong went on to state that if this was happening to him, he could only imagine what's happening to others in the community targeted by the PRC. He felt Canada was badly lagging behind its Five Eyes partners (US, UK, Australia and New Zealand) in how it deals with foreign interference. The country's neglect of national security has made it vulnerable, he added. It was the "weak link" in the chain and puts undue pressure on Canada's allies as a result.[28]

In response to the uproar surrounding the revelations about Chong and other interference stories, the PM contended there were "many inaccuracies" in the reporting, though he did not clarify what those were. The PM's security adviser stated more or less the same, and for months nothing happened. At one point the PM suggested that "anti-Asian" racism may have been driving interest in the interference narrative. Dong, Chan, Ke and Xian all filed lawsuits against the various media outlets that had reported on them. As of this writing, all are before the courts except Dong's case, which was settled. If the government had any information that could set the record straight and clear other people's reputations, it was not offering it.[29]

After Trudeau's awkward confrontation with President Xi in 2022, the government did put forward an Indo-Pacific strategy that called China a "disruptive global power." But as a statement of strategy, it was hazy on how Canadian interests would be protected and served, let alone how success was going to be measured or what it would look like. The government claimed it was "clear eyed" about China, but that just seemed to suggest that Canada would continue watching but not acting on PRC interference. The government also seemed to rely on the "intelligence is not evidence" dilemma that faces Canada's court system. Often, intelligence cannot be entered into evidence in courts because of how it was collected or what it would reveal about sources and methods. It could also be prevented from being used as evidence if it came from an allied partner that shared it on condition it not be used in court. But this legal dilemma seemed to be in play mostly as a means of avoiding action on the serious allegations appearing in the press. As this logic had it, because "intelligence is not evidence," even if the media reports were accurate, the intelligence itself could not be relied upon.

———

Calls grew for some type of investigation or inquiry. The government named former governor general David Johnston to serve as a "Special Rapporteur" and asked two intelligence review bodies, the National Security Intelligence Review Agency (NSIRA) and NSICOP, to look into the intelligence and what the government knew and did about it. Johnston investigated the media reports and undertook interviews with national security heads. In his first report, made public in May 2023, he concluded that no inquiry could ever be held on the subject of PRC interference in Canada because the risk was too great that adversaries would discern sources and methods of intelligence collection. As an intelligence historian I didn't buy this. Canada has held several inquiries in the past that dealt with intelligence, including the one that led to the creation of CSIS. Johnston's reasons struck me as an attempt to find reasons to not act. On the issue of how intelligence was shared, Johnston did conclude that there were serious problems with how the "machinery of government" disseminated information. For instance, the reported targeting of Chong was apparently missed because CSIS had sent the information securely in an email to the public safety minister, who stated he didn't receive it. Johnston was mixed in his assessment of the accuracy of the media reporting, even discounting Conservative Party claims that some riding outcomes were influenced by PRC interference.

Opposition parties were not in the mood to trust a family friend of Pierre Trudeau who had gone on trips with the family, including a young Justin Trudeau. Johnston was even a member of the Trudeau Foundation. Overwhelmingly, the opposition, the press and the public were unwilling to accept the independence of his report. Johnston resigned from his position, the two committees would still do their work, and in September 2023 the government appointed a judge of the Quebec Court of Appeal, Justice Marie-Josée Hogue, as commissioner of its Public Inquiry into Foreign Interference in Federal Electoral Processes and Democratic Institutions.

Hogue held numerous interviews and public hearings on the subject of PRC interference in the 2019 and 2021 elections, and the inquiry viewed tens of thousands of documents. The inquiry opened with controversy, as the deputy mayor of Markham, Michael Chan, and former Liberal MP Han Dong were given full standing status, allowing them to question witnesses and access evidence. Senator Yuen Pau Woo received intervenor status, allowing him to participate in the fact-finding hearings in addition to having standing in the second phase of the inquiry, tasked with recommending policy options. Community groups opposed these inclusions, citing Pau Woo's public opposition to a foreign agent registry, which he likened to the Chinese Exclusion Act, a comparison the groups found unreasonable, to say the least. They feared the inquiry "risk[ed] becoming a taxpayer funded platform to disseminate disinformation and propaganda for the CCP."

The inquiry heard from the SITE task force, which was created by the government in 2019 to monitor for electoral threats. It is part of a series of measures to monitor and report on interference in elections. The other measures include the Critical Election Incident Public Protocol (CEIPP), which outlines how to communicate to the public an incident that threatens an election during the electoral period. The protocol is overseen by the Panel of Five, which is made up of five senior civil servants. The inquiry heard that the SITE task force had in its possession classified intelligence that detailed PRC operations in Canadian democracy, but the information was never shared by SITE with the political party representatives who had received security clearances. A SITE-produced document written during the 2021 federal election campaign noted how PRC proxies were targeting Conservative candidates, but again, this information had not been shared. The SITE briefings that did take place with party officials had offered nothing of substance, according to the party reps, and instead sounded like "cybersecurity 101." To make matters worse, the Conservative Party wrote to the committee after the election detailing what they said took place in some ridings, but an October 2021 SITE document dismissed their concerns contending that the Conservatives were unhappy SITE didn't declare that foreign interference had cost them the election. The party had never held this position, and Justice Hogue noted as much in her first report.

The SITE committee appeared plagued with other issues, some cultural, some structural. It wasn't surprising that no classified information was shared with the party reps. No matter the country, intelligence being siloed is a problem, with intelligence sometimes not even being shared between government departments, let alone with parties outside government. A report on the 2021 election commissioned by the Trudeau government, written by former CEO of the Trudeau Foundation Morris Rosenberg and published in early 2023, found another issue that review bodies also picked up on: Because even just announcing a possible instance of political interference could influence an election, the threshold for announcing any findings was so high that no announcement was likely to be made.[30]

The NSIRA review made public on May 27, 2024, put it this way: Intelligence about foreign interference was a priority for the government and CSIS, but "CSIS was sensitive to the possibility that the collection and dissemination of intelligence about elections could itself be construed as a form of election interference. A basic tension held: any action—including the dissemination of intelligence—taken by CSIS prior to or during an election must not, and must not be seen to, influence that election." This was never "addressed in policy or guidelines." The conclusions were clear: A focus on hypothetical outcomes and people's perceptions of them created a made-in-Canada prison, where no action could be taken for fear of how it might be interpreted.

During the first round of public hearings for the Hogue Inquiry, members of the SITE task force made so many mentions of the US elections that one had to wonder whether the committee was primed to look for and recognize interference in Canada at all. In Trudeau's testimony, the PM stated that his government created the electoral monitoring system in part because of what the government witnessed in the US in 2016—where the PM stated that "Russia certainly threw misinformation and disinformation online and attempted to interfere" in the US election—and because of "Russian disinformation" in the 2017 French election.

The election monitoring system seemed doomed to fail. It was trapped structurally—by the undefined threshold for coming forward with evidence of foreign interference—and culturally by fears of the consequences of sharing intelligence and publicly reporting on interference. NSIRA ended up recommending "a basic accountability mechanism" for CSIS and Public Safety to track documents, as well as establishing "thresholds and practices" for communicating intelligence. "This would include levels of confidence, corroboration, contextualization and characterization necessary for intelligence to be reported." In addition, NSIRA said any new policy should "clearly articulate CSIS' risk tolerance for taking action" against interference threats.

The Hogue Inquiry revealed more that Johnston seems to have breezed past or overlooked altogether. Johnston's report notes "irregularities" in Dong's nomination to be the Liberal party candidate in 2019 in Don Valley North. It claims there was "well-grounded suspicion" that the irregularities were connected to the PRC Toronto consulate but that Dong did not know of any issues. Meanwhile, media were reporting that Chinese international students with fake addresses were bused into the riding and compelled to vote for Dong's nomination under threat of losing their student visas. A declassified summary released in the inquiry claims that "intelligence reported after the election indicated that veiled threats were issued by the (People's Republic of China) Consulate to the international students." As it turns out, Dong testified at the inquiry that he did meet with international students at a private school called the NOIC Academy. He encouraged them to volunteer for him and to vote for his nomination. He didn't mention this to inquiry lawyers when first interviewed by them in February 2024. Nor did he mention busloads of students showing up for his nomination vote, because he "didn't understand it as an irregularity." He claimed he didn't think of this information until his wife reminded him of it. But perhaps Dong didn't see it as an irregularity because at the time in Liberal party nomination races, a person could vote for the nominee (who could eventually become an MP) without even being a Canadian citizen and being as young as fourteen. When discussing this practice with the Hogue Inquiry, the Liberal party national director, Azam Ishmael, saw no issue with it.

More controversy emerged in the late stages of the first phase of the inquiry, with the PM's inner circle in the PMO, such as his chief of staff, deputy chief of staff and senior advisers, claiming they were not briefed in early 2023 about PRC interference during the 2019 and 2021 elections. They were referring to a top-secret CSIS document about a briefing dated February 2023 and made public by the inquiry. It was reportedly drafted in response to all the media attention that year, and it stated that the PRC had "clandestinely and deceptively interfered in both the 2019 and 2021 general elections." The document was prepared for the PMO and claimed that interference would continue unless the government "impose[d] consequences on perpetrators," and it would persist until viewed "as an existential threat to Canadian democracy and governments forcefully and actively respond." Even still, Katie Telford, the PM's chief of staff, articulated that the PMO did not "take CSIS intelligence at face value."

The PM's testimony at the Hogue Inquiry largely centred on actions he claimed his government took to counter election interference and his frustration with intelligence leaks to the media. When faced with the subject of the Dong nomination irregularities, the PM claimed he didn't always trust the intelligence he received. "I didn't feel there was sufficient or sufficiently credible information that would justify this very significant step as to remove a candidate." Trudeau then addressed the suggestion that he should not have let Dong become the Liberal nominee in 2019. He claimed that when it came to nomination races, "my concern was more that perhaps the service didn't understand as deeply as political actors do the prevalence of busing different community groups in nomination campaigns." It was no "smoking gun," the PM claimed. Trudeau went on to say he was skeptical that any kind of foreign interference against Kenny Chiu and the Conservatives cost them any seats. The Liberals won the ridings, he claimed, because they "had better candidates, ran better campaigns, and because the rhetoric of the CPC towards China had an impact on the ground— not because of a disinformation campaign."

CSIS director David Vigneault was recalled to testify after these comments from Trudeau and his inner staff. When asked about briefing the PMO and the PM himself about PRC interference in elections, Vigneault said, "It is indeed something that's been communicated." He continued: "I can say with confidence this is something that has been conveyed to the government, to the ministers, the prime minister, using these words and other types of words." The briefing note in question, made public by the inquiry, stated there had been thirty-four previous briefings for the PMO, senior ministers, top civil servants and election integrity officials. They were held from 2018 to December 2022, with Trudeau having attended at least two of those, one in February 2021 and another in October 2022. The inquiry also heard testimony that Liberal party officials were briefed by CSIS on the "irregularities" in the Dong nomination on September 28, 2019. Two days afterwards, Trudeau was told of the situation by one of his staff.

Questions swirled about contact between the CSIS director and the PMO because the inquiry also heard that intelligence reports provided to the government were recalled twice, once after a meeting with Trudeau. In the first case, a report that suggested interference by PRC proxies in a 2019 Liberal nomination race was circulated to government officials in charge of election integrity in 2019 but later recalled. In the second, after similar details were provided in a meeting with Trudeau, changes to an intelligence assessment were made and a recall was issued as well. Interviews with analysts at CSIS were released by the inquiry with their names redacted. The inquiry summary mentions that "witness 2 noted that it was not common for the NSIA [national security and intelligence adviser] to request a recall of a report." Another stated that changes happened "based on that meeting," and were for CSIS internally. A government official said the PMO did not request a correction, but instead pointed out a factual error in an assessment. Asked about the 2019 recall, the CSIS director could not remember the reason for it.[31]

Divisions existed not only between the intelligence community and the government, but within the intelligence community itself. A rift had emerged between a CSIS regional office and CSIS HQ. Trouble had been brewing since at least 2019. NSIRA and NSICOP found that in one regional office, officers collecting intelligence on PRC interference would share it with a CSIS HQ unit dedicated to the subject. The HQ unit was to analyze the intelligence and share it with the government, except the intelligence often didn't reach the people who "needed to know," and in some cases it never left CSIS. According to NSIRA, "one CSIS analyst wrote emails to spy agency headquarters demanding to know why unidentified reports he had prepared on PRC foreign interference were not being disseminated. As one email opined, 'If we are not going to inform and share what we know, why are we collecting it.'" The email NSIRA quoted appeared to effectively capture the disconnect that the review body was trying to describe.

Media reports documented numerous examples of intelligence on PRC interference that was "delayed, downplayed" or straight-up "buried." But even worse, when intelligence about PRC interference did make it to the government, bureaucrats in turn downplayed its importance. How bad did their dismissive approach become? Bad.

———

In June 2021, an unnamed CSIS senior analyst assembled a detailed draft report on PRC interference. The intelligence service viewed it as "the most complete and detailed analysis of PRC foreign interference directed against political actors produced to date." Nothing came of it. In October 2022 the author of the report contacted CSIS management to push for the report's release, given the public interest in foreign interference. The author, and CSIS superiors, arranged to have it published on an internal intelligence archive. It was uploaded in February 2023 but was then removed. The director had ordered it pulled down, and he said he did so because the prime minister's national security adviser, Jody Thomas, told him to. Two days later, a meeting took place in the Privy Council Office (PCO) with the author of the report and the top brass of Canada's intelligence community. Thomas reportedly wanted the report "sanitized," meaning she wanted names removed, and she wanted to reduce how many people could read it. A new version was created, but it was not shared with Trudeau.[32]

———

What were the conclusions of the Hogue inquiry's fact-finding mission?

Foreign interference has been a "stain" on Canada's electoral process. China was the "most persistent and sophisticated foreign interference threat to Canada." Hogue added that the "government must re-establish" trust in the electoral process by "informing the public of the threat of foreign interference, and by taking real concrete steps to detect, deter and counter it." She agreed with all parties—including the Conservative Party—that interference in the 2021 election did not ultimately change the results, but said that there was indeed "ample evidence that some foreign states engaged in foreign interference in the past two Canadian elections." She wrote that when it came to ridings like Chiu's, "there are strong indications of PRC involvement and there is a reasonable possibility that these narratives could have impacted the results of this riding." Hogue was critical of SITE and wrote that "based on the intelligence collected by Canada's intelligence agencies, the People's Republic of China stands out as a main perpetrator of foreign interference against Canada." She viewed foreign interference meddling in nomination contests as "significant" because meddling in nominations could determine who wins the seat in a safe riding. She wrote that the Dong nomination incident "makes clear the extent to which nomination contests can be gateways for foreign states who wish to interfere in our democratic processes."

Perhaps, then, CSIS's perception of interference in the elections didn't stem from the agency's failure to understand the nomination process, as the PM had suggested in his testimony, but from processes that were ripe for abuse as presently structured and yet were somehow still acceptable to the PM. Hogue questioned the Liberal party rules around nomination contests and contended that while Trudeau had claimed he would revisit the Dong incident after the election, she saw no evidence of him following up. The government introduced Bill C-70, which finally put forth the creation of a foreign agent registry and new foreign interference laws, among other measures.[33] But the timing was curious, as the NSICOP final report examining foreign interference had not yet emerged. It soon would, and it would add a little bit of "treason" to the discussion of foreign interference.

On June 3, 2024, NSICOP released its final report into foreign interference, focused specifically on the activities of China and India. NSICOP had been created by the Trudeau government, and the PM expressed confidence in its ability to get to the bottom of any outstanding questions around foreign interference. He might have wished otherwise. The final report declared that some MPs were "wittingly assisting" foreign governments and that the government had been too slow to deal with the threat of foreign interference. It went on:

> The slow response to a known threat was a serious failure and one from which Canada may feel the consequences for years to come. The implications of this inaction include the

undermining of the democratic rights and fundamental freedoms of Canadians, the integrity and credibility of Canada's
parliamentary process, and public trust in the policy decisions made by the government.

NSICOP's review of 33,000 pages of documents unearthed examples of MPs "communicating frequently with a foreign mission
before or during a political campaign" in order to have community
organizations back them, with the foreign mission promising to
"quietly mobilize in a candidate's favour." Some candidates had
received money from foreign missions, while others provided "privi-
leged information" about parliamentary work, knowing it would
be used for influence operations. Others "responded to requests
or direction" by foreign officials to influence Parliament for the
benefit of a foreign government. A former MP also met with a
foreign intelligence official abroad.

The NSICOP committee noted that, though some of the afore-
mentioned activities may be illegal, Canada's outdated laws were
unlikely to lead to prosecutions. Nonetheless, the committee found
the actions "deeply unethical and . . . in breach of the oaths and
affirmations that parliamentarians take." The report called for
changes in the nomination process. It noted that problems still
exist, with differing interpretations across government departments
of what foreign interference is or how much of a threat it presents.
The committee had harsh words for the leakers who caused the
slew of media stories, but added:

> on the other hand, the Committee acknowledges an uncom-
> fortable truth. Prior to the leaks, there was little sense of
> urgency between elected officials and senior decision-makers

to address outstanding gaps to this important and well-documented threat to national security. Regrettably, the leaks were the principal catalyst for the government to start considering key legislative reforms and to take meaningful actions against particular states . . . [I]t is unfortunate that it took leaks to do so.

Opposition party leaders have viewed the classified version of NSICOP's report. Green party leader Elizabeth May was "relieved" it had no "lists" of the names of MPs who had seemingly betrayed their country. NDP leader Jagmeet Singh stated he was "more alarmed" after reading it. He referred to the MPs in it as "traitors." Singh stated that "the prime minister has had access to intelligence that raises concerns about MPs . . . knowingly benefiting from foreign interference." By failing to punish some MPs, he said, the PM had accepted a certain level of foreign interference. While May was softer in tone, she effectively agreed with Singh's take.

Parliament voted to pass the findings of the NSICOP report to the Hogue Inquiry to find a way to deal with them. It ultimately concluded that it wouldn't release the names of the MPs if the government was unwilling to do so.[34]

———

Robert McNamara, secretary of defence for the United States during the Vietnam War, once appeared in a documentary entitled *The Fog of War*. He discusses the feeling of certainty that had seized the United States when it became embroiled in Vietnam. He says, "We were wrong. But we had in our minds a mindset that led to that action . . . and it carried such heavy costs. We see incorrectly or we see only half of the story at times." The host, Errol Morris, adds, "We see what we want to believe." McNamara replies, "You're absolutely right. Belief and seeing, they're both often wrong." I can't think of a more precise description of the mindset of the Canadian government since 1970, as it failed repeatedly to deal with PRC interference and espionage activities in Canada.

The Trudeau Liberals were perpetuating a mindset and government culture that appeared to predate them. While my interviews were convincing, I could never verify if they were true or not, but the totality of my research, especially the testimony of government officials at the inquiry suggested that Canada had been determined to historically see China one way, and it was the wrong way. The PRC appeared to be a potential partner on the Asian continent, a place where Canadians could do business, a trading partner that could help Canada be less reliant on the US, and a country that would eventually be seduced by our freedoms to adopt our democratic values. Security concerns never seemed to be able to disrupt these views, which meant that no amount of intelligence would change people's minds. Indeed, the Trudeau Liberals had access to any and all of the intelligence presented to the Hogue Inquiry, to NSIRA, to NSICOP and in any of the thirty-four briefings it had received. It could have asked for follow-ups, for more information and so on. But unless the government has become a lot better at keeping secrets, none of those things appeared to have happened. Instead, the PM has publicly stated he questioned intelligence from CSIS and refused to believe disinformation and foreign interference had cost an opposition party seats in the 2021 election. Even faced with NSICOP's report, which his own government arranged, he questioned its findings.

To people who have not studied intelligence, this may all seem incredible—that a government could operate in such a state of denial—but to those of us familiar with intelligence history, the government's attitude is quite familiar. There is a substantial difference between choosing not to see what you know (a type of willful blindness) and truly believing that something isn't happening, or at least that it is not as bad as people think it is, or even a problem at all. Many historical examples come to mind, but for me the one that stands out is Joseph Stalin ignoring the intelligence of the impending Operation BARBAROSSA, Germany's invasion of the Soviet Union in 1941. Why did he ignore it? Because he didn't believe it. There was no smoking gun, one could say, or perhaps the intelligence wasn't evidence. In the end, he thought the circulating rumours were just another British plot against him. They weren't.

Intelligence is meant to inform policy-making. It is meant to give advance warning to government. It is selectively dismissed or ignored to the detriment of the country and its institutions. To invoke "intelligence is not evidence" when the government finds the intelligence uncomfortable, or disagrees with it, is as short-sighted as it is stupid.

The PM questioned NSICOP's findings, and even the public safety minister stated that the findings lacked "proof." They were not meant to provide proof. They were likely meant, as intelligence is meant, to inform; to provide the government with advance warning of a threat, to provide it with information that has gone through an intelligence cycle, in order to allow it to create policy or—if reasonable doubt remains—ask for more intelligence. Instead, by failing to understand what intelligence is, what it's for and how to act on it, the government has left Canada less secure.[35]

While no one can condone intelligence leaks to the press, no one can deny, as NSICOP could not, that in their absence there would very likely have been no action on this long-standing threat to Canada's democracy and sovereignty—a threat that NSICOP acknowledges has caused serious damage to the country that will be felt for years. Reporting on the topic of foreign interference could be viewed as not only spurring the creation of no fewer than four investigations tasked with examining issues brought up in reports, but also in the creation of new laws and even the creation of a foreign agent registry.

What of the role of public servants? How do we account for incidents like news of the threats to Michael Chong being shared with the minister via an email from CSIS? Or the paralysis that NSIRA identified when it came to announcing threats to elections? Or the revisions to security assessments, an issue on which the public still has little information? Perhaps some answers can be found in a report created by the Institute on Governance, titled "Top of Mind." Its publication was covered by the *Ottawa Citizen*. The report found that public service leaders in Canada feel "ill-equipped" to present policy advice and, worse, appear to be "afraid to tell their political masters the hard truths" when they are uncovered. It found that the public service felt too isolated from the outside world, too "isolated from Canadians and not independent enough from politics," and that "speaking truth to power" seemed less possible among the study's participants, especially if what they were speaking was unpopular or "not in tune with their government's political position." But these problems are old ones, the study found, dating back to the Harper and Chrétien years, when public servants were dragged into the politics of their governments.[36] Intelligence, as I was once told, is in the bad news business. You can imagine that if the findings of this report were applied to the past thirty years of Canadian intelligence operations around PRC interference, you might have some of the ingredients for a full-blown public inquiry.

In the fall of 2024, the inquiry had its second round of hearings to investigate information flows between intelligence services and the government. The testimony was unsurprising. What emerged from high-ranking public officials and even the PM reaffirmed my findings. David Morrison, the deputy minister of foreign affairs, testified that when the news broke about Zhao Wei and the targeting of Michael Chong, the government asked the then Chinese ambassador to withdraw the diplomat. In other words, it was the news story that led to his expulsion, not the discovery of his actions by a government agency. Eventually the government sent Zhao Wei packing after China refused to withdraw him, but Morrison's testimony revealed that he didn't consider China's targeting of Chong and his relatives to be foreign interference. He considered it normal for diplomats to collect information on legislators. Perhaps unsurprisingly, the PM's second round of testimony said much the same, that the PM did not consider Chong's targeting by China to be foreign interference.

The public also heard that the office of Jody Thomas, Trudeau's national security and intelligence adviser (NSIA), was given a draft of an intelligence assessment produced by the PCO and CSIS. It was delivered in January 2022, and it looked at China's foreign interference in 2021. It was meant to get discussion going amongst senior government officials, including the PM and his cabinet. Martin Green, who was a senior intelligence official in the PCO, told Thomas the report should be widely shared. That didn't happen. Green repeatedly raised the lack of movement on this report with Thomas's office, but it never received final approval and never made it to the PM. The document was reportedly leaked to Global News and was part of the network's foreign interference reporting. Thomas would later testify that she thought the report "useful" but it didn't "come to any new conclusions." She said it wasn't her job to make sure the report was no longer a draft and to ensure it was distributed. Trudeau also testified that he had a close relationship with his NSIAs, he trusted their judgment, and that when he eventually did see the report, he thought the same as Thomas.

What about the targeting paper produced by that CSIS analyst that Thomas wanted "sanitized" and redistributed on a shorter distribution list? What happened to it? According to Hogue's final report, a sanitized version was prepared by CSIS, but the distribution list was never updated and so it never went anywhere. Thomas claimed she never received a revised version to give to anyone. Apparently it just "fell through the cracks." Canada's taxpayer-funded intelligence service unearthed information about an adversarial country's efforts to interfere in our political process—a process integral to Canada's very sense of its democratic self—but the public is told that the reason no one was able to see it was because, in essence, things just got misplaced.

Trudeau thought that Zhao Wei was engaged in "influence" when it came to Chong rather than "direct interference." The PM said that when it came to collecting information on MPs, "it is part of what diplomats do in every country around the world." This was a false distinction. As this book has repeatedly shown, covert influence attempts are a type of interference when undertaken by a foreign power. But the PM's statements were in line with those of his national security advisers. NSIRA's and NSICOP's reports that highlighted the tension between a regional CSIS office and CSIS HQ noted that when intelligence on PRC foreign interference finally did make it to the government, the Liberal government's national security advisers described the actions in the intelligence reports as "standard diplomatic activity," as the PM seemed to be doing in his testimony. NSICOP, the government's own review body, rejected this reasoning outright. There was nothing "standard" going on in the activities reported as foreign interference. "In almost all cases," they said, "the activities could not be construed as regular diplomatic activity."

For Trudeau, it was instead Zhao's interference in other cases that led to his removal; because Zhao Wei had been "outed," he wasn't going to be useful as a diplomat for anyone. The obvious question that arises, but was not asked, is, if Zhao hadn't been "outed" does that mean he could have remained in Canada? Even though CSIS regarded Zhao Wei's activities against Chong as a "threat" and conducted a Threat Reduction Measure by briefing Chong about it after the news broke, the PM didn't see a threat. Hogue's final report also states that the CSIS director thought things were sensationalized in the press because there was no "physical threat" to Chong. One wonders if a Russian intelligence service—the FSB, SVR or GRU—collecting information on a Canadian politician and their family so they can act on it later might have elicited a different response. Indeed, the PM used his time at the inquiry, and was permitted to do so by inquiry lawyers, to go off on other issues involving other countries, like his public statements on the removal of Indian diplomats from Canada and his claims of foreign interference at work in the Conservative Party.

While interference by India should of course not be tolerated, he was never asked why his government was so mobilized and engaged on interference by India but not by China. Signs of that lack of urgency were everywhere, from the inability to acknowledge interference to information not being passed on to the PM to no action being taken against diplomats until media stories appeared. The inquiry even heard that the office of then–public safety minister Bill Blair had allowed a CSIS warrant application concerning PRC interference to sit for fifty-four days. Testimony from government officials stated the usual turnaround time was ten days. Urgency is often given to warrants to ensure operations are not affected. The media claimed the warrant was on Michael Chan, though the government wouldn't confirm this. Rob Stewart, the former deputy minister of public safety, said Blair and his staff took "some time" to get "comfortable" with this warrant because of the nature of it, though he didn't elaborate. Blair's chief of staff offered no clarity as to why this warrant application mysteriously sat in Blair's office for almost two months. Blair simply said he signed it when he saw it.

What about investigating criminal elements linked to PRC foreign interference, especially given the India investigations by the RCMP and what has been revealed about PRC foreign interference ties to organized crime in other countries? At the inquiry, documents revealed the RCMP was made aware of a PRC "money laundering network that was connected to organized crime and PRC (foreign actor interference) activity," but Deputy Commissioner Mark Flynn testified that he made the decision not to investigate because it wouldn't make a difference, since "multiple backup" networks could be called upon to keep the money moving. Basically, there's so much money laundering going on, shutting down the activity of Chinese organized crime wouldn't make a significant difference.[37]

The final report by Justice Hogue didn't shed much light on anything. There was no explanation for the delay on the warrant in Blair's office, and no one was held accountable for it. Hogue claimed she didn't believe there were "traitors" in Parliament in regard to the NSICOP report (though they never used this term), but said some politicians did engage in "problematic" and "concerning conduct," though this wasn't elaborated on. She didn't believe people had malicious intent, but she didn't explain how she had come to this conclusion, and she took no questions from the press after summarizing her final report to them. The final recommendations had little to offer communities faced with transnational repression, other than the suggestion of a "hotline" to report activity. Some of the most important recommendations concerned adding sections to the Canada Election Act to deal with the undue influencing of an elector's potential vote, even outside of election periods. Canadian citizenship should also be a requirement for voting in nomination races, Hogue said, although she never offered any suggestion for how to verify someone's citizenship in these races other than a declaration made by an individual. Other notable recommendations included the need to improve tracking of intelligence and for increased transparency by the government about foreign interference. Oddly, she cited disinformation as the greatest threat to democracy, though it was unclear why; documents filed as evidence cited interference networks and how threat actors were interfering in elections, and aside from the disinformation used against the Conservatives, it remains difficult to understand how she arrived at the disinformation threat as her biggest takeaway. Hogue did acknowledge that the government's response to foreign interference was not timely and was generally poor. But ultimately, the inquiry's final report seemed to mostly blame faceless systemic issues, such as things getting misplaced or falling through the cracks. It essentially leads one to a conclusion that if everyone is to blame, no one is to blame.

In the end, the greatest success of much of the PRC's foreign interference and secret operations since 1970 is that they have been mostly legal. This may finally change with the creation of foreign interference laws. But having new laws is one thing; enforcing them is another. What this story has reinforced so far is Michael Kinsley's law that "the scandal isn't what's illegal, the scandal is what's legal." Except, I would argue, to see it as a scandal, you have to believe it first.

CONCLUSION

I LEFT THE world of Canadian intelligence in 2022. I left to pursue that fabled unicorn of a tenure-track teaching position, but I also felt there was little more I could do in my position. I had moved into an advisory role and had left the world of operations. Operationally, I felt I had done all I could. I decided to take my bow and move on.

Sometimes I reminisce. My colleagues and I came from different walks of life. We had different life experiences. We had different political views. We not only surpassed all the expectations of our supervisors, we blew past them. It's fair to say we were leaders on our file and really carved a path forward for the future. We were recognized by our department for "the innovation, commitment, relevance and professionalism," working on counter-intelligence and advancing high-profile and sensitive work. I think our contributions to the field will stand the test of history.

We experienced moments of pure joy, something like the scene in *The Imitation Game* where Turing's character and his team first crack the Enigma code. If you worked in intelligence and were lucky enough to have experienced a breakthrough, that feeling of the hard work finally paying off, it stays with you. We had our lows and our frustrations and arguments. One thing remains indisputable, though: We worked extremely hard to serve our country and its people, and we did damn good work. There is a story to be told about those years. Perhaps one day.

It should never have taken the public revelations that some MPs had engaged in what some have called "treason" to compel the government to create legislation for a foreign interference registry and laws, but it did. All of this has left me wondering what the cost of PRC covert actions against Canada has been over the past fifty years. It's impossible to answer, but it's worth thinking about. We certainly frustrate our American neighbours. The US is surely far more knowledgeable about the threat the PRC poses to Canada than we would like to admit. The uncomfortable truth is that the threat of the PRC to Canada has been and remains a direct threat to the national security of the United States. How could it not be? Given all that the US shares with Canada, the more Canada dithers on acting against PRC operations, the larger the risk to the US. This is not to say that the US has always been forward leaning on China. It sought business and trade in the '90s the same as Canada. Historically the US has been quicker to act on threats from China. Trump's second term in office, at the time of writing, has been more complex than his first term. Tariffs were applied on countries across the globe, but China was hit the hardest. Trump permitted TikTok extra time to find a buyer in spite of the US Supreme Court upholding TikTok's ban, but the tariff war with China makes it unlikely a deal will ever be secured. Even if one could be reached someday, any deal that emerges that allows any PRC control over TikTok's algorithm could still be a security threat to the US. At the same time, with the appointment of Marco Rubio as secretary of state, the US has successfully pressured Panama to not renew its commitment to China's Belt and Road Initiative.

This book has illustrated the damage done in terms of technical and advanced research stolen from the United States by the PRC, at times with the aid of operatives in Canada. Canada was excluded from the recent US/UK/Australian partnership AUKUS, which is intended to counter China. The Canadian government took the position that it wasn't bothered by our exclusion because we weren't in the market for nuclear submarines anyway. That position was childish and nonsensical. We have three coastlines to protect, and share an Arctic coveted by both China and Russia. The government later announced that it was indeed in the market for twelve nuclear submarines. I have no way of knowing whether Canada was excluded because of its PRC problem or because it has sought to nearly completely ignore the challenge of defending itself, but I wouldn't be shocked if both reasons played a role in our allies' decision.

———

Canada has to get a handle on its security and defence problem. *It has to.* Countries are waging covert wars against Canada and Canadians on Canadian soil, and Canada has only recently begun to recognize this. For far too long, Ottawa has taken it as fact that the US would come to Canada's aid were it ever attacked. Perhaps, but if the United States did have to enter Canada to protect it, it could also choose to remain in Canada. Government after government has made empty announcements about defence. They generate photo ops and headlines, but government priorities quickly move elsewhere. When missiles are one day pointed at us, when guns are put in our face, no camera or headline will save us. When it comes to Canada's lack of action on intelligence and security, historically, it's the Americans who have been far too polite a neighbour. I say historically, because Canadian complacency is now coming home to roost.

Trump's second term in office began with his use of arguments about defence spending to justify the implementation of tariffs on Canada. He contended that Canada's inability to control fentanyl entering the US was one reason for them, but also accused Canada of freeloading on US security and even threatened annexation, essentially making the argument that Canada was not a "viable country" without what he called US "subsidies." Canada's inaction on defence doesn't justify tariffs or threats of annexation. But regardless of whether Trump was using these arguments as a pretext for extracting concessions or to justify dreams of a new Manifest Destiny, Canada's weakened military and security position and its dependency on the US both economically and for security gave him and his supporters the ammunition and opportunity to make these arguments.

Trump's threats reinforced why Canada should not have neglected its defence and needed to rebuild its security and military and economic independence. Turning to adversaries of the West, like China, was never a viable option, because the US was using national security as a justification for its proposed tariffs. Canada needs to begin building its defence sector and decrease American dependence, not to satisfy Trump, but so it can protect and defend its own interests in the world without having to be so reliant on others for its security.

But was Trump's position his alone? What did other Americans in the security sector think of Canada? In researching this book, I got a small taste of how Canada is viewed by others south of the border. I interviewed two individuals connected to US congressional and Senate committees on China and the CCP. These were not people I would regard as prone to partisan politics—far from it. I consider them well-connected, professional and knowledgeable in our shared subject area. I am not identifying them for the same reasons I haven't identified some sitting politicians who spoke to me for this book: Guaranteeing anonymity is a way for me to hear what people really think without them having to worry about professional repercussions. I asked them for an honest assessment of how the US interprets its northern neighbour when it comes to PRC foreign interference. It's worth mentioning that these comments were made before Trump's election win and during Biden's time in office, a so-called more friendly US administration in regard to Canada.

"I don't want to say 'joke,'" one of them replied, "but the saying you get a lot of times here is, 'Look to Canada if you want to see what could happen here.'"

I asked them to elaborate.

"Can I be blunt?" one replied.

"Of course," I said. "Please."

The response was, "Canada is . . . overrun. I know some of the people I work with in the malign influence space say 'Canada is trying to stay afloat.'"

I asked why they thought that was.

Here they hesitated, saying it might have to do with "certain perceptions of the Canadian government about China and Chinese influence."

The subject changed quickly after that. Our brief exchange left me with a feeling that they might know more than they were letting on, or maybe they just didn't want to offend. They needn't have worried: I was too embarrassed to take offence.

While we talked, one of the Americans seemed confused about Canada's lack of response on interference. In their eyes, the Canadian media coverage appeared to be richer than in the US. They thought it was great that Canadians were more attuned to the issue. But they were perplexed why the government response was "so quiet." I asked them what effect this would have, if any, on Canada's partnership with the US. I was told, "Eventually, [the lack of action] will come to have an impact." The issue of PRC interference was gaining prominence for Congress and the executive. Indeed, in spite of Trump's recent mixed messaging on China, security was cited by Trump as one of the reasons for his tariffs on Canada.

Even worse was the American view of sharing intelligence with Canada. The level of PRC interference in Canada has led to a growing worry among US policy-makers. My interview subjects said there is a "growing realization [within the US] that the situation in Canada is maybe not as secure as we have been taking for granted all these years," though they admitted PRC interference is a problem shared by all Western nations. The two Americans expressed these opinions to me before NSICOP's most recent report dropped. Based on Trump's comments when he took office in January 2025, perceptions haven't improved since.

When we discussed sharing intelligence with Canada, they didn't raise the issue of leaks to the media. Instead, they were concerned about the government's inaction on PRC interference. The conclusion was obvious to me. The Americans that I spoke to were worried that intelligence shared with Canada was in danger of being compromised because of unchecked PRC espionage efforts. When Canadian review bodies are stating publicly that Canadian MPs have "wittingly" helped foreign states, how could *anyone* not hesitate to share intelligence with us, let alone our security-conscious neighbours? The Americans have stated that China's assistance to Russia has helped Russia in its war against Ukraine, which directly undermines the funding and support Canada and the United States have provided to Ukraine. What route have so many American secrets taken to reach Beijing? More worrying yet, a secret document obtained by *The New York Times* details how the United States was preparing for a coordinated nuclear confrontation with Russia, China and North Korea, so much more dangerous has the world become. Canada needs to take a more aggressive stance on its own defence and security because, even after Trump, I am skeptical that these concerns will go away anytime soon. If it wasn't Trump making these statements and threats, it could easily be another president. In other words, these issues will return again.[1]

Bill C-70, An Act Respecting Countering Foreign Interference, received royal assent on June 20, 2024. The measures it contains will not end Canada's foreign interference problem, but they can be refined as time goes on. The question that remains is whether the government will use the foreign agent registry. Consider how recently the subject of interference in elections was not taken seriously. When speaking at the Liberal convention in 2023, Jean Chrétien joked about the news coverage on foreign interference, to much applause and laughter. Would that applause and laughter still come after NSICOP's findings about some MPs and their assistance to foreign governments? How does the wisecrack by the captain of Team Canada look in hindsight? Even in the middle of a federal inquiry on foreign interference, Canadian MPs and senators travelled to China. During the same inquiry, after former Opposition leader Erin O'Toole had testified, Trudeau was asked about O'Toole's testimony, and his response left me shaking my head: "I can understand where someone who lost an election is trying to look for reasons other than themselves why they might have lost an election." More shocking yet was the fact that he said this when the government *already had all the intelligence that went to the inquiry, that went to NSIRA and that went to NSICOP*, and even more intelligence if cabinet documents are included. And to date, only once NSICOP's report was concluded was anything done and legislation finally tabled. Even with the prospect looming over Parliament that MPs have assisted a foreign government, and no real clarity provided by the Hogue Inquiry, no action appears to have been taken regarding those individuals. What kind of message does inaction send to our Five Eyes partners, to the US in particular, when an internal review finds that some MPs wittingly assisted a foreign power, and the response is to punt the issue to the justice heading an inquiry?

NSICOP claimed the effects of government inaction will be damaging for years to come. Without seeing the unredacted version of its report, it's difficult to tell why its members think so. Is it because of the degree to which PRC interference networks have become ingrained in Canadian communities and in political and party machinery, or because of the damage to Canada's reputation abroad, or because of the mistrust the scandal has bred in Canadians of our own politics and democracy, or because of a combination of all these things?

There have certainly been personal and political costs. While the Justin Trudeau government is not solely to blame for Canada's compromised state, it's clear that Trudeau's government failed miserably on countering China's intelligence plays, even when alarm bells were ringing everywhere about the direction President Xi was leading his country. While defence and security are historically not top issues for voters, the subject has no doubt broken voters' trust with the government. The Liberal Party's poll numbers faced a significant drop in the summer of 2023 after months of media reports on foreign interference hammered the government's handling of the issue. Across the post-COVID Western world, incumbent governments were being pummelled by voters, even in the United States, leading to the re-election of Donald Trump in 2024. While Trudeau's government was undeniably hit by that same wave, the effect of the foreign interference issue, I would argue, was a significant contributor in Trudeau's early decline in popularity. Any legacy left by his government will be forever scarred by the perceived inaction or foreign interference. Some may have been tempted to think that once Trudeau left office, and once the inquiry was completed, foreign interference from the PRC would die down or even fall flat and fail. But that thinking runs counter to everything this book has exposed. With no firm deterrence mechanisms yet in place, interference continues. This is exactly what happened after Trudeau stepped down.

During the Liberal Party leadership race in early 2025, the SITE task force reported that a blog linked to the PRC was putting out disparaging comments about leadership candidate Chrystia Freeland, which was being amplified on WeChat. Up to three million people saw the posts. Her competitors in the race, such as Mark Carney, could have stood to benefit from the negative posts about her.

The 2025 Canadian federal election cycle saw more controversy. On March 28, 2025, the Toronto Association for Democracy in China (TADC) reported that Paul Chiang, the Liberal MP and candidate in the Markham–Unionville riding, held a press conference in January with Chinese media in Canada. At the event, the TADC claimed Chiang told reporters that Joe Tay, the Conservative candidate running in Don Valley North, had a PRC bounty on him and that if anyone wanted to claim it, they could bring him to the PRC Toronto Consulate. Chiang issued a public apology for his comments, but the public outrage was intense. Chiang was a former police officer, an MP in a predominantly ethnically Chinese riding, he was likely well aware of the sensitivity around PRC harassment and repatriation since Tay did indeed have a bounty on his head for his Hong Kong pro-democracy activism. When media confronted now-Prime Minister Mark Carney with Chiang's comments and asked if he would continue to keep Chiang as a Liberal candidate, Carney issued his full support for Chiang. Carney claimed it was a "teachable moment" and said that Chiang had his "full confidence."

I remember watching this in real time and being completely stunned that the PM would support a candidate that made these comments. But the situation would worsen just days later. Chiang again expressed remorse for his comments and did resign. But after that resignation, SITE made another announcement, this time during the federal election, the PRC was interfering by boosting online content about Mark Carney.

The SITE group made a public announcement that the same PRC media site that was connected to the PRC government and which had posted negative comments about Freeland, and previously about MP Michael Chong, was boosting content about

Carney. Some of the content spoke highly of him, referring to him as a "rockstar candidate" and as "the only adult in the room" in the election and praising his ability to deal with Trump.

SITE claimed the boosting of the content online was from the PRC and "inauthentic," a sign it was connected to a foreign state. It reached between one and three million views and was directed at Chinese Canadians on WeChat.

While the public awareness of interference had certainly increased since the Hogue Inquiry, China would likely not have engaged in interference if it didn't think the payoff was worth the risk. And despite all that Canadians learned from the inquiry, that the PM could still support Chiang and have full confidence in him after his inflammatory comments, seemed to be a continuation of Canadian leaders not paying enough attention to the dangers communities face. Even the SITE task force's statement that the online influence attempts were aimed at the Chinese-Canadian community does not capture the real problem, which is that the interference targets Canada as a whole. The Chinese-Canadian community is a part of Canada; it doesn't exist in isolation. If even a small portion of those one-to-three million WeChat viewers were influenced by the PRC's operation, those could go on to influence others inside and outside of their community. The posts were likely designed to be as authentic looking as possible so as not to alert anyone's attention that their amplification was not legitimate. The incident also begged the questions of whether the PRC was using AI for the articles and boosting, other apps, or using human operatives alongside the online ones, as part of this influence campaign.

Although little seemed to have changed in the government's official response to these influence attempts, a shift showed in that SITE was finally making public statements about interference. This was a positive development even though the announcements were somewhat lacking in the way of conclusions. It was a sign that, in some respects, things were beginning to change.[2]

There was no evidence Carney welcomed or was complicit in any interference but the glaring question that lingered was why the PRC was boosting content in support of him. He would face more questions from the press after the Liberals put forth a new candidate to replace Chiang. *The Globe and Mail* reported on April 10 that Chiang's replacement was former Toronto police officer Peter Yuen. The *Globe* reported that Yuen appeared to have a "strong relationship" with the PRC mission, which had held a celebration for him in 2014 when he became Toronto police superintendent. They reported that he attended other consulate celebrations and events held by groups that advocated for the "peaceful reunification" of Taiwan and China, which is a phrase that is rejected by the Taiwanese government. He was also an honorary director of the Jiangsu Commerce Council of Canada (JCCC), a Toronto-based organization that the *Globe* reported had "clear ties" to the UFWD. In response to the *Globe* Yuen claimed his role with the JCCC ended a decade ago but he declined to answer the *Globe's* questions about whether he supported Taiwan's self-determination, or disapproved of UFWD activities and condemned China's actions against Uyghurs. The JCCC still listed Yuen as an honorary director in early April 2025. Yuen claimed his former service as a police officer demonstrated his suitability to be a candidate.

In an interview with the *Globe*, Cheuk Kwan pointed out that two members of the JCCC also attended the CPPCC, the united front affiliated conference that takes place in the PRC. The *Globe* also reported that Carney met with the group during the Liberal Party leadership race. When confronted with this on the campaign trail, Carney defended Yuen, saying he was "proud to have him as a candidate." He flat-out denied he met with the group saying "I didn't have a setup meeting with this group. Full stop." He also stated that "you can't believe everything you read in *The Globe and Mail*," and advised the reporter that people should "check their sources." Carney claimed he "never heard of this group [the JCCC]." The problem for Carney was that it certainly looked like he did meet the executives of the group which is all the *Globe* claimed he did. On its website the JCCC showcased pictures of their meeting with Carney and claimed that during "an in-depth exchange" between Carney and two of their leaders, Carney "highly praised the pioneering role of the Chinese business community." The group claimed Carney's entry into politics marked "an important turning point in the upgrading of China–Canada relations." But in a bizarre turn of events the Liberal Party claimed it was inaccurate that Carney had any in-depth discussion with the group leaders, denied a meeting took place and they instructed the JCCC to remove these claims. And just like that, the article from the JCCC about this event was deleted and scrubbed, complete with the pictures, though it was archived online.

Carney's denials and explanations of these events, including his lack of condemning (or even discussing in any depth) the PRC boosting content about him, his defence of a candidate that made abhorrent comments and defending another that had questionable relations with PRC mission, felt unsatisfactory in the post–Hogue Inquiry era. Rather than answers, the incidents seemed to provoke more questions that may never be answered.

———

My focus in this book has been on the actions of the PRC government and its governing party, the CCP, not the people of China.
This should go without saying, yet it needs to be said. Oddly enough,
as much as I oppose what the CCP and PRC have waged in terms
of interference, I have respected them as an adversary. Respect does
not mean overestimating them. It is far too common for people to
think that everyone is a spy and that spies are everywhere. It's not
true. Occam's razor applies more often than not—most people
are just what they say they are. We need to remember this to avoid
running into conspiracy theory headwinds and making racist
assumptions about communities. The PRC would love to make the
argument that Canada is being racist. Not everything is united front,
not everyone a UFWD officer. Not everyone who has had contact
with the PRC mission has been captured. It is even true that the
UFWD doesn't always function as an intelligence collection body.
Sometimes community events and community building and cultural sharing are exactly that and nothing more. And besides,
interference in communities is more important than electoral interference, because the latter is not possible without the former.
Interference happens year-round, not just during election cycles,
and we need to take action against it to protect innocent Chinese
communities targeted by China.

Nuances can too conveniently be ignored to suit grand conspiracy narratives. People do not behave as if they are some kind of
Manchurian candidate, and even if in an isolated case someone
really is secretly working for China, this would be a rarity, not the
norm. People who have been "co-opted" or convinced to assist
adversaries—that, I think, is a more accurate depiction of reality.

Ultimately, things do not have to continue in an adversarial way
with the PRC. Leaders could find their way to a ceasefire on the

interference front, but they cannot do this with inaction and constant acquiescence. Canada could also look to NATO and have it occupy a new role in the future with respect to interference. It could help build multilateral support to counter this threat. My concern about rapprochement with the current PRC regime is that it may simply no longer be possible. Ultimately, though, it's up to them— and to us to become too difficult a target for their interference strategies to continue to succeed. But remember that the bulk of this book has been about PRC interference before Xi Jinping. Canada has been under assault by the CCP for decades, so even when Xi eventually leaves, things are unlikely to change with the CCP still controlling the PRC. What needs to change? I outline a number of recommendations on the following pages, and many are in keeping with what others have advocated over the years.[3]

Recommendations

- Foreign interference laws and the new registry need to be enforced and used. There is no sense in creating interference laws without ever intending to expose or prosecute individuals engaged in foreign interference.

- Capacity needs to be improved in Canada's security services, and with respect to financial crimes and investigations.

- Canada needs to get serious about money laundering. These crimes are often connected to other serious criminal offences, and the RCMP has confirmed that money laundering is tied to foreign interference and foreign states. We need a better form of the American RICO (Racketeer Influenced and

Corrupt Organizations) laws that can target international drug cartels and money launderers presently at work in Canada. These laws in the US have had a major effect on taking down high- and low-level organized-crime members, while Canada's laws focus on specific and individual crimes, making it harder to connect them to the bosses.

- Canada's political nomination process needs oversight from Elections Canada. Political parties may not like it or want to hear it, but at this point, who cares? They need the oversight. Nomination votes are vectors for foreign interference. There is no reason why the same requirements for voting in an election are not applied to voting in nomination processes. If something is not allowed in an election, why is it allowed in a nomination vote? I would also concur with the Hogue Inquiry that portions of the Canada Election Act around undue influence on electors should apply at all times. I agree that the Canada Elections Act should be amended to close loopholes around foreign entities and third-party financing.

- The most necessary changes are cultural ones. The communities targeted by the PRC are Canadian, and they need to be protected against foreign threats the same as any other citizens. Politicians cannot court the "ethnic vote" and then walk away, oblivious to what the community faces. This means more outreach to build trust and engender awareness of foreign interference, more bridge-building with non-CCP-affiliated groups, and more solutions implemented from what the communities themselves propose and want.

- In the realm of security and intelligence, Canada needs to grow up. It needs an intelligence culture and more cooperation with academia and society, and not just within Ottawa. It is also a leader's job to receive and consider reports from the country's intelligence services. It is not the role of public servants to shield a leader from things they or the leader may disagree with. It is not the leader's job to look the other way when they see reports they'd rather not believe are true. What intelligence is and what it is not needs to be understood. If more intelligence is needed to fill out the picture, the government can direct their services to go collect it. Unless a leader or public servant has direct knowledge of why some intelligence may be wrong, they have no place discounting it outright based on their personal opinions. Challenging is one thing, ignoring is another. Intelligence is in the bad news business, and leaders in Canada's intelligence community need to be comfortable delivering bad news whether their political bosses want to hear it or not. Consistent and documented information flows can help here, and I would agree with the Hogue Inquiry and NSIRA on that, along with record-keeping as to what things were approved and what were denied and why. An option could be considered to allow security services to work directly with the federal court to submit warrant applications when investigating sensitive foreign interference cases.

- Where possible, Canada needs to act on intelligence, not bury it in silos and hide it in archives. Leaders need to meet regularly. The new National Security Council that the government created in 2023 is a start, but it needs to meet in a routine and defined way, lest it fall by the wayside when governments change.

- Canada needs a regularly published national security strategy, and it needs to clarify its interests in the world and work to protect them alongside like-minded states. It could also use a foreign interference strategy, as the Hogue Inquiry suggested. It can work with NATO on foreign interference as well, but to do that, it needs to show that it is a member that NATO can count on by spending its due share on defence and security.

- The intelligence community and the government need to be better at transparency. The US reveals far more information about national security threats to the public, even in criminal prosecutions and during elections, than Canada does. Canada doesn't have to wait for smoking guns to emerge before acting on intelligence and telling the public about it. That's not how intelligence works; it will never provide 100 percent certainty. Probability matters. This will change when Canada gets more serious about acting on intelligence rather than hoarding it. Canada should not be looking for alternatives to public disclosures for threats to elections; it should instead set clear parameters to make public disclosures, and get more comfortable with actually making them. Intelligence about counter-intelligence files needs to be shared between departments at least as well as information is shared on the counterterrorism file. The SITE public disclosures during the 2025 election and Liberal Party nomination race were a step in the right direction but they could still benefit from being more direct in their releases.

- The intelligence-to-evidence dilemma needs to be addressed as well. We need to avoid unnecessary overlap in institutions and routinely meet evidence collection standards. Another method of addressing this could be for the RCMP to handle domestic counterterrorism and counter-intelligence files (now that Canada has foreign interference laws), just as the FBI does, leaving CSIS to operate as a foreign intelligence service. This is a contentious idea, but it is a real option. It would also allow for Canada to be less dependent on its allies for intelligence.

In the late summer of 2025 the government indicated it would adopt many of the Inquiry's recommendations. It is a positive step, but the true test will be proper resourcing and monitoring effectiveness in the years to come. There appear to be some glimmers of hope. Canada is finally waking up to the threat it sleepwalked into. We are waking up later than our allies, but waking up nonetheless. Even the Desmarais family is shutting down its investment management operations in China and pulling out of its "public equities strategy in the country."[4] The China foreign interference threat also presents itself as one where countries need domestic protections, but like the threat of terrorism years ago, multilateral solutions and co-operation may be necessary.

Any obstacle, though, no matter how daunting, can be overcome. A saying I learned from community members is worth repeating now, and worth ending on: "No matter how tall the mountain is, it cannot block the sun."

ACKNOWLEDGEMENTS

THIS BOOK MATERIALIZED after I recognized that Canada lacked a comprehensive and detailed study and assessment of PRC espionage and interference in Canada as part of its diplomatic history. Canada's allies, such as the US, the UK, New Zealand and Australia, all have richer studies in this area and are much farther ahead in having an intelligence culture within their respective countries. Canadians have had much in the way of media coverage on the subject, based on intelligence leaks. The focus of this book is not on leaks (which I do not condone); the intention has been to take a broader and deeper view in order to inform the Canadian public about what it needs to know with respect to espionage and foreign interference by China. Canadians were getting their information on the subject from multiple sources, voices and online sites, and they lacked a comprehensive study and explanation for how and why Canada is where it is on this subject. Everything has a history, and this one needed to be told.

I have taken great care to ensure that this book is as accurate, detailed and concise as it can be, and that it does not use classified information. No such material appears in this book. All the analysis and information is sourced directly from interviews and publicly available sources and my conclusions and analysis are derived from such. I amassed hundreds if not thousands of publicly available documented source materials that had to be meticulously combed. I hope I have done them and my interview subjects justice. My discussion of media stories involving intelligence leaks is not to be interpreted as confirming or denying the information within those stories; they are presented only as part of the historical record of events, nor am I able to confirm the veracity of the statements of interview subjects. Notes at the end of, and within paragraphs, generally cover all information since the previous note.

The book would not have been possible without the assistance of many people, including my interview subjects. Some of them I cannot thank by name, in order to protect their safety and security, but all of them will recognize their contributions and have my gratitude.

I am grateful for the support of my peers and colleagues, some of whom agreed to review early drafts of this book, as well as researchers who assisted with the book. I would like to thank Grace van Vliet, John Pearce at Westwood Creative Artists, Library and Archives Canada and the ATIP staff at csis, Craig Pyette, John Sweet, Deirdre Molina and the staff at Random House Canada, and most of all my network of friends and family, who assisted me through some tough times and whose support was instrumental in allowing me to complete this book. My family has been unwavering in their support. This book is for them.

NOTES

INTRODUCTION

[1] *Guardian* Staff and Agencies, "FBI and MI5 Leaders Give Unprecedented Joint Warning on Chinese Spying," *Guardian*, July 7, 2022. For how the PRC engages in interference, see Anne-Marie Brady, "'Magic Weapons': China's Political Activities Under Xi Jinping," Wilson Center (Washington, DC), September 2017; Clive Hamilton, *Silent Invasion: China's Influence in Australia* (Hardie Grant Books, 2018). For a definition of foreign interference and summary of PRC activities in Canada see Government of Canada, CSIS Public Report 2024, June 2025.

CHAPTER ONE: OTTAWA GUARANTEES

[1] Anthony B. Chan, *The Chinese in the New World* (New Star, 1983); Ninette Kelly and Michael Trebilcock, *The Making of the Mosaic: A History of Canadian Immigration Policy* (University of Toronto Press, 2010); Peter M. Mitchell, "The Missionary Connection," in Paul Evans and Michael Frolic, *Reluctant Adversaries: Canada and the People's Republic of China 1949–1970* (University of Toronto Press, 1991); Jonathan Manthorpe, *Claws of the Panda: Beijing's Campaign of Influence and Intimidation in Canada* (Cormorant Books, 2019), ch. 3.

[2] Benjamin Yang, *From Revolution to Politics: Chinese Communists on the Long March* (Routledge, 1990); Maochun Yu notes how Chiang was unable to control the many foreign interventions and operations in China over the course of the war, from the Soviets to the British, French and Americans. They decreased his legitimacy and ability to control rival political factions and weakened his position as a leader of "a sovereign state." This failure contributed to the CCP's victory in

1947. See Maochun Yu, *The Dragon's War: Allied Operations and the Fate of China, 1937–1947* (Annapolis: Naval Institute Press, 2013), 202–8.

[3] Dennis Molinaro, "Calculate Diplomacy: John Diefenbaker and the Origins of Canada's Cuba Policy," in Robert Wright and Lana Wylie, eds., *Our Place in the Sun: Canada and Cuba in the Castro Era* (University of Toronto Press, 2009); G.A.H. Pearson, *Seize the Day: Lester B. Pearson and Crisis Diplomacy* (McGill-Queen's University Press, 1993), ch. 8; Greg Donaghy and Michael D. Stevenson, "The Limits of Alliance: Cold War Solidarity and Canadian Wheat Exports to China, 1950–1963," *Agricultural History* 83, no. 1 (Winter 2009): 29–50; Chester Ronning, *A Memoir of China in Revolution* (Pantheon Books, 1974); Manthorpe, *Claws of the Panda*, ch. 4; Patrick Kyba, "Hamilton and Sino-Canadian Relations," in Evans and Frolic, *Reluctant Adversaries*. Paul Martin Sr. was a strong proponent of recognizing China; see Greg Donaghy, "Red China Blues: Paul Martin, Lester B. Pearson and the China Conundrum, 1963–1967," *Journal of American East Asian Relations* 20 (2013): 190–202.

[4] Cheng Yinghong, "向世界输出革命——'文革'在亚非拉的影响初探,"*Modern China Studies* 3 (2006), modernchinastudies.org/cn/issues/past-issues/93-mcs -2006-issue-3/972-2012-01-05-15-35-10.html.

[5] Michael Pillsbury, *The Hundred-Year Marathon: China's Secret Strategy to Replace America as the Global Superpower* (St. Martin's Griffin, 2015), 21–27; Wu Chunqiu, *On Grand Strategy* (Current Affairs Press, 2000); Evan A. Feigenbaum, *China's Techno-Warriors: National Security and Strategic Competition from the Nuclear to the Information Age* (Stanford University Press, 2003).

[6] Henry Kissinger, *On China* (Penguin Press, 2011), 211; Pillsbury, *Hundred-Year Marathon*, 54–60.

[7] Michael Frolic, *Canada and China: A Fifty Year Journey* (University of Toronto Press, 2022), 49. For examples of anti-Americanism at the time, see also the transcript of Ivan Head's conversation with Kissinger, November 26, 1971; J.L. Granatstein, *Yankee Go Home: Canadians and Anti-Americanism* (Harper-Collins, 1996), 165–69, 181.

[8] Pierre Trudeau and Jacques Hébert, *Two Innocents in Red China* (Douglas & McIntyre, 2007), ch. 4 and 5.

[9] Ibid., 75.

[10] Hollander's work is useful for trying to understand why Western intellectuals were taken with regimes like the Soviet Union and China during the Cold War. See Paul Hollander, *Political Pilgrims: Travels of Western Intellectuals to the Soviet Union, 1928–1978* (University Press of America, 1981).

[11] Frolic, *Canada and China*, 30, 31, 36.

[12] Files from the PRC Ministry of Foreign Affairs presented by Ambassador Mei Ping, Lu Congmin, Vice Chairman of the Foreign Affairs Committee of the 10th National People's Congress of China, and Ambassador Chen Wenzhao, at "Past and Future in Canada–China Relations," a conference hosted by UBC and the Institute of Asian Research and the Shanghai Institute for International Studies, Shanghai, November 10–12, 2010; Frolic, *Canada and China*, 37, 40, 44.

[13] Frolic, *Canada and China*, 37–44; Mitchell Sharp, House of Commons, July 21, 1969.

[14] Mitchell Sharp, "Memorandum to the Cabinet: Implementation of Canadian China Policy," January 30, 1969, Library and Archives Canada (LAC) RG 25-A-3-c, vol. 8815, file 20-1-2-CHINA-1.

[15] Paul T.K. Lin with Eileen Chen Lin, *In the Eye of the China Storm* (Queen's University Press, 2011); Manthorpe, *Claws of the Panda*, 87–94; 中加关系：过去和未来 https://zhuanlan.zhihu.com/p/634326943?utm_id=0; Richard H. Soloman, "Soloman to Scowcroft," June 13, 1973, Central Intelligence Agency, file LOC-HAK-35-2-6-4.

[16] Canadian Embassy in Stockholm to Undersecretary of State for External Affairs, "Chronology of Events Relating to Efforts of Canadian Embassy in Stockholm to Establish Contact and Negotiate with Embassy of People's Republic of China: Twentieth Installment," August 10, 1970, file 20-1-2-CHINA-1.

[17] Trudeau and Hébert, *Two Innocents*, ch. 10. Lin did not "directly" admit to being an intermediary, and Trudeau claimed he never met Lin at that time. See Frolic, *Canada and China*, 407–12.

[18] Lin, *In the Eye of the China Storm*, 164–67.

[19] "Stockholm to External," August 5, 1970, file 20-1-2-CHINA-1.

[20] "Starnes to Wall," August 14, 1970; "Parent to Beavis," January 5, 1971; RCMP Security Service, "Re: Paul T.K. Lin," May 2, 1973; "Dare to Hall," November (ND), 1976.

[21] "Canada Likely to Recognize Communist China Next Month, Government Source Says," Tokyo Shimbun, September 6, 1970, file 20-1-2-CHINA-1.

[22] Mitchell Sharp, *Which Reminds Me: A Memoir* (University of Toronto Press, 1994), 203–4; Frolic, *Canada and China*, 51.

[23] Yonglin Chen interview, 2023; Chen WenZhao, "On the Uniqueness and Far-Reaching Significance of the Establishment of Diplomatic Relations Between China and Canada," paper presented at the "Past and Future in China–Canada Relations" conference, November 10–12, 2010, Shanghai. The term "old friends" appears to be used by China publicly with respect to some international leaders. Henry Kissinger was also referred to publicly as an "old friend" based on his role in the US recognition of China. See Fan Wang, BBC News, "Henry Kissinger: China Mourns a 'most valued old friend,' BBC News, November 30, 2023. Given China's referral to Kissinger and even Jean Chrétien publicly as "old friends," it is likely Pierre Trudeau may have also been referred to in this way. See PRC Ministry of Foreign Affairs, "Han Zheng Meets with Former Canadian Prime Minister Jean Chretien," November 1, 2023.

[24] Secretary of State Translation Bureau, Bureau 2223, August 4, 1970, "The Communists Are Using the University Settlement House Which Is Financed by the United Appeal to Camouflage Their Illegal Activities. We Urge That Our Fellow Chinese Not to Believe in Their Propaganda," file 20-1-2-CHINA-1; "Across Canada," *ChinaTown News* (Vancouver), November 3, 1970, file 20-1-2-CHINA-1.

[25] La Vong, "Chiang Clique Weeping, Their American Master Aching," *National Salvation,* October 25, 1970; "Recognition of Red China," *Progress* (Winnipeg), October 25, 1970; "Recognition of the Peking Regime Will Not Interfere with the Lives of Immigrants," *Chinese Voice*, November 10, 1970, file 20-1-2-CHINA-1.

[26] A.J. Andrew, "Activities of Chinese Diplomatic Mission," November 26, 1970, file 20-1-2-CHINA-1.

[27] A.J. Andrew, "Opening of the Chinese Embassy," November 16, 1970, file 20-1-2-CHINA-1; E.R. Rittie, "PSI to GFE, Opening of the Chinese Embassy," December 8, 1970, file 20-1-2-CHINA-1.

[28] Chen interview; Cheuk Kwan interview, 2023; Mark Bourrie interview, 2023; Doug Young, *The Party Line: How the Media Dictates Public Opinion in Modern China* (John Wiley & Sons, 2013); Joël-Denis Bellavance, "Chinese Journalists in CSIS's Crosshairs," *La Presse*, May 1, 2017; Dave Naylor, "Ottawa Press Gallery Expels Chinese Agency," *Western Standard*, March 8, 2021.

CHAPTER TWO: A SYMBIOTIC RELATIONSHIP

[1] Frolic, *Canada and China*, ch. 3. The actual number killed in the Tiananmen Square massacre continues to be debated, but is likely in the thousands. For more on the debates and voting on UN Resolution 2758, see United Nations, "General Assembly Twenty-sixth Session Official Records," October 25, 1971, A-PV-1976, digitallibrary.un.org/record/735611?In=en&v=pdf; Frolic 65-66.

[2] Frolic, *Canada and China*, ch. 3; "ICTDET to EXTERNALOTT, Subj Recognition of PRC," October 15, 1970, LAC, file 20-1-2-China-1, vol. 19, part 3, 000754; "CBC Says Diplomat Was Spying in US," *Globe and Mail*, May 2, 1975, 4.

[3] Xu Guoqi, "The Montreal Games: Politics Challenge the Olympic Ideal," in *Olympic Dreams: China and Sports, 1895–2008* (Harvard University Press, 2008), 164–96; Donald Mackintosh and Michael Hawes, "Trudeau, Taiwan, and the 1976 Montreal Olympics," in *Sport and Canadian Diplomacy* (McGill-Queen's University Press, 1994), 37–58; Lord Killanin, *My Olympic Years* (Secker and Warburg, 1983); James Worrall, *My Olympic Journal* (Canadian Olympic Association, 2000); Frolic, *Canada and China*, 67–81.

[4] Frolic, *Canada and China*, 89.

[5] Peter C. Newman, "Epitaph for the Two-Party State: Trust Canadians to Invent a New System of Government: Elected Dictatorship," *Maclean's*, November 1993, 14; Peter C. Newman, "King Paul," *The Canadian Establishment: The Titans, How the Canadian Establishment Seized Power*, vol. 3 (Viking Canada, 1998), 164–89, 166–72; Robert A. Hackett and Richard Gruneau with Donald Gutstein, Timothy A. Gibson, and NewsWatch Canada, *The Missing News: Filters and Blind Spots in Canada's Press* (Garamond Press, 2000), 131–32; Peter C. Newman, *The Canadian Revolution, 1985–1995: From Defence to Defiance* (Viking, 1995), 389; Murray Dobbin, *Paul Martin: CEO for Canada?* (James Lorimer, 2003), 11; Frolic, *Canada and China*, 95–98; Lee Harding, "Power Corp's 50+ Years Behind Quebec Prime Ministers," *Niagara Independent*, May 31, 2024.

[6] "A Brief History of Canada–China Partnerships in Forestry," *Forestry Chronicle* 88, no. 2 (March/April 2013); Frolic, *Canada and China*, 106, 108, 111–12.

[7] Robin Sears interview, 2023; IAC Assessment—Chinese Interference, February 27, 1986, LAC RG24 BAN 2002-00892-2, box 67, file 15324; IAC Assessment—Soviet Union, Eastern Europe, January 5, 1989, PCO National Security Branch Special Registry Files, ATIP A-2017-00250.

[8] Canada, "Canadian Strategy for China," Memorandum to the Cabinet of Canada, PNRE-0194, File 20-1-2 China, Volume 38, 1987; Brian Mulroney, *Memoirs, 1939–1993* (McClelland & Stewart, 2007), 439–45; Frolic, *Canada and China*, 140.

[9] Sheng Xue interview, 2023; Lin, *In the Eye of the China Storm*, 254–57; Frolic, *Canada and China*, 180–96, 212–20; John Fraser, "The Terror Is Remorseless," *Globe and Mail*, June 5, 1989; Paul Gecelovsky, "Explaining the Canadian Response to the Tiananmen Square Massacre: A Comparative Study of Canadian Foreign Policy" (PhD diss., University of Alberta, 2000); Kim Richard Nossal, *Rain Dancing: Sanctions in Canadian and Australian Foreign Policy* (University of Toronto Press, 1994); George Bush and Brent Scowcroft, *A World Transformed* (Alfred A. Knopf, 1998), ch. 4; Earl Drake, *A Stubble-Jumper in Striped Pants: Memoirs of a Prairie Diplomat* (University of Toronto Press, 1999), 216.

[10] Richard Cleroux, "Clark Says Chinese Spying on Their Students in Canada," *Globe and Mail*, June 17, 1989.

[11] Chen interview; Mulroney, *Memoirs*, 996; Editorial, "Remembering Tiananmen," *Globe and Mail*, June 4, 1994.

[12] Alexandre Trudeau, introduction to Trudeau and Hébert, *Two Innocents*. For a picture of the pair in the square, see Alexandre Trudeau, "Barbarian Lost Excerpt: When the Trudeaus Went to China," *Maclean's*, September 4, 2016; Charles Trueheart, "Canada, Eyeing Vast Chinese Market, Deemphasizes Rights Issues," *Washington Post*, March 29, 1994; Frolic, *Canada and China*, 245–51.

[13] Senior public servant interview, 2023; the individual was giving their opinion on what they felt was the "mood" or "prevailing logic" of the time, not referring to official government policy or documents; Howard Balloch, *Semi-Nomadic Anecdotes* (Lulu Publishing, 2013), 358–59; Frolic, *Canada and China*, 254–55; "Canada, China Approve Trade Worth $6.3 Billion," Reuters, November 9, 1994.

[14] Canadian Press, "Canadair, China Discuss Spy Plane Sale," *Windsor Star*, July 11, 1994; John Solomon, "China Learned Secrets of U.S. Nuclear Weapons," *Ottawa Citizen*, May 15, 1999.

[15] Statistics Canada, "Canada's Trade with China," *The Daily*, June 8, 2004.

[16] Sears interview. See also Robin V. Sears, "China In-Between: Ensconced in the Diaoyutai and Meeting an 'Immortal,'" *Policy: Dispatches* 11, no. 4 (July–August 2023); Chris George, "The Ties That Bind Trudeau Liberals to Communist China," *Niagara Independent*, February 19, 2021.

[17] Paul Palango, *Dispersing the Fog: Inside the Secret World of Ottawa and the RCMP* (Key Porter Books, 2008), 441.

[18] Reuters, "Canada, China Approve Trade Worth $6.3 Billion," November 9, 1994; Frolic, *Canada and China*, 272–84; Michel Juneau-Katsuya, Special Committee on Canada–China Relations, Parliament of Canada, House of Commons, 43rd Parliament, 2nd session, April 19, 2021. See also an interview Juneau-Katsuya did with *The Epoch Times* on October 14, 2023: theepochtimes .com/epochtv/michel-juneau-katsuya-inside-communist-chinas-network-of -dormant-spies-5509751?&utm_medium=AmericanThoughtLeaders&utm _source=SocialM&utm_campaign=MichelJuneauKatsuya&utm_content=10 -14-2023; "Chinese Intelligence," LAC RG18, vol. 16592, file 010120-92-213, January 2, 1992–August 10, 1992.

[19] "Chinese Intelligence," LAC.

[20] Sears interview; Senior public servant interview, 2023; Liberal MP interview, 2023; Senior Liberal party official interview, 2023; the individual gave their opinion on intelligence but was not a member of government, elected official or involved in intelligence; PRC Ministry of Foreign Affairs, "Han Zheng Meets with Former Canadian Prime Minister Jean Chretien," November 1, 2023.

CHAPTER THREE: "WE WERE OUR OWN WORST ENEMIES"

[1] Lawrence Surtees, "Nortel Breaks Market Value Record," *Globe and Mail*, January 21, 2000; "International People: Northern Telecom," *Financial Times*, June 6, 1995; Natalie Obiko Pearson, "Did a Chinese Hack Kill Canada's Greatest Tech Company," *Bloomberg Businessweek*, July 1, 2020; Dealbook, "Nortel Faces Possible Delisting from NYSE," *New York Times*, December 12, 2008; Li Na, "Huawei's Net Profits up More than 130%," *Global Times*, March 31, 2010.

[2] Timothy Fogarty, Michel L. Magnan, Garen Markarian, and Serge Bohdjalian, "Inside Agency: The Rise and Fall of Nortel," *Journal of Business Ethics* 84, no. 2 (January 2009): 165–87; Jonathon Calof, Gregory Richards, Laurent Mirabeau, et al., "An Overview of the Demise of Nortel Networks and Key Lessons Learned: Systemic Effects in Environment, Resilience and Black-Cloud Formation," Telfer School of Management, University of Ottawa, 2014; Brian Shields interview, 2023.

[3] Brian Laghi, "Harper Promises He Won't 'Sell Out' on Rights," *Globe and Mail*, November 16, 2006; Frolic, *Canada and China*, 334–40.

[4] David Mulroney, *Middle Power, Middle Kingdom: What Canadians Need to Know About China in the 21st Century* (Allen Lane, 2015); Paul Evans, "Harper's Turn," in *Engaging China: Myth, Aspiration and Strategy in Canadian Foreign Policy from Trudeau to Harper* (University of Toronto Press, 2014); Kim Richard Nossal and Leah Sarson, "About Face: Explaining Changes in Canada's China Policy, 2006–2012," *Canadian Foreign Policy Journal* 20, no. 2 (2014): 146–62; Charles Burton, "Canada's China Policy Under the Harper Government," *Canadian Foreign Policy Journal* 25, no. 1 (2015): 45–63; Campbell Clark, "Hawkish Trade Minister Beijing Trip Signals Policy Shift," *Globe and Mail*, April 8, 2009; Frolic, *Canada and China*, 332–41.

[5] Gordon Lubold, Warren P. Strobel, and Aruna Viswanatha, "Chinese Gate-Crashers at U.S. Bases Spark Espionage Concerns," *Wall Street Journal*, September 4, 2023.

[6] Mulroney, *Middle Power*, ch. 4. For the joint statement text, see canada ca/en /news/archive/2009/12/canada-china-joint-statement.html; Frolic, *Canada and China*, 341–60.

[7] For Harper's speech, see alicewong.ca/2009/12/. Wong travelled to the PRC with Harper. "PM Doesn't Shy Away from Human Rights in China," CTV News, December 4, 2009; Frolic, *Canada and China*, 358–63; Jane Taber, "Harper 'Reaping What He Has Sown,'" *Globe and Mail*, December 3, 2009.

[8] "What Richard Fadden Told the CBC," *Globe and Mail*, June 25, 2010; Michelle Shephard, "Explain Yourself or Resign, Critics Tell Top Spy," *Toronto Star*, June 25, 2010; Susan Delacourt, "Olivia Chow Slams 'Baseless Spy Fiction,'" *Toronto Star*, June 25, 2010; Anthony Reinhart and Colin Freeze, "NDP MP Slams 'Baseless Spy Stories,'" *Globe and Mail*, June 24, 2010.

[9] Bourrie interview; Steve Chase, Mark Mackinnon, and Colin Freeze, "Journalist in Bon Dechert Affair Returns to China," *Globe and Mail*, September 15, 2011.

[10] Shields interview.

[11] Shields interview; Sam Cooper, "Inside the Chinese Military Attack on Nortel," Global News, August 25, 2020; Tom Blackwell, "Did Huawei Bring Down Nortel? Corporate Espionage, Theft, and the Parallel Rise and Fall of Two Telcom Giants," *National Post*, February 20, 2020.

[12] Shields interview.

[13] Shields interview; Cooper, "Inside the Chinese"; Pearson, "Did a Chinese Hack."

[14] Pearson, "Did a Chinese Hack"; Greg Weston, "Chinese Firm's Canadian Contracts Raise Security Fears," CBC News, May 15, 2012.

[15] Yun Wen, "The Rise of Chinese Transnational ICT Corporations: The Case of Huawei" (PhD diss., Simon Fraser University, 2017), 63–67; Scott Livingston, "Huawei, HONOR, and China's Evolving State Capitalist's Tool Kit," Center for Strategic and International Studies, December 11, 2020, 1–8.

[16] Shields interview.

[17] Ibid.

[18] Yuan Yang, "China's Tsinghua University Linked to Cyber Espionage, Study Claims," *Financial Times*, August 17, 2018; InsikT Group, "Chinese Cyberespionage Originating from Tsinghua University Infrastructure," *Recorded Future*, August 16, 2018; US Government, "Report of the Select Committee on U.S. National Security and Military Commercial Concerns with the People's Republic of China," US Government Printing Office, Washington, 1999. For Desmarais's role on the board, see CITIC Pacific 1999 Annual Report, citic.com/en/investor_relation/financial _reports/ and citic.com/uploadfile/2017/0525/20170525110441o419.pdf. CITIC announced Desmarais was leaving as a "non-executive director" of the company in 2014. See citic.com/ar2014/English/corporate-governance/corporate-governance /board-of-directors.html. CITIC Pacific Limited is a wholly owned subsidiary of CITIC Limited. For the history of the company, see "About Us" at citicpacific.com.

[19] Shields interview; Pearson, "Did a Chinese Hack"; "Background Information on an Incident at Nortel's Beijing Campus," unpublished, 2012.

[20] Shields interview; The Register, "Canada: Nortel Helps Build China's Surveillance Technology," *Corpwatch*, October 22, 2001; Cooper, "Inside the Chinese."

[21] Shields interview; Jack Swearingen, "The FBI Ran a Sting on Huawei While a *Bloomberg* Reporter Watched," *Intelligencer*, February 4, 2019.

[22] Heather Zieger, "Why Do Huawei's Inventions Look Oddly Familiar?," *Mind Matters*, April 9, 2021; Chuin-Wei Yap, Dan Strumpf, Dustin Volz, Kate O'Keeffe, and Aruna Viswanatha, "Huawei's Yearslong Rise Is Littered with Accusations of Theft and Dubious Ethics," *Wall Street Journal*, May 25, 2019.

[23] Shields interview; Cooper, "Inside the Chinese"; Dan Ciuriak and Mara Ptashkina, "Quantifying Trade Secret Theft: Policy Implications," Centre for International Governance Innovation, CIGI Papers No. 253, May 2021.

[24] David Pugliese, "The Mystery of the Listening Devices at DND's Nortel Campus," *Ottawa Citizen*, October 18, 2016; "DND May Abandon $1B Move to Former Nortel Site Because of Surveillance Bugs," CTV News, September 30, 2013; David Pugliese, "DND Losing Staff Because of Move to Former Nortel Campus but Numbers Unknown So Far," *Ottawa Citizen*, November 14, 2019.

[25] Shields interview; Weston, "Chinese Firm's."

CHAPTER FOUR: COUNTING THE SU BINS

[1] Garrett M. Graff, "How the US Forced China to Quit Stealing—Using a Chinese Spy," *Wired*, October 11, 2018.

[2] Vito Pilieci, "GhostNet Buster," *Ottawa Citizen*, April 25, 2009; Amy Hawkins, "Huge Cybersecurity Leak Lifts Lid on World of China's Hackers for Hire," *Guardian*, February 23, 2023.

[3] Stewart Bell, "War on the Web," *National Post*, January 2, 2008; Julie Ireton, "Hackers Stole Secret Canadian Government Data," CBC News, January 2, 2011; Stephen Starr, "Cyberattacks a Global Threat to Energy Industry," *Financial Post*, January 4, 2013; Matthew Fisher, "Time for the Gloves to Come Off When Dealing with China," *Ottawa Citizen*, February 22, 2013.

[4] David Pugliese, "Quebec Firm Seeks China Deal," *Windsor Star*, November 30, 2014. China made significant investments in Canadian oil and gas in this period. The PRC acquired the Canadian gas and oil company Nexen Inc. for $15 billion through its state-owned enterprise CNOOC Ltd., giving the PRC a foothold in the North American gas and oil sector. See Frolic, *Canada and China*, 354, 370.

[5] Andrew Duffy, "Alleged Spy Can Reapply to Stay," *Times Colonist* (Victoria), April 29, 2000.

[6] Tom Blackwell, "Ensnared in China's Espionage Web," *Gazette* (Montreal), August 2, 2017.

[7] CBC News, "Defectors Say China Running 1,000 Spies in Canada," June 15, 2005.

[8] Stewart Bell, "RCMP Allege Man Offered Patrol Ship Documents," *National Post*, December 2, 2013; Joseph Brean, "Co-workers Shocked by Charges," *National Post*, December 2, 2013; Jim Bronskill, "Secrecy Shrouds Sluggish Spy Case," Canadian Press, June 29, 2019; "Man Accused of Trying to Spy for China Has Case Stayed," *National Post*, December 16, 2021; Canadian Press, "Case of Hamilton Man Allegedly Spying for China Tangled in Secrecy," June 28, 2019; Colin Freeze, "Prosecutors Stay Charges Against Qing Quentin Huang in Probe of Naval Leaks to China," *Globe and Mail*, September 18, 2020.

[9] Graff "How the US"; Jessica Murphy, "Kevin and Julia Garratt on Their Experience as Detainees in China," BBC News, January 29, 2019; Julia and Kevin Garratt, *Two Tears on the Window* (First Choice Books, 2018); "'We Only Came Here to Help': Canadian Couple Imprisoned in China, Accused of Spying," *The Current*, CBC Radio, December 8, 2016; Michael Pillsbury has made the argument that China seeks to overtake US hegemony in the world; see Pillsbury, *Hundred-Year Marathon*.

[10] Touria Izri, "Singh Mulls Tiktok Return as U.S. Nears Potential Ban over Security Fears," Global News, April 24, 2024; Mike Wending, "Canada Bans TikTok on Government Devices," BBC News, February 27, 2023; Kari Paul, "Senate Passes Bill Banning Tiktok if Parent Company Does Not Sell It," *Guardian*, April 24, 2024; dot.LA, "TikTok Timeline Update: The Rise and Pause of a Social Video Giant," July 8, 2022; Sophia Harris, "Federal Government Departments Have Green Light to Advertise on TikTok—Despite Security

Concerns," CBC News, November 13, 2024; Holly Cabrera, "What the Federal Ban on TikTok's Canadian Operations Means for You," CBC News, November 7, 2024; Lily Jamali and Peter Hoskins, "Delay to TikTok Ban Gets Trump Sign-off," BBC News, January 21, 2025.

[11] Robert Fife and Steven Chase, "FBI Tells Parliamentarians They Were Targets of Chinese Hackers in 2021," *Globe and Mail*, April 29, 2024; Christopher Nardi, "CSIS Director Expected House Leadership to Warn MPs of Attempted Cyberattack in 2021," *National Post*, June 11, 2024.

[12] "Suspected China-Linked Hack on US Telecoms Worst in Nation's History, Senator Says," Reuters, November 22, 2024; Cybersecurity & Infrastructure Agency and FBI, "Joint Statement from FBI and CISA on the People's Republic of China (PRC) Targeting of Commercial Telecommunications Infrastructure," CISA, November 13, 2024.

[13] Justin Ling, "A Brilliant Scientist Was Mysteriously Fired from a Winnipeg Virus Lab. No One Knows Why," *Maclean's*, February 15, 2022; Canada, "National Research Council Contribution Plays Key Role in Newly Approved Ebola Vaccine," National Research Council Canada, March 20, 2018.

[14] CSIS, "CSIS Act Security Assessment of Ms. Xiangguo Qiu," June 30, 2020, File 8530-441-35-e, Sessional Paper Document, House of Commons, released February 28, 2024; CSIS, "CSIS Act Security Assessment of Mr. Keding Cheng," July 7, 2020, File 8530-441-35-e, Sessional Paper Document, House of Commons, released February 28, 2024; Robert Fife, Steven Chase, and Nathan Vanderklippe, "Infectious-Disease Scientist Fired from Winnipeg Laboratory Surfaces in China," *Globe and Mail*, March 19, 2004.

[15] Katherine Eban, "Secret Warnings About Wuhan Research Predated the Pandemic," *Vanity Fair*, November 21, 2023; Elaine Dewar, *On the Origins of the Deadliest Pandemic in 100 Years* (Biblioasis, 2021), ch. 2–4; David Klepper, "The CIA Believes COVID Most Likely Originated from a Lab but Has Low Confidence in Its Own Finding," Associated Press, January 26, 2025.

[16] CSIS Assessment Qiu; CSIS Assessment Cheng; Nathan Vanderklippe, Steven Chase, and Robert Fife, "Fired Winnipeg Scientists Use Pseudonyms in China as RCMP Probe Continues," *Globe and Mail*, March 20, 2024.

[17] CSIS Assessment Qiu; Canadian Press, "'It Was Political': China Actively Blocked Development of CanSino Vaccine, MPs Learn," *National Post*, March 11, 2021; Sam Cooper, "Canadian Spy Suspect Qiu Led WIV's 'Synthetic Bat Filovirus' Project with Wuhan Institute's Vice-Director: CSIS Document Investigation," *Bureau*, March 3, 2024.

[18] Vanderklippe, Chase, and Fife, "Fired Winnipeg Scientists."

[19] Jack Ewing, "U.S. Accuses Two Men of Stealing Tesla Trade Secrets," *New York Times*, March 19, 2024; Office of Public Affairs, Department of Justice, "Owners of China-Based Company Charged with Conspiracy to Send Trade Secrets Belonging to Leading U.S.-Based Electric Vehicle Company," March 19, 2024; Ben Penn, "Tesla Trade Secrets Stolen by Chinese Company's Owners, US Says," *Bloomberg News*, March 19, 2024; Blake Brittain, "Canadian National Pleads Guilty in Stealing Tesla Trade Secrets," Reuters, June 13, 2024.

CHAPTER FIVE: RED CARPETS AND PYROTECHNICS

[1] PRC, "Notice Declaring the 2019 High-End Foreign Expert Recruitment Plan," Translation by CSET, March 17, 2020; Yun Jiang, "Winning Hearts and Minds: The PRC's Efforts to Attract Scientific Talent," *China Matters*, Australian Institute of International Affairs, December 7, 2022; Manthorpe, *Claws of the Panda*, 192–200; CSIS Assessment Qiu; Benjamin Fung interview, 2023.

[2] CSIS Assessment Qiu; CSIS Assessment Cheng; Jiang, "Winning Hearts and Minds"; PRC, "Notice Declaring the 2019 High-End."

[3] Robert Fife and Steven Chase, "CSIS Warns About China's Efforts to Recruit Canadian Scientists," *Globe and Mail*, August 6, 2020; Lele Sang, "US Universities Secretly Turned Their Back on Chinese Professors Under DOJ's China Initiative," *Michigan News*, University of Michigan, March 29, 2024.

[4] Fung interview; Ryan Tumilty, "Ottawa Says It Doesn't Screen Out China-Affiliated Researchers in Federal Grants," *National Post*, March 9, 2024.

[5] Fung interview; Chris Sorensen, "U of T, Huawei Extend Research Partnership," *U of T News*, September 14, 2018.

[6] Douglas Quan, "'Significant and Clear' Threat: What Canada's Spy Chief Says About China Behind Closed Doors," *National Post*, August 13, 2019; Media

Relations, "Huawei and University of Waterloo Partner for World-Class Research and Innovation," *Waterloo News*, November 11, 2016; Sean Silcoff, Robert Fife Steven Chase, and Christine Dobby, "How Canadian Money and Research Are Helping China Become a Global Telecom Superpower," *Globe and Mail*, May 26, 2018

[7] Robert Fife and Steven Chase, "Canadian Universities Conducting Joint Research with Chinese Military Scientists," *Globe and Mail*, January 30, 2023.

[8] Fung interview; Robert Fife and Steven Chase, "Ottawa Clamps Down on University Research Partnerships with China, Iran and Russia," *Globe and Mail*, January 16, 2024.

[9] Fung interview; Benjamin Fung, evidence to Standing Committee on Science and Research, Parliament of Canada (Ottawa: King's Printer, September 20, 2023).

[10] Academic interview, 2023.

[11] Manthorpe, *Claws of the Panda*, 192–200; Mukhammadsodik Donaev, "A Closer Look at the Growing Chinese Presence in Uzbekistan," *Diplomat*, May 2, 2023; Sophia Nina Burna-Asefi, "China and Uzbekistan: An Emerging Development Partnership?," *Diplomat*, May 13, 2022; Ambassador Mark A. Green, "Debt Distress on the Road to 'Belt and Road,'" *Stubborn Things* (blog), Wilson Center (Washington, DC), January 16, 2024.

[12] Bob Pickard interview, 2023; Pedro Allende, "What Do the Asian Infrastructure Investment Bank's Recent Forays Outside of Asia Mean?," Center for Strategic and International Studies, October 28, 2022; Reuters, "Canada Freezes Ties with Chinese Bank AIIB over Claim It Is 'Dominated by Communist Party,'" *Guardian*, June 15, 2023.

[13] Manthorpe, *Claws of the Panda*, 192–200.

[14] Manthorpe, *Claws of the Panda*, 192–200; "Confucius Institutes Rebrand on Canadian Soil Under New Name," *Vision Times*, January 23, 2023; Jacques Poitras, "Cardy Cut New Brunswick's Education Ties with China Before Resignation," CBC News, January 4, 2023; "Chinese Culture Program Removed from 18 New Brunswick Schools," CBC News, August 26, 2019; Lin Yang, "Controversial Confucius Institutes Returning to U.S. Schools Under New Name," *Voice of America*, June 27, 2022.

[15] Fung interview; Fung, evidence to Standing Committee.

[16] Wendy Stueck and Xiao Xu, "Universities, School Boards Across Canada Defend Ties with China's Confucius Institute," *Globe and Mail*, October 21, 2020; "Confucius Institutes Rebrand," *Vision Times*.

[17] Yang, "Controversial Confucius Institutes."

[18] Ruth Hayhoe, "China's Universities Since Tiananmen: A Critical Assessment," *China Quarterly* 134 (June 1993): 296–99.

[19] Suisheng Zhao, "The Patriotic Education Campaign in Xi Jinping's China: The Emergence of a New Generation of Nationalists," *China Leadership Monitor* 75 (Spring 2023): 1–6.

[20] Academic of Chinese descent interview, 2023; Academic interview, 2023; US Department of State, "The Chinese Communist Party on Campus: Opportunities & Risks," September 2020; Chen interview; Chen has given numerous public interviews about the connections between the CSSAs and PRC mission see for example Michael Conway, "Diplomat Turned Whistleblower Claims China Controls Students at Scots Universities," *The Ferret*, March 28, 2021; Craig Desson and Nick Murray, "Chinese Students in Canada Say They've Been Targeted by Beijing's Campaign of Fear," CBC News, September 28, 2024. For more on China utilizing WeChat for censorship and surveillance, see Miles Kenyon, "WeChat Surveillance Explained," *Citizen Lab*, May 7, 2020; Seth Kaplan, "China's Censorship Reaches Globally Through WeChat," *Foreign Policy*, February 28, 2023; Jeanne Whalen, "Chinese Censorship invades the U.S. via WeChat," *Washington Post*, January 7, 2021.

[21] Fung interview; Fung, evidence to Standing Committee; Kate O'Keeffe, "Barred Huawei Secretly Backs US Research, Awarding Millions in Prizes," *Bloomberg*, May 2, 2024; Kate O'Keeffe, "Optica CEO Departs Amid Probes into Society's Links to Huawei," BNN Bloomberg, August 26, 2024; Kate O'Keeffe, "Optica Cuts Ties with Huawei After Secret Funding Exposed," *Bloomberg*, June 6, 2024.

CHAPTER SIX: "YOUR EXISTENCE BECOMES POLITICAL"

[1] Cheuk Kwan interview, 2023.

[2] Brady, "Magic Weapons;" Hamilton, *Silent Invasion*, ch. 3 and ch. 8; Chen interview; Alex Joske and Jeffrey Stoff, "The United Front and Technology

Transfer," in William C. Hannas and Didi Kirsten Tatlow, eds., *China's Quest for Foreign Technology: Beyond Espionage* (Routledge, 2020), 260. UFWD took control of OCAO in 2017 with the official announcement taking place in March 2028. See Cheryl Yu and Peter Mattis, "Q&A: What Was the Relationship Between the United Front System and the Overseas Chinese Affairs Office?," Jamestown Foundation's *China Brief*, October 7, 2024 and s.15 of "中共中央印发《深化党和国家机构改革方案》_中央有关文件_中国政府网". Government of China. Archived.

[3] Brady, "Magic Weapons"; Kwan interview. Kwan also described the idea of "astroturfing" organizations to Joanna Chiu; see Joanna Chiu, *China Unbound: A New World Disorder* (House of Anansi, 2021), 106–8; Chen interview. Chen uses "UFWD" and "United Front" interchangeably; Chen has given interviews and testified to the US Congress about how PRC missions engage in interference and are connected to some community groups. See "Confessions of a Chinese Consular Official," Faluninfo, July 21, 2005; Jichang Lulu, "Antipodica 2: Chen Yonglin: Australia as China's Backyard," February 26, 2018; The NCCC denies it has a pro-Beijing stance and receives any money from the PRC Consulate stating that its position is politically neutral. See Craig Offman and Steven Chase "Canada Fields Controversial Delegate in China Trip," *Globe and Mail*, November 7, 2014; "How China Turns Members of Its Diaspora into Spies," *Economist*, December 2024; Wong interview, 2023; Katherine Leung interview, 2023; Xue interview, 2023; Activists interview, 2023; Falun Gong interview, 2023.

[4] Mehmet Tohti interview, 2023; Steven Chase, "Parliament Votes to Help Uyghurs and Condemn Genocide in China," *Globe and Mail*, October 25, 2022; Edward Lemon, Bradley Jardine, and Natalie Hall, "Globalizing Minority Persecution: China's Transnational Repression of the Uyghurs," *Globalizations* 20, no. 4 (2023): 565–67; Chemi Lhamo interview, 2023; "Toronto Police Investigating Online Abuse of Student Leader at U of T," CBC News, February 28, 2019.

[5] Mehmet Tohti interview; Lhamo interview, 2023; Cheng-Tian Kuo, "The PRC and Taiwan: Fujian's Faltering United Front," *Asian Survey* 32, no. 8 (August 1992): 683–95; King-Yi Hsu, "Taiwan's Response to Peking's United Front Tactics," *Asian Affairs: An American Review* 8, no. 2 (Nov.–Dec. 1980): 89–112.

[6] Samson Yuen and Edmund W. Cheng, "Deepening the State: The Dynamics of China's United Front Work in Post-handover Hong Kong," *Communist and Post-Communist Studies* 53, no. 4 (2020): 136–54.

[7] Lemon et al. "Globalizing Minority Persecution"; Thomas Hylland Eriksen, "Some Questions About Flags," in *Flag, Nation, and Symbolism in Europe and America* (Routledge, 2007); "The Battle over Which Flag to Fly in America's Chinatowns," BBC News, January 20, 2020; "China Holds Flag Raising Ceremonies Across Occupied Tibet to Mark China's National Day," *Tibet News*, October 3, 2022; Lynette Ong, *Outsourcing Repression: Everyday State Power in Contemporary China* (Oxford University Press, 2022).

[8] Yongnian Zheng, *Contemporary China—A History Since 1978* (John Wiley & Sons, 2014), 106–7.

[9] Thomas Gold, Doug Guthrie, and David Wank, eds., introduction to *Social Connections in China: Institutions, Culture, and the Changing Nature of Guanxi* (Cambridge University Press, 2002). Scholars have also debated to what degree guanxi is a uniquely Chinese cultural element; Peng Wang, "Military Corruptions in China: The Role of Guanxi in the Buying and Selling of Military Positions," *China Quarterly* 228, no. 12 (2016): 970–91; Xiaoting Li, "Cronyism and Military Corruption in the Post–Deng Xiaoping Era: Rethinking the Party-Commands-the-Gun Model," *Journal of Contemporary China* 26, no. 107 (2017): 696–710; James Mulvenon, "'Comrade, Where's My Military Car?': Xi Jinping's Throwback Mass-Line Campaign to Curb PLA Corruption," *China Leadership Monitor* 42, no. 10 (2013): 1–5; James R. Gorrie, *The China Crisis: How China's Economic Collapse Will Lead to a Global Depression* (John Wiley & Sons, 2013), 74–78, 110.

[10] Gorrie, *China Crisis*, 74–78, 110.

[11] "Chinese Capital Controls Reflect Changing Political Priorities in Beijing," *GSI*, August 31, 2017.

[12] Sidhartha Banerjee, "Ex-RCMP Office Charged with Foreign Interference Looks to Quash Charges," CBC News, April 22, 2024; Laura Harth and Yenting Chen, "Chasing Foxhunt," *Safeguard Defenders*, April 15, 2024; "Interpol: Address China's 'Red Notice' Abuses," Human Rights Watch, September 25, 2017; Robert Fife and Steven Chase, "CSIS Warns China's Operation Fox Hunt

Is Targeting Canada's Chinese Community," *Globe and Mail*, November 10, 2020; Norimitsu Onishi, "A Retired RCMP Officer Is Charged with Spying for China," *New York Times*, July 21, 2023; Andrew Hartnett, Nicole Morgret and Rachael Burton, China Economic and Security Review Commission, December 13, 2023, 10 "China's Global Police State: Background and U.S. Policy Implications," U.S.-China Economic and Security Review Commission, December 13, 2023, 10.

[13] Scott Anderson, Bob McKeown, and Matthew Pierce, "How Canada Has Been Helping China Hunt Fugitives for Decades," CBC News, October 21, 2023

[14] "14 Governments Launch Investigations into Chinese 110 Overseas Police Service Stations," Safeguard Defenders, November 7, 2022; Leyland Cecco, "Canada Issues 'Cease and Desist' Warning to China over 'Police Stations' in Ottawa," *Guardian*, December 1, 2022; Julian Borger, "FBI Arrests Two New Yorkers Accused of Running Covert Chinese Police Station," *Guardian*, April 18, 2023; Catherine Tunney, "RCMP Commissioner Says Mounties Have 'Credible' Info About Alleged Chinese 'Police Stations,'" CBC News, March 8, 2024; Christopher Nardi, "Group Suspected of Hosting Chinese 'Police Station' Received up to $200,000 in Federal Funding," *National Post*, May 18, 2023.

[15] Stewart Bell and Jeff Semple, "Foreign Interference: RCMP Investigate Death of B.C. Man Targeted by China," Global News, September 21, 2023; "FBI Chief Warns of Beijing Plot to Compel Overseas Critics to Return to China," ABC News, July 7, 2020; "Involuntary Returns: China's Covert Operation to Force 'Fugitives' Overseas Back Home," Safeguard Defenders, January 2022, 51; Cheuk Kwan interview and Yonglin Chen interview, 2023.

CHAPTER SEVEN: BELIEF AND SEEING

[1] Frolic, *Canada and China*, 373–84; Nathan Vanderklippe, "China Pushed Hard for a Wide-Ranging Extradition Treaty for Years Prior to Meng Arrest," *Globe and Mail*, October 5, 2020; David Mulroney interview, 2023; Diplomat interview, 2023; Michael Kinsley, "Psst! Inside Information! It's the Scandal—and the Norm," *Washington Post*, June 4, 1986.

[2] Colin Freeze, Access to Information and Privacy request, Global Affairs Canada, "Canada–China: Proposed Initiatives," EDT-16-Printroom-KM554E-20180528161055; Pillsbury, *Hundred-Year Marathon*.

[3] Robert Fife and Steven Chase, "Trudeau Attended Cash-for-Access Fundraiser with Chinese Billionaires," *Globe and Mail*, November 22, 2016; Robert Fife and Steven Chase, "The Murky Beginnings of a New Canadian Bank," *Globe and Mail*, November 24, 2016; Robert Fife and Steven Chase, "Influential Chinese-Canadians Paying to Attend Private Fundraisers with Trudeau," *Globe and Mail*, December 2, 2016; Jacob Serebrin, "Montreal University to Keep Donation Linked to Chinese Government Influence Effort," CBC News, April 21, 2023; Craig Offman and Nathan Vanderklippe, "Cash-for-Access Organizers Sought Payments That Exceeded Federal Contribution Limits," *Globe and Mail*, December 22, 2016.

[4] Brady, "Magic Weapons"; Hamilton, *Silent Invasion*, ch. 3 and ch. 8. Alex Joske has also written about how China's MSS has utilized community groups to aid in interference and espionage; see Alex Joske, *Spies and Lies: How China's Greatest Covert Operations Fooled the World* (Hardie Grant Books, 2018); Michael Shoebridge, "Editors' Picks for 2018: 'It's Time to Get Things Straight with China,'" *Strategist* (blog), Australian Strategic Policy Institute (ASPI), December 31, 2018 Kwan interview; Activist interview, 2023.

[5] Wong interview; Activist interview, 2023; John Dotson, "China Explores Economic Outreach to U.S. States via United Front Entities," Jamestown Foundation's *China Brief* 19, no. 12 (June 26, 2019); NSICOP, "Special Report on Foreign Interference in Canada's Democratic Processes and Institutions," June 2024, 26,–29; Brady, "Magic Weapons." For a recent example see Michael Forsythe, "Threats and Cash: How China Meddles in U.S. Local Elections," *The New York Times*, August 28, 2025.

[6] Robert Fife, Steven Chase, and Xiao Xu, "Security Experts Question Political Influence of Toronto Developer with Ties to Beijing," *Globe and Mail*, December 3, 2018.

[7] Agence France-Presse, "Meng Wenzhou and the Two Michaels: A Timeline," *Guardian*, September 24, 2021; Paul Wells, "Who Lost China? And How Was Canada Supposed to Win It?," *Maclean's*, January 3, 2019; Terry Glavin, "What Jean Chrétien Has Done to Canada on the Meng Wenzhou Case," *Maclean's*, June 19, 2019; Omid Ghoreishi, "The Man Behind McCallum's Controversial Press Conference That Led to His Removal as Ambassador to China," *Epoch Times*, January 31, 2019; Scott McGregor and Ina Mitchell, *The Mosaic Effect: How the*

Chinese Communist Party Started a Hybrid War in America's Backyard (Toronto: Optimum Publishing International, 2023), 184; Matt Schrader, "'Chinese Assistance Centers' Grow United Front Work Department Global Presence,'" Jamestown Foundation's *China Brief* 19, no. 1 (January 5, 2019); Office of the Conflict of Interest and Ethics Commissioner, "List of Sponsored Travel Presented to the House of Commons 2013," March 2014; Terry Glavin, "Glavin: Canada's China Policy in 2020—Continue to Kowtow," *Ottawa Citizen*, December 27, 2019; website for the HuaZhu association, www.huazhu.ca/?page_id=280 (archived), http://huazhu.ca/?cat=8 (archived), http://huazhu.ca/?cat=9 (archived). It is not clear if being an adviser or consultant to HuaZhu meant playing any type of major role or if an individual was just selected for it. It is not known if any advisers or members knew the organization was tied to OCAO and the UFWD. Even if such information was known, it does not imply individuals acted inappropriately by being affiliated with the group. It is unknown if the group continues to operate today.

[8] Stephen Foley, Ryan McMorrow, and Demetri Sevastopulo, "McKinsey Website Touted Its Advice to Chinese Government Ministries," *Financial Times*, February 27, 2024; Dan De Luce and Yasmine Salam, "Advising Both Chinese State Companies and the Pentagon, McKinsey & Co. Comes Under Scrutiny," NBC News, November 13, 2021; Walt Bogdanich and Michael Forsythe, *When McKinsey Comes to Town: The Hidden Influence of the World's Most Powerful Consulting Firm* (Doubleday, 2022); Lloyd Green, "When McKinsey Comes to Town Review: The Book to Consult on Opioids, China and More," *Guardian*, October 29, 2022; "McKinsey Agrees $573m Opioid Settlement in US," BBC News, February 4, 2021; Robert Fife, Steven Chase, and Bill Curry, "Ottawa Contracts Comprise up to 10 Per Cent of McKinsey Canadian Revenue," *Globe and Mail*, January 31, 2023; Ben Mussett, "Justin Trudeau and I Had 'a Professional Relationship,' Former McKinsey Head Dominic Barton Tells Contracts Probe," *Toronto Star*, July 19, 2023; Prime Minister's Office, "Prime Minister Announces Appointment of Dominic Barton as Ambassador to China," press release, September 4, 2019.

[9] Christian Paas-Lang, "Michael Kovrig and Michael Spavor Arrive in Canada After Nearly 3-Year Detention in China," CBC News, September 25, 2021; Clare Duffy and Evan Perez, "Huawei CFO Meng Wanzhou Reaches Agreement with US to Resolve Fraud Charges," CNN, September 25, 2021; "The Meng Wanzhou Huawei Saga: A Timeline," CBC News, September 24, 2021.

[10] Catharine Tunney, "RCMP Says It's Running Check on Equipment Purchased from Company Linked to China," CBC News, January 30, 2023; Motorola Solutions, "Hytera Pleads Guilty to Felony for Conspiring to Steal Trade Secret Information from Motorola Solutions in U.S. Department of Justice Prosecution," January 14, 2025; Hytera, "FCC Rules Do Not Include Hytera Radios," https://www.hytera.us/news/fcc-rules-do-not-include-hytera-radios; Ahmad Hathout, "Hytera and Huawei Respond to FCC Blocking Chinese Equipment as U.S. Players React," Broadband Breakfast, September 21, 2021; Catharine Tunney and Richard Raycroft, "Canada Bans Chinese Tech Giant Huawei from 5G Network," CBC News, May 19, 2022; Government of Canada, "China's Intelligence Law and the Country's Future Intelligence Competitions," May 17, 2018; Rush Doshi prepared statement, "China's New National Security Laws: Risks to American Companies and Conflicts of Interest," US Senate Committee on Homeland Security and Government Affairs," September 24, 2024.

[11] Keith Doucette, "Canada's Defence Minister Says China Is Not an Adversary," Canadian Press, November 22, 2019; Murray Brewster, "Canada's Ties to China's Military Underscore the Weird Contradictions in Its Foreign Policy," CBC News, December 12, 2020; "Liberals Dismayed That Military Exercises with China Were Cancelled, Secret Documents Reveal," National Post, December 9, 2020; Tom Blackwell, "Why Ottawa Let Chinese Forces Attend a 'Military Science' Meet in Canada," National Post, November 15, 2022; Rob Gillies, "Canada's Defence Minister Says China Is Not an Adversary," Associated Press, November 22, 2019.

[12] Ryan Tumilty, "Chinese 'Influence' and 'Intelligence Threat' Outlined in Declassified 25-Year-Old CSIS-RCMP Report," National Post, September 18, 2023. For more on organized crime and PRC connections, see Sam Cooper, Willful Blindness: How a Network of Narcos, Tycoons and CCP Agents Infiltrated the West (Optimum Publishing, 2021); Salmaan Farooqui, "Dozens Charged, Millions in Property and Cash Seized in Alleged Illegal Casino Bust: York Police," Global News, September 30, 2020; Tom Blackwell, "Alleged Mastermind of Lavish Mansion Casino Raided by Police Met Twice with Prime Minister Trudeau," National Post, October 7, 2020.

[13] Alex Boutilier, "RCMP Nixed Probe into Suspected PRC-Linked Money Laundering Network," Global News, October 3, 2024; Catherine Tunney and Racy Rafique, "Trudeau Accuses India of Supporting Violent Crimes in Canada,"

CBC News, October 14, 2024; Mark Galeotti, "Gangster's Paradise: How Organized Crime Took Over Russia," *Guardian*, March 23, 2018; Sebastian Rotella, "Outlaw Alliance: How China and Chinese Mafias Overseas Protect Each Other's Interests," ProPublica, July 1, 2023; Sebastian Rotella and Kirsten Berg, "The Globetrotting Con Man and Suspected Spy Who Met with President Trump," ProPublica, October 11, 2022. Cheryl Yu and Peter Mattis, "Q&A: What Was the Relationship Between the United Front System and the Overseas Chinese Affairs Office?," Jamestown Foundation's *China Brief*, October 7, 2024; Blackwell, "Alleged Mastermind."

[14] "Vote Passes Recognizing China's Treatment of Uyghurs as Genocide," Global News, February 22, 2021; Tom Blackwell, "Chinese-Canadian Tories Urge O'Toole to Resign, Saying Tough-on-China Platform Alienated Voters," *National Post*, October 13, 2021.

[15] Sam Cooper, "International Students and Offshore Banking Flagged in Canadian Real Estate Money Laundering," Global News, November 25, 2021; Fife and Chase, "Trudeau Attended."

[16] Fife and Chase, "Trudeau Attended"; Steven Chase, "Canadian Businessman Cuts Record $60 M Forfeiture Deal with New Zealand Police over 'Profits from Pyramid Scheme,'" *Globe and Mail*, June 16, 2021; Gong (Re), 2024ONCMT 24 (CanLII), https://canlii.ca/t/k7m8d; Aisling Murphy, "Who Is Edward Gong, Was His Company a Pyramid Scheme, and Why Is He on So Many Campaign Signs in Toronto?" CTV News, June 21, 2023.

[17] Alex Boutilier, "Conservatives Believe 13 Ridings Were Targeted by Foreign Interference in 2021 Election," Global News, December 15, 2021; Andy Blatchford, "O'Toole Blames China for Conservative Election Results," *Politico*, June 9, 2022.

[18] Sam Cooper, "Canadian Intelligence Warned PM Trudeau That China Covertly Funded 2019 Election Candidates: Sources," Global News, November 7, 2022; Sam Cooper, "Toronto Businessman Allegedly Focus of Chinese Interference Probes: Sources," Global News, November 16, 2022.

[19] Cooper, "Toronto Businessman"; Robert Fife and Steven Chase, "CSIS Briefed Trudeau That China Targeted Federal Candidates in 2019 Election, but No Evidence of Covert Funding," *Globe and Mail*, December 21, 2022; Cooper, "Wei Chengyi Statement." The *Globe* also reported that the CTCCO had ties

to UFWD. The *Globe's* attempts to reach the group for comment about the TD "debanking" and UFWD ties were unsuccessful. Robert Fife and Steven Chase, "TD Bank closed accounts of pro-China group, ex-Liberal MP Han Dong, records show," *The Globe and Mail*, April 16, 2025. I was unsuccessful in reaching CTCCO for comment.

[20] Robert Fife and Steven Chase, "CSIS Documents Reveal Chinese Strategy to Influence Canada's 2021 Election," *Globe and Mail*, February 17, 2023; Victoria Bela, "'Smears and Baseless': China Rejects Canadian Election Meddling Claims," *South China Morning Post*, May 4, 2024; David Carrigg and Derick Penner, "Chinese Consulate in Vancouver Rejects Allegations It Interfered in Federal Election in B.C.," *Vancouver Sun*, February 19, 2023.

[21] Kenny Chiu interview, 2023; Marcus Kolga and Ai-Men Lau, "Influence Operation Targeting Canadian 2021 Federal Election," *DisinfoDigest* (blog), DisinfoWatch, December 1, 2021; Kenton Thibaut, "China-Linked WeChat Accounts Spread Disinformation in Advance of 2021 Canadian Election," *Medium*, November 4, 2021.

[22] Craig Offman, "The Making of Michael Chan," *Globe and Mail*, June 17, 2015; Craig Offman, "CSIS Warned This Cabinet Minister Could Be a Threat. Ontario Disagreed," *Globe and Mail*, June 16, 2015; Robert Fife and Steven Chase, "CSIS Warned Trudeau About Toronto-Area Politician's Alleged Ties to Chinese Diplomats," *Globe and Mail*, February 13, 2023; Sam Cooper, "Liberals Ignored CSIS Warning on 2019 Candidate Accused in Chinese Interference Probe: Sources," Global News, February 25, 2023; Alex Boutilier, "Ontario Court Dismisses Michael Chan's 2015 Lawsuit Against the *Globe and Mail*," Global News, December 10, 2024.

[23] Chen interview. PRC Consular and Embassy positions in a host nation can be found on the consular or embassy websites. Chen has given interviews and testimony before the US congress about how the PRC Mission and its positions have engaged in interference. See "Confessions of a Chinese Consular Official," Faluninfo, July 21, 2005; David Kilgour, "Former Chinese Diplomat Chen Yonglin Reveals Secret Documents that Show How the CCP Exports Its Persecution of Falun Gong Abroad," August 6, 2007. For examples of the various position titles, see PRC Toronto Consulate, "Consulate General of China in Toronto Seeks Assistance in Preventing Telephone Fraud," July 14, 2018

(archived); "Mr Xian Was Invited to Chinese New Year Gala Hosted by the Chinese Consulate General in Toronto," Shenglin Financial, January 17, 2020 (archived). In public interviews, Yonglin Chen has cited that the second deputy-consul positions are tasked with preventing defections but also dealing with "orders from the Ministry of State Security"; see Jichang Lulu, "Antipodica 2: Chen Yonglin: Australia as China's Backyard," February 26, 2018. Zhao Wei appears as heading the "political office" or "political and new affairs," per Google Translate; see "2019 Canadian Shenzhen Community Association Federation 'Shenzhen Good Voice' New Year Masquerade Ball Concluded Successfully," *Easyca*, March 4, 2019.

[24] Robert Fife, Steven Chase, and Nathan Vanderklippe, "China's Vancouver Consulate Interfered in 2022 Municipal Election, According to CSIS," *Globe and Mail*, March 16, 2023; Sam Cooper, "Ontario Legislature Member Is Part of Alleged Beijing 2019 Election-Interference Network: Sources," Global News, March 10, 2023; "Ontario MPP Resigns from PC Caucus, Denies Alleged Link to Foreign Election Interference," CBC News, March 10, 2023; Sam Cooper, "Liberal MP Han Dong Secretly Advised Chinese Diplomat in 2021 to Delay Freeing Two Michaels: Sources," Global News, March 22, 2023; Robert Fife and Steven Chase, "Trudeau Government Decided CSIS Transcript of MP Han Dong Provided No 'Actionable Evidence,'" *Globe and Mail*, March 23, 2023.

[25] Robert Fife and Steven Chase, "CSIS Uncovered Chinese Plan to Donate to Pierre Elliott Trudeau Foundation," *Globe and Mail,* February 28, 2023; James Griffiths, "Meet the Chinese Billionaire Who Donated to the Trudeau Foundation," *Globe and Mail*, April 16, 2023.

[26] Robert Fife and Steven Chase, "Chrystia Freeland Rings National Security Alarm About Founders of Canadian Bank with Suspected Ties to China," *Globe and Mail*, February 23, 2023; Robert Fife and Steven Chase, "Freeland Imposes Extraordinary Measures to Force Out Founding Investors of Wealth One Bank with Alleged Ties to China," *Globe and Mail*, September 2, 2023; Steven Chase and Robert Fife, "Wealth One Fined $676500 for Failing to Comply with Anti-Money Laundering Law," *Globe and Mail*, March 6, 2023; Judy Trinh, "Banking Mogul Suing Government After Intelligence Leaks Leave Him Shut out of Canadian Economy," CTV News, May 17, 2024; Robert Fife and Steven Chase," Ottawa Ties Wealth One Founders to Possible Chinese Interference," *Globe and Mail*, September 6 , 2024.

[27] Robert Fife and Steven Chase, "China Views Canada as a 'High Priority' for Interference: CSIS Report," *Globe and Mail*, May 1, 2023; Steven Chase and Robert Fife, "CSIS Head Tells MP Michael Chong That He and Family Were Targeted by China," *Globe and Mail*, May 2, 2023; "CSIS Has Begun Offering Other MPs Briefings on Foreign Interference," CBC News, May 12, 2023.

[28] Michael Chong interview, 2023.

[29] None of the allegations against Chan, Dong, Ke, Xian, Majacher or others in relation to foreign interference media reports discussed in this chapter have been proven. As of this writing, lawsuits filed by all of these individuals are before the courts, with Dong and Ke's lawsuits recently being allowed to proceed as anti-SLAPP motions were dismissed by courts. See Bruce Livesay, "Lives Ruined, No 'Traitors' Found: The Cost of Baseless Reporting on Chinese Interference," The Breach, January 30, 2025. Dong and Global News settled with Global saying it "recognizes the findings of the Final Report of the Public Inquiry into Foreign Interference, including that the classified information reviewed by Justice Marie Josée Hogue corroborates that Mr. Dong did not suggest that the PRC extend the detention of Michael Kovrig and Michael Spavor." See Staff, "Global News and Former MP Han Dong Settle Lawsuit," Global News, June 15, 2025.

[30] John Ibbitson and Salmaan Farooqui, "Canada's Indo-Pacific Strategy Sees China as a 'Disruptive Global Power,'" *Globe and Mail*, November 27, 2022; Robert Fife and Steven Chase, "Former Governor-General David Johnston Named as Special Rapporteur on China's Election Interference," *Globe and Mail*, March 15, 2023; Alex Boutilier, "The Unanswered Question at the Heart of David Johnston's Foreign Interference Report," Global News, May 26, 2023; Robert Fife and Steven Chase, "Foreign Interference a 'Stain' on Canada's Electoral Process, Hogue Inquiry Concludes," *Globe and Mail*, May 3, 2024; Robert Fife and Steven Chase, "Second Diaspora Group Won't Take Part in Foreign-Interference Inquiry," *Globe and Mail*, February 20, 2024; Robert Fife and Steven Chase, "Political Parties Kept in Dark About Chinese Foreign Interference in 2019 and 2021 Elections," *Globe and Mail*, April 2, 2024; Public Inquiry into Foreign Interference in Federal Electoral Processes and Democratic Institutions, "Public Hearing," Volume 11, April 5, 2024, English interpretation; Spencer Van Dyk, "Rosenberg Says Foreign Interference Inquiry Should Be 'On the Table': Read the Full Interview," CTV News, March 5, 2023.

[31] Jim Bronskill, "Spy Watchdog's Foreign Interference Review Finds 'Unacceptable Gaps' in Accountability," Canadian Press, May 28, 2024; NSIRA, "Review of the Dissemination of Intelligence on People's Republic of China Political Foreign Interference, 2018–2023," May 28, 2024; Andrew Coyne, "The Foreign Interference Inquiry Features a Parade of Senior Liberals Protesting Too Much," *Globe and Mail*, April 19, 2024; Robert Fife and Steven Chase, "Foreign Interference Did Not Affect Outcome of 2021 Election, Report Says," *Globe and Mail*, February 28, 2023; Laura Osman and Dylan Robertson, "Han Dong Sought Support from International Students, Foreign Interference Inquiry Hears," Canadian Press, April 2, 2024; Robert Fife and Steven Chase, "CSIS Director Recalled After PMO Staff Say They Weren't Told About China Interference in 2019 and 2021 Elections," *Globe and Mail*, April 9, 2024; Jim Bronskill and Laura Osman, "Prime Minister Justin Trudeau 'Expressed Frustration' About 'Sensationalized' Leaks of Intelligence," Canadian Press, April 10, 2024; Justin Trudeau, "Testimony at the Public Inquiry into Foreign Interference," *Globe and Mail*, April 10, 2024; Catherine Tunney, "CSIS Chief Defends His Spies' Work After PM Casts Doubt on Reliability of Agency's Reports," CBC News, April 12, 2024; Robert Fife and Steven Chase, "Liberal Party Member Warned MP Dong of CSIS Surveillance, National Security Source Says," *Globe and Mail*, April 10, 2024; Robert Fife and Steven Chase, "PMO, Top Ministers and Senior Officials Received 34 Briefings on Foreign Interference Since 2018, CSIS Says," *Globe and Mail*, April 8, 2024; Catherine Lévesque, "Five Big Takeaways from Justin Trudeau's Testimony About Foreign Interference," *National Post,* April 10, 2024; Stephanie Levitz, "Canada's Spy Agency Recalled Intelligence About Suspected Chinese-State Interference, Inquiry Documents Reveal," *Toronto Star,* April 5, 2024; Christopher Nardi and Catherine Lévesque, "Trudeau Doubted Intelligence Officials' Ability to Spot Interference in Liberal Nomination Contest: Testimony," *National Post,* April 10, 2024; Public Inquiry into Foreign Interference in Federal Electoral Processes and Democratic Institutions, "Initial Report," May 3, 2024.

[32] Andrew McIntosh, "Friction Among Regional Spies, Shadowy CSIS HQ Unit a Challenge for New Intelligence Boss," Global News, August 16, 2024.

[33] Fife and Chase, "Foreign Interference a 'Stain'"; Andrew Coyne, "The Foreign-Interference Scandal Shows It's Time to Clean Up Canada's Party Nomination

Races," *Globe and Mail*, May 10, 2024; Public Inquiry into Foreign Interference in Federal Electoral Processes and Democratic Institutions, "Initial Report," May 3, 2024. Government of Canada, "Legislation to Counter Foreign Interference Receives Royal Assent," press release, June 21, 2024.

[34] Catherine Tunney, "NDP Leader Says He's More Alarmed After Reading Unredacted Intelligence Report," CBC News, June 12, 2024; NSICOP, "Special Report on Foreign Interference in Canada's Democratic Processes and Institutions," 2024; Campbell Clark, "Despite Softer Tone, Elizabeth May Agrees with Jagmeet Singh's Searing Assessment of Secret Foreign Interference Report," *Globe and Mail*, June 14, 2024; Ryan Tumilty, "Some MPs 'Wittingly' Helped Foreign Agents, Liberals Too Slow to Respond to Threat: Intelligence Report," *National Post*, June 3, 2024; Robert Fife and Steven Chase, "Commissioner Won't Name Parliamentarians Allegedly Collaborating with Foreign Powers," *Globe and Mail*, September 16, 2024.

[35] Robert McNamara, *The Fog of War: Eleven Lessons from the Life of Robert S. McNamara* (film), Sony Pictures Classics, 2004; "LeBlanc Downplays Intelligence in NSICOP Report: 'Long Way Away from Proof,'" Global News, June 14, 2024; Annie Bergeron-Oliver, "Trudeau Calls into Question Findings of Stunning Watchdog Foreign Interference Report," CTV News, June 15, 2024. "Liberals Blocking Access to 1,000-Plus Documents, Says Intel-Oversight Panel Reviewing Foreign Interference," *National Post*, June 5, 2024; Robert Fife and Steven Chase, "Trudeau Cabinet Withholding Documents on Foreign Interference from Inquiry," *Globe and Mail*, May 23, 2024; Coyne, "The Foreign-Interference Scandal"; Robert Fife and Steven Chase, "Trudeau Welcomes Inquiry Decision to Probe Allegations of Parliamentarians Colluding with Foreign States," *Globe and Mail*, June 17, 2024.

[36] Kathryn May, "Speaking Truth to Power Discouraged in Public Service," *Policy Options*, May 11, 2022.

[37] Robert Fife and Steven Chase, "Revelations Forced Ottawa to Respond to Foreign Interference, Hogue Inquiry Hears," *Globe and Mail*, October 4, 2024; Alex Boutilier, "A 2021 Chinese Interference Analysis Stalled with Trudeau Security Advisor," Global News, October 7, 2024; Alex Boutilier, "Trudeau's National Security Advisor Says There Are No 'Traitors' in Parliament," Global

News, October 9, 2024; Justin Trudeau, "Trudeau Testimony Foreign Interference Inquiry," CNN News18, October 16, 2024, youtube.com/live/fKPIW6dgZ6Q?si =viepuvpRIBWW31G2; Andrew McIntosh, "Friction Among Regional Spies. Shadowy CSIS HQ Unit a Challenge for New Intelligence Boss," Global News, August 16, 2024; Christopher Nardi, "Poilievre Demands Names After Trudeau Claims Conservatives Compromised by Foreign Interference," *National Post*, October 16, 2024; Robert Fife and Steven Chase, "Former Public Safety Minister, Staff Needed Time to Get 'Comfortable' with Warrant Targeting Liberal Powerbroker, Inquiry Hears," *Globe and Mail*, October 8, 2024; Robert Fife and Steven Chase, "Blair Says He Never Knew CSIS Warrant Sat in His Office for 54 Days," *Globe and Mail*, October 11, 2024; Alex Boutilier, "RCMP Nixed Probe into Suspected PRC-Linked Money Laundering Network," Global News, October 3, 2024; Public Inquiry into Foreign Interference in Federal Electoral Processes and Democratic Institutions, "Final Report," January 28, 2025, 79–88, 111–121; The Editorial Board, "The Hogue Report Keeps Canadians Where They Were—in the Dark," *Globe and Mail*, January 30, 2025; Norimitsu Onishi, "Trudeau Government Left Canada Vulnerable to Foreign Interference, Report Finds," *New York Times*, January 28, 2025.

CONCLUSION

[1] Canada, "Certificate of Appreciation," Dennis Molinaro; Sean Boynton, "As AUKUS Looks to Collaborate with Other Allies, Why Is Canada Not Mentioned?," Global News, April 10, 2024; Touria Izri and Sean Boynton, "Canada to Unveil NATO Spending Plan, Details 'First Step' on New Submarines," Global News, July 10, 2024; US interviews, 2023; Dan De Luce and Owen Hayes, "In Ukraine War, China Is Helping Tilt Momentum in Russia's Favor, Top U.S. Spy Says," NBC News, May 2, 2024; David E. Sanger, "Biden Approved Secret Nuclear Strategy Refocusing on Chinese Threat," *New York Times*, August 20, 2024; Michael Drummond, "President Trump Threatens Canada over Trade War—Saying It Should Become 'Cherished 51st State,'" Sky News, February 2, 2025; Nicole Johnston, "China Has Avoided the Same Tariffs as Mexico and Canada for Now—and Is Taking Trump in Its Stride," Sky News, February 1, 2025; Didi Tang and Ken Moritsugu, "After Talking Tough During Campaign, Trump Appears to Ease Up on China at Start of Presidency," Associated Press, January 29, 2025; Ben Blanchard, "Responding to Trump Tariff Threat, Taiwan Says Chip Business Is 'Win-Win,'" Reuters, January 28, 2025.

[2] Ryan Tumilty, "Jean Chrétien Dismisses Foreign Interference in Liberal Convention Speech," *National Post*, May 5, 2023; Matt Gurney, "O'Toole Passed the Statesmen Test. Trudeau Flunked," *Line*, April 5, 2024; NSICOP, "Special Report on Foreign Interference; Editorial Board, "Forget Inflation. Justin Trudeau's Real Sins in 2023 Involved Elections and Ethics," *Globe and Mail*, December 28, 2023.

[3] Ismail Shakil, "Canada task force says ex-Finance Minister Freeland target of China-linked campaign," Reuters, February 7, 2025; TADC, "China election Interference in This Year's Federal Election," March 28, 2025; Tom Blackwell, "Liberal MP apologizes for suggesting Tory Candidate Be Turned Over to Chinese Consulate for Hong Kong Bounty," *National Post*, March 28, 2025; Bill Curry, Steven Chase, Stephanie Levitz, "Carney Stands by Liberal Candidate Who Said Conservative Rival Should Be Turned in For Chinese Bounty," *Globe and Mail*, March 31 2025; "Canada MP Quits Election Race Over Chinese Bounty Comments," BBC News, March 31, 2025; Christopher Nardi, "Chinese Government Boosted Carney Posts On Popular Social Media Platform," *National Post*, April 7, 2025.

Robert Fife and Steven Chase, "Liberal Candidate Peter Yuen, Chosen To Replace Paul Chiang, Linked To Pro-Beijing Groups, Events," *Globe and Mail*, April 10, 2025; CBCNNLIVE, "Mark Carney Liberal Party Leader Live," 11:44 am, April 10, 2025 "Financial Giant Takes Charge of the Maple Leaf Country, and the China-Canada Strategic Breakthrough Ushers in Hope," JCCC, https://www.thejccc.com/newsinfo/8127529.html; Robert Fife and Steven Chase, "Carney Says He Never Heard of Pro-Beijing Group Despite Photos With Its Leaders," *Globe and Mail*, April 10, 2025. My attempts to reach the JCCC for comment were unsuccessful.

Dennis Molinaro, "A Foreign Agent Registry Won't Be Enough—We Need to Reform How We Handle Interference," *Globe and Mail*, March 20, 2023; Thomas Juneau and Vincent Rigby, "Regular Renewal of Canada's National Security Policy Will Be Worth the Effort," *Globe and Mail*, May 6, 2024; Thomas Juneau and Stephanie Carvin, "Canada's Intelligence Providers and Policymakers Don't Understand Each Other," *Globe and Mail*, May 30, 2024; Alexandra Wrage, "Canada Needs a RICO Law. Can We Do It Better than the U.S.?," *Globe and Mail*, August 18, 2023; Vincent Rigby and Thomas Juneau, "Some Advice for the Prime Minister upon the Creation of His New National Security Council," *Line*, July 31, 2023; Philippe Lagassé and Justin Massie, "How Canada Can Reach NATO's 2-Per-Cent Target—and Quickly," *Globe and Mail*, December 27, 2024.

[4] Derek Decloet, "Desmarais' Power Sustainable Gives Up on China's Equities Strategy," Bloomberg, May 9, 2024; Elizabeth Thompson and Aloysius Wong, "Foreign Interference watchdog to be named next month, public safety minister says," CBC News, August 19, 2025.

GLOSSARY

ADS – approved destination status

AIIB – Asian Infrastructure Investment Bank

AMMS – Academy of Military Medical Sciences

BCIT – British Columbia Institute of Technology

BRI – Belt and Road Initiative

CBSA – Canada Border Services Agency

CCBC – Canada China Business Council

CCDI – Central Commission for Discipline Inspection

CCFA – Canadian Confederation of Fujian Associations

CCNC – Chinese Canadian National Council

CCP – Chinese Communist Party

CEIPP – Critical Election Incident Public Protocol

CI – Confucius Institute

CIA – Central Intelligence Agency

CIDA – Canadian International Development Agency

CITIC – China International Trust and Investment Company

CPPCC – Chinese People's Political Consultative Conference

CSC – China Scholarship Council

CSE – Communications Security Establishment

CSIS – Canadian Security Intelligence Service

CSSA – Chinese Students and Scholars Association

CTCCO – Confederation of Toronto Chinese Canadian Organizations

DND – Department of National Defence

DOJ – Department of Justice

FBI – Federal Bureau of Investigation

FG – Falun Gong

FINTRAC – Financial Transactions and Reports Analysis Centre of Canada

FIPA – Foreign Investment Protection Agreement

FSB – Federal Security Service (Federal'naya Sluzhba Bezopasnosti)

GOF – gain of function

GRU – Main Intelligence Directorate (Glavnoye Razvedyvatelnoye Upravleniye)

HUMINT – human intelligence (human sources working for states)

IOC – International Olympic Committee

IP – Intellectual Property

JCCC – Jiangsu Commerce Council of Canada

MFA – Ministry of Foreign Affairs

MP – member of Parliament

MPS – Ministry of Public Security

MSS – Ministry of State Security

MTA – Material Transfer Agreement

NCCC – National Congress of Chinese Canadians

NCNA – New China News Agency

NGO – Non-Governmental Organization

NHFERP – National High-End Foreign Experts Recruitment Plan

NML – National Microbiology Laboratory

NSA – National Security Agency

NSC – National Security Council

NSIA – National Security and Intelligence Adviser

NSICOP – National Security and Intelligence Committee of
    Parliamentarians
NSIE – Network Security Information Exchange
NSIRA – National Security Intelligence Review Agency
NUDT – National University of Defense Technology
OCAO – Overseas Chinese Affairs Office
PCO – Privy Council Office
PHAC – Public Health Agency of Canada
PLA – People's Liberation Army
PMO – Prime Minister's Office
PRC – People's Republic of China
PSPC – Public Services and Procurement Canada
RCMP – Royal Canadian Mounted Police
RICO – Racketeer Influenced and Corrupt Organizations
ROC – Republic of China
SITE – Security and Intelligence Threats to Elections
SOE – state-owned enterprise
SVR – Foreign Intelligence Service (Sluzhba Vneshney Razvedki)
TADC – Toronto Association for Democracy in China
TDSB – Toronto District School Board
TTP – Thousand Talents Plan
UBC – University of British Columbia
UFWD – United Front Work Department

INDEX

DENNIS MOLINARO is a former national security analyst and policy adviser for the Canadian federal government. He has advised the UK and Canadian governments on matters of foreign interference and economic security. An author and academic, he earned his PhD from the University of Toronto in 2015 and studies the history of security, counter-intelligence and foreign interference. His research on wiretapping and the government's use of emergency powers in the 1970s received national media coverage. A frequent media commentator on intelligence and foreign interference issues, he has taught courses on modern espionage, human rights law and national security at several Canadian universities, including the University of Toronto. He is the president and founder of CipherCore Consulting, specializing in analytical and research solutions.